D0150964

THE COMMUNIST SUBVERSION OF CZECHOSLOVAKIA, 1938-1948

BY THE SAME AUTHOR

Tito's Communism. Denver: University of Denver Press, 1951

Danger in Kashmir. Princeton: Princeton University Press, 1954

THE COMMUNIST SUBVERSION OF CZECHOSLOVAKIA 1938-1948

The Failure of Coexistence

PRINCETON, NEW JERSEY
PRINCETON UNIVERSITY PRESS
1959

London: Oxford University Press

L.C. Card: 59-11080

Printed in the United States of America
by Princeton University Press, Princeton, New Jersey

To the Memory of my Parents

PREFACE

In this age of all but unbearable tension between the communist and the free world, it is small wonder that the possibilities of the coexistence of these two antagonistic ways of life are being thoroughly explored. The danger of such a resolution of this tension lies in the possibility that one side or the other may use coexistence as a weapon, not of peace, but of conquest.

This book is an attempt to present a case study of a thoroughly democratic nation, Czechoslovakia, which embraced coexistence as a method of resolving the bitter clash of democratic and communist forces within its own borders. The results were tragic to all lovers of freedom. The story of Czechoslovakia must give all thoughtful people who are drawn to this properly attractive process of coexistence some cause for grave thought.

There is no attempt in this study to assert that all instances of communist conquest parallel in every way the history of the communist coup in Czechoslovakia. Nevertheless, nearly all the traditional methods of communist takeover are found to one degree or another in this narrative.

Ten years is too short a period in which to pass final judgment on the role of the persons involved, or the events which slowly but inexorably destroyed the forces of democracy in Czechoslovakia. Ten years is, however, a long enough time to record and review these factors with some detachment, particularly in the light of numerous new sources which the Communist Party of Czechoslovakia made public—after the struggle had reached the final stage.

A definitive study of the process of the communization of Czechoslovakia will have to await the day when Soviet documents and those of the Communist Party of Czechoslovakia will have been made available, as well as the archives of the late President Edvard Beneš. The latter are now in the possession of the Communist Party, which seized them a few hours after his death.

I am indebted to many persons for their assistance in the preparation of this book: to Mr. C. Dale Fuller, former Director of the Social Science Foundation, for his generous understanding; to Dr. Jaroslav Drábek, Mr. Arnošt Heidrich, and Professor Jaroslav Stránský for reading the manuscript; to Professor S. Harrison Thomson for reading the manuscript and for opening his unique library to research; to the exiled Czechoslovak leaders —Vratislav Bušek, Jaroslav Drábek, Ladislav Feierabend, Arnošt Heidrich, Ivan Herben, Vladimír Krajina, Václav Majer, Ján Papánek, Hugo Skala, Juraj Slávik, Jaromír Smutný, Jaroslav Stránský, Pavel Tigrid, Petr Zenkl—for making their personal knowledge of the critical events in Czechoslovakia available through their unpublished materials, correspondence, and interviews; to Mrs. Irene Hairgrove, Mr. Arnold Nachmanoff, and my wife for their research contribution; to Mrs. Helen Huling for her untiring efforts in typing the manuscript; to Miss Ruth Davis and Mrs. Lavonne Delahunty for typing the preliminary materials; to Miss Miriam Brokaw, the Managing Editor of the Princeton University Press, for her most skillful piloting of the manuscript to its final stage. I am most grateful to my friend and colleague, Professor R. Russell Porter, who edited the work with his customary skill and warmth. The responsibility for the book is, needless to say, solely mine.

Due acknowledgment is given to the sources used in the work. In particular, my thanks go to the publishers of the following works for their permission to excerpt materials: *Memoirs of Dr. Eduard Beneš* (translated by Godfrey Lias. London: George Allen & Unwin, 1954. Boston: Houghton Mifflin Co.); Jozef Lettrich, *History of Modern Slovakia* (New York: F. A. Praeger, 1955); Hubert Ripka, *Le coup de Prague* (Paris: Plon, 1949; copyright Opera Mundi, Paris); Ivo Duchacek, *The Strategy of Communist Infiltration: The Case of Czechoslovakia* (New Haven, Conn.: Yale Institute of International Studies, 1949); E. Taborsky, "Beneš and the Soviets," *Foreign Affairs*, Vol. 27, pp. 302-15; E. Taborsky, "Beneš and Stalin, Moscow, 1943 and 1945,"

Journal of Central European Affairs, Vol. 13, pp. 154-81; E. Táborský, "Benešovy moskevské cesty," *Svědectví*, Vol. 1, No. 3-4, pp. 193-214; E. Taborsky, "The Triumph and Disaster of Eduard Beneš," *Foreign Affairs*, Vol. 36, No. 4, pp. 669-84.

Denver, Colorado J.K.
June 1959

CONTENTS

THE COMMUNIST SUBVERSION OF CZECHOSLOVAKIA, 1938-1948

EPILOGUE

On the morning of June 7, 1948, between nine and ten o'clock, in the small village of Sezimovo Ústí in southern Bohemia, the President of the Czechoslovak Republic, Dr. Edvard Beneš, performed the last official act of his thirty years of statesmanship. He abdicated.

The event was marked by neither ostentatious ceremony nor the ugly sounds of revolution. It was a quiet scene. A broken man affixed his signature to a document, presented it for delivery to Jaromír Smutný, his Chancellor, and then, with him, stepped out onto the grounds of his unpretentious villa, to watch the quiet striking of the presidential flag. And that was all. The act of abdication had taken place.

But this was more than an act of abdication. It was, in a sense, a certificate of death, his death, though three months were to elapse before his body gave up the battle for survival and was lowered into its grave. Even more than this, it was a certificate of death for the democratic hopes and dreams and struggles of a nation, born only thirty years before with high aspiration, now brought to its grave by the violence and terror of militant communism, its democratic institutions in ruins and in their place the somber and soulless architecture of communist totalitarianism.

Did such thoughts race through the mind of this statesman as on that day of June 7 he stepped into the bleak morning air to watch the lowering of his official flag? One cannot say with certainty what is in any man's mind, but one may surmise that they did. He knew now that the long struggle was finally and completely over, the last barricade had fallen, the last compromise had been made, and there was left nothing but the resignation of death.

He must, of course, have seen beyond the trees the neighboring villa of Zdeněk Fierlinger; Fierlinger, whom he had lifted to high places in government, only to see him betray his country to communism.

He was alone now, completely alone; his democratic comrades who had fought by his side dead or scattered like leaves before the communist hurricane. Jan Masaryk, his devoted friend, son of an illustrious father, dead. Prokop Drtina, tough defender of justice and his loyal follower, near death by his own hand. The many others, in their graves or fled beyond the borders of their country.

These thoughts, these sights, these events may have appeared for a moment, but distant now and dim, for the light in this great statesman's eyes was already fading out.

The text of the letter of resignation, addressed to the Prime Minister of the communist government, Klement Gottwald, would reveal little, if anything, about the profound reasons which had led President Beneš to this final step. It spoke vaguely of "the problems of the general political situation" and the doctor's recommendations concerning his health. It ended with a moving wish "to all dear fellow countrymen, their representatives and their government, that the Republic be spared from all calamities, that all citizens live and work in mutual tolerance, love and forgiveness, that they wish for others the freedom which they themselves should conscientiously enjoy."[1]

Only a handful of his close associates knew that President Beneš, as a final act of protest, had first prepared a draft letter of abdication which was different from the final copy. In that draft he had expressed a strong protest against certain clauses of the new Constitution. He had stated "that his conscience and his convictions about democracy and [his] understanding of human and civil rights precluded his agreement" with the Constitution

[1] J. Smutný, *Únorový převrat 1948* (The February 1948 Upheaval), 5 vols., mimeographed, London, Ústav dr. Edvarda Beneše, 1953-1957. Vol. v, p. 1.

and his ability to sign it; he, therefore, had decided to resign.[2] The letter was to be addressed not to the Prime Minister, Gottwald, but to the Chairman of the Constitutional Assembly. This in itself was meant to be something of an affront to the communist Prime Minister.

But at the last all this was changed. The letter went to Gottwald, and Beneš' objections to the Constitution were omitted. The battle finally lost, even his last act was the product of his concept of the democratic process, of his regard for other people's viewpoint, of compromise—the characteristics which had accompanied his activities for thirty long years.

When Dr. Beneš on February 25, 1948 succumbed to the violence of the communist putsch and nominated a new communist government, he knew that the day signaled the end of Czechoslovak freedom and the end of his political life. Yet he decided on this action because above everything else he wanted to avoid chaos in his country, which stood at the brink of civil war. He could have resigned rather than appoint a communist government, the product of "the street," of violent mobs. However, as he put it in his address to the new government, "the State must be administered and led"[3]—a statement open to severe scrutiny.

After he had made the necessary arrangements for the communist administration of the country, he wished to dissociate himself from the developments which would follow. On February 27, after having received the new government, he left Hradčany Castle, the Prague seat of the President and the centuries-old symbol of the nation's noblest achievements, for his private home at Sezimovo Ústí. Stepping into the car he glanced through the draft of the official communiqué prepared in a routine manner and announcing his departure. He substituted the words "he retired" from Prague Castle for the word "left."[4] He wished to give through this wording, which probably impressed only linguists and others trained in the niceties of political thinking,

[2] *Ibid.*, pp. 58-59. [3] Smutný, *op.cit.*, vol. IV, p. 169.
[4] *Ibid.*, p. 173.

an expression of his attitude toward the new regime. More importantly, he also instructed his Chancellor Smutný to prepare a letter of resignation. After he had reached his home he ordered that the presidential flag not be raised.

Two days passed. Then Dr. Beneš, now the head of state in name only, changed his mind. He shelved the draft letter of resignation and thought instead of "remaining as President but not to function." On March 7 he received Gottwald and in conversation with him revealed some of the reasons which had led him to remain in office for the time being. Stating again that he had appointed the present government "to avoid bloodshed and conflict within the nation," he pointed out to Gottwald that he was now waiting to see "what will happen next and what [Gottwald] will do. I will continue," he said, "to work toward an agreement to avoid a complete split in the nation. If I do not succeed, I'll leave. . . . I dislike to see what you are doing, how you fire many people from their jobs."[5]

Gottwald assured him that the Communist Party of Czechoslovakia would not conduct any mass trials, that it would punish only those people who had acted against the law. He asked the President to let the flag be raised over his home. Beneš agreed.

But promises having been given and concessions secured from the President, the communist revolution went on, the persecutions continued uninterrupted. Thousands of people were arrested, tens of thousands deprived of employment.

The President, broken in health by two strokes and exhausted to the point of collapse by the hectic events of the recent past, became increasingly a lonely figure, cut off from any direct contact with his nation.

He received numerous letters asking him to speak to the nation. One of them read, "If there is something, Mr. President, for which we should be chastized, do it; we can take it more easily than your silence."[6] But he did not speak. There was little to say of which the communist censorship would have approved.

[5] Smutný, *op.cit.*, vol. v, pp. 10, 11-12. [6] *Ibid.*, p. 49.

On one occasion only did he raise his voice. On April 6 he participated at the celebration of the six-hundredth anniversary of the foundation of Charles University, the oldest institution of higher learning in Central Europe. Gravely, speaking slowly, he reminded his people that Czech universities "have always stood on the side of truth, freedom, and morality." Speaking then about the need for peace he continued: "To achieve this natural longing of mankind [for peace] and to have it accompanied by freedom of conscience, of science, of thought, and of religion, it is necessary to cultivate constantly and to employ an all-embracing spiritual freedom. This is the condition of every real spiritual life and of all intellectual work. This freedom, based on the respect of man for man and on general tolerance . . . will, God permitting, lead . . . us all toward a happy prosperity and a truly happy future."[7] It was President Beneš' last public statement.

A few days later, the government submitted to him the text of a new election law and of the new Constitution. He studied the documents and reached the conclusion that the first provided for the conduct of totalitarian elections, the latter went "against [his] understanding of democracy."

On May 4 he again received Gottwald. The audience lasted two and one-quarter hours. It was typical of Beneš' reasoning and his methods of procedure. Until the last moment he remained faithful to his democratic convictions, but also to his quiet ways of applying them, his inclinations to compromise. He first told Gottwald that his decision to abdicate was final. Then he stressed that just as he had always been loyal to the Prime Minister he wanted now, too, to speak with him "clearly, frankly, and as a friend. . . ." He could not, he said, affix his name to the Constitution which defined "the will of the people" in such a way that it could be easily supplanted by "the will of the street," as was the case in the February events. He did not seek for discord: "he loves this country above everything else and will do nothing damaging to it." He would not undertake "any action against

[7] *Ibid.*, p. 24.

his own state, nor would he go against communists or [partake in] an action which would be aimed against the USSR."

Gottwald, in answer, said that the Communist Party would have preferred not to do anything about the presidential question. However, he respected the President's reasons for abdication. If, therefore, a parting of the ways was necessary, the communists would like to do so on good terms. Gottwald was, of course, aware of the power Beneš still held, even in silence, and he could not brush it lightly aside, particularly because only two and one-half months had passed since the communists had taken over the government.

But, reasoned Gottwald, Beneš' resignation before the elections and before the promulgation of the Constitution would be understood as a political demonstration, which the Communist Party would have to answer. "You are throwing us the gauntlet," he stated, "and we will be compelled to pick it up." He suggested that the President take a leave for reasons of health (as was provided for in the Constitution); meanwhile the elections would take place and the new Constitution would be signed in his absence.

Dr. Beneš in answer stressed his good will and his desire to reach an agreement acceptable to both sides.[8] It was reached. The new Constitution was adopted May 9, and was to be signed by the President within thirty days.

Meanwhile the elections were held on May 30 according to the new law which Dr. Beneš had signed, and the National Front ticket, the only one which, as he had anticipated, was presented to the electorate, received the familiarly high figure of 89.3 per cent.

Eight days after the elections, on June 7, his signature not affixed to the new Constitution, Dr. Edvard Beneš resigned. When Gottwald's government met in extraordinary session that same afternoon, the Prime Minister made a solemn speech of thanks in which he highly praised Dr. Beneš' contributions to

[8] For a detailed memorandum about the conversation, see *ibid.*, pp. 31-39, 41.

the country and rendered honor to him "as a distinguished successor to the President Liberator [T. G. Masaryk], as the leader of the struggle for liberation and also as the co-creator of the new order."

After Beneš' death, however, communists had different words for his undemonstrative withdrawal from office. They said that his explanation of his abdication was "typically Beneš-like, neither salty, nor greasy." To them Beneš was a "democrat-formalist."[9]

Obviously, what Beneš considered to be the essence of democracy, communists ridiculed with disdain; what he cherished and respected, they abused.

And so, on this morning of June 7, there came to all but its physical end the life of this great democratic statesman; there came to a close the democratic life of his freedom-loving people. Though the end came with some suddenness, the infection had been evident for many years. Against it Beneš and his nation had struggled, but always in a way apparently unequal to the virulence of the disease.

Herewith is the narrative of those dreary and seemingly inexorable events.

[9] Jindřich Veselý, *Kronika únorovych dnů 1948* (The Chronicle of the February 1948 Days), Prague, Státní nakladatelství politické literatury, 1958, pp. 221, 218.

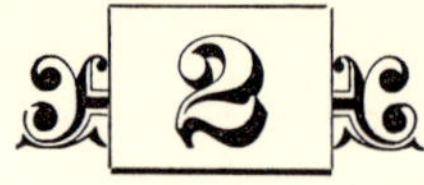

LOOKING BACK

THE conviction is widespread among social scientists that communism's fertile soil is economic misery and social injustice, that its roots seek the nourishment of political dictatorship. The accumulated evidence of the recent past would seem to validate this belief.

In all countries in which the Communist Party is in power today these economic, social, and political factors existed to a greater or lesser degree. Even if the intervention of Soviet armed forces brought about the final act of communization, as was undoubtedly the usual case with the exception of China and Yugoslavia, vast social injustices and the absence of a vitally democratic spirit facilitated the process. There is one exception to this observation: Czechoslovakia.

The Republic of Czechoslovakia rose phoenix-like from the ashes of the Austro-Hungarian empire on October 28, 1918. On that day a century-old dream and struggle for independence became a reality. On that day a nation, rich in its heritage of freedom which had persisted through centuries of domination, was reborn.

Its first years were not easy. The shadow of servitude still hung over it. The true spirit of freedom is the habit of free men, and for three hundred years the people of Czechoslovakia had not been free. Mistakes were inevitable as this reborn nation began once more to build for its people a free way of life.

Strong national emotions, the by-product of war and independence, caused misunderstandings between Czechs and Slovaks. More seriously, the German minority of more than two and a half millions was estranged from their new government in these first years of the Republic.

Looming over the whole of Central and Eastern Europe was the menacing shadow of the October Revolution in Russia and of the unscrupulous agitation of the Third International. Germany appeared ripe for a communist upheaval in 1919. Hungary experienced a communist rule for a half a year in 1919. Poland was exposed to Soviet propaganda and military pressures. Austria was in chaos. Nor was Czechoslovakia spared from the turbulence of those revolutionary times.

Her finances, too, were disturbed, not only by the complex consequences of the dismemberment of the Austro-Hungarian empire and the disruption of its economic and financial unity, but also by a general inflation. Nevertheless, after a few years, her people became acclimated to the heady air of freedom. Nationalism subsided, to be replaced by quiet self-confidence. Her most vexatious problem, that of the German minority, was well under way to peaceful, loyal solution, and one may reasonably speculate that the problem would have found a final and satisfactory solution had the rise of Hitlerism in neighboring Germany not reversed the promising trend.

The postwar revolutionary wave dissipated, too, against the solid structure of a quickly recuperating economy and sound financial measures. On the whole, political writers and statesmen of the free world agree that Czechoslovakia became a thoroughly democratic and progressive country. Indeed, as reporters of the world's woes hurried in those days from one area of crisis to another, Czechoslovakia enjoyed the doubtful privilege of neglect; "this island of democracy and peace," as she was frequently called, offered little of interest to the men who write the headlines. Her future, though not untroubled, seemed secure. And yet, less than three decades were to pass before this vigorous young democracy was to sink beneath the dark waters of communist dictatorship, a servitude far more deadly than that from which she had emerged.

Why? Was there here the soil from which the social scientists tell us communism springs—reactionary dictatorship, economic misery, and social injustice? A quick look at the political life of Czechoslovakia in this interwar period and at her social and economic policies reveals a far different picture.

Politics

Czechoslovakia entered upon her new political life with several traditional political parties in existence. The first elections, held in June 1919, were local and showed a marked trend to the left. A coalition government, led until then by a conservative party, the National Democrats, responded immediately to the wishes of the people and relinquished leadership to the Social Democratic Party. Meanwhile, the Constitutional National Assembly, composed of appointed delegates, prepared and in February 1920 voted a new Constitution. It was a strictly democratic document, the principles of which were a combination of the French and American Constitutions.

The first elections for the Parliament were held in April of 1920 and confirmed the continuation of a tendency toward the left. There was as yet no communist party; the Social Democrats, from whom eventually most of the communists were to split away, secured seventy-four seats in the Chamber of Deputies. On the right, the Agrarian Party, supported by masses of small and middle farmers but controlled by powerful interest groups, received forty seats; gaining in support, however, it became in five years, and thereafter remained, the strongest party in the Parliament and the government. The third largest party was the Czechoslovak National Socialists, with a program somewhat left of the center. Then followed other minor parties, some with conservative, some with progressive programs, but all of them devoted to basic principles of democracy.

In the next general elections, in November 1925, the Communist Party of Czechoslovakia appeared through a schism in the ranks of the Social Democrats' principal constituency, the united workers movement. Communists won forty-one seats. As a consequence of the elections, the two socialist parties, the Social Democrats and the National Socialists, abstained for three years from the coalition government. On the other hand, however, the process of consolidation in state affairs was demonstrated by the entry into the government of two German minority parties, and at a later date a third one.

In the 1929 elections the trend toward the radical left was halted. Social Democrats and National Socialists gained substantially in strength; communists were reduced to thirty seats, only 10 per cent of the three hundred members of the Chamber of Deputies. Never during the interwar period did they exceed this number, and the elections, in May 1935, confirmed the stability of forces among the Czechoslovak (though not the German) political parties.[1]

Never throughout the interwar period did a fascist movement achieve any significance. Nor was there in existence, even for a single day, a political dictatorship. The country was ruled by a coalition government which was controlled by a freely elected Parliament. Certainly, then, this one element of the traditional soil of communism—political dictatorship—did not exist.

Economics and Social Welfare

Before the Czechoslovak people regained independence in 1918, the land had for the most part come under the ownership of a few landlords. Indeed, some one thousand individuals were in possession of 26 per cent of the total land area which later became Czechoslovakia. Many of the large estates were in the hands of German or Germanized aristocracy, as a result of a centuries-old process of political and economic Germanization of the country.

The injustice of land distribution was obvious. Soon after

[1] See the table of party strength in Czechoslovakia in the Parliament, 1920-1946, in U.S. Congress, 81st Cong., 1st Sess., *The Strategy and Tactics of World Communism*, Committee on Foreign Affairs, Report of Subcommittee No. 5, Supplement III, p. 7.

the foundation of the Republic this inequality was largely remedied, though admittedly not without some mistakes, by a series of legislative acts. In April 1919, only five months after the liberation, a land reform law was enacted which broke up large estates, which were defined as those which exceeded 150 hectares (370.65 acres) of arable or 250 hectares (617.75 acres) of any kind of land. The released land, for the loss of which the original owner had been compensated, was distributed among agricultural workers, small farmers, war invalids, and Czechoslovak legionaries. A popular cooperative movement was considerably helpful to the small farmers, who constituted most of the 33 per cent (according to 1930 census) of the agricultural population.

The land reform was not a sweeping, revolutionary measure. Hunger for land was not fully satisfied. However, observers and agricultural experts agree that the reform was an important step forward in removing injustices of the past and in laying solid foundations for an economic democracy. There was neither the political nor economic climate among the farming population for more extreme measures. In fact, farmers steadily supported the Agrarian Party, known for its conservative policy.

Subcarpathian Russia, the eastern tip of the Republic, was an exception. Burdened by poverty, economic and cultural backwardness, its impoverished population, for the most part dependent upon the land, had reasons for dissatisfaction. In the 1935 national elections, 25.6 per cent of its voters cast their ballots for the Communist Party. Out of Czechoslovakia's total population of 14,500,000, however, only some 700,000 lived in Subcarpathian Russia.

The relationship between agriculture and industry was balanced. Approximately the same ratio of people earned a living from industry as from the land—34.9 per cent (according to the 1930 census); 12.9 per cent of the population was active in commerce, transportation, and finance; 17.4 per cent found employment in public service and the professions.

Mines and industries were in private ownership. Railroads,

the postal service, the telephone, and the telegraph were run, as in some other European countries, by the state. Utilities services and local communications were owned by local communities. Industry combined a mixture of private ownership and public enterprise, with emphasis on the first.

To a considerable extent, the prosperity of the country depended on foreign trade. Capital goods formed an important part of its export. The products of light industry, such as textiles, gloves, glass, sugar, and ceramics, were exported to countries the world over; 80 per cent of the products were sold abroad.

Labor was protected by progressive legislation, finding a powerful and constructive spokesman in the two socialist parties, the Social Democrats and the National Socialists. Trade unions, which were organized along party lines, defended workers' interests in the Parliament, in collective contract negotiations and, if necessary, by organizing strikes. Three weeks after the proclamation of independence the Parliament enacted an eight-hour working day. Social and health insurance, retirement plans, paid vacations were all guaranteed by law.

Certainly there was still some room for complaints. On the whole, however, Czechoslovakia had succeeded in establishing, particularly by comparison with many other European countries, a sound balance between employers and the working class, between industry and agriculture, between the city and the village.[2]

Apparently then, the other ingredient of communism's favorite soil—economic misery, social injustice—did not exist. But communism did grow, like a cancer, at last consuming the healthy tissues of this democratic state.

Atypical, then, as was the communization of Czechoslovakia, the story of the process is one that particularly merits examination. It is a story of deliberate intent, of unscrupulous design, in which no falsehood was too great, no betrayal too vicious, no

[2] The data are compiled from V. Busek and Nicolas Spulber, eds., *Czechoslovakia*, New York, F. E. Praeger, 1957; J. Kerner, ed., *Czechoslovakia, Twenty Years of Independence*, Berkeley, University of California, 1940.

treachery too infamous, no deceit too contemptuous to be avoided if its employment could advance in any way or to any extent the subversion of this democratic state to the totalitarian authority of communism. The tracing of this process is the burden of this study.

THE COMMUNIST PARTY OF CZECHOSLOVAKIA

On October 28, 1948, V. Kopecký lectured before the functionaries of the Central Committee of the Communist Party of Czechoslovakia. It was a day of special significance, the thirtieth anniversary of the foundation of the Czechoslovak Republic. The speaker came from the ranks of the Politburo. An old-time communist, he was known as one of the more vocal and noisy ideologists of the party. Since April of 1945 he had been the permanent Minister of Information in the Czechoslovak government.

Kopecký opened his speech with the startling, albeit frank statement that the interpretation of the historical significance of this anniversary depended on "who writes the history" and asserted that the communists were now writing it "from the point of view of [their] class truth."[1]

Kopecký then proceeded to unravel "the legend" that the country's independence was due to the efforts of such men as Woodrow Wilson, T. G. Masaryk, E. Beneš, and R. Štefánik. The Western imperialists were against the idea of freedom for the Czechoslovak people, he stated, and continued, "The truth is that without the Soviet October of 1917 there would be no Czechoslovak October of 1918."[2]

The misstatement of historical facts is, of course, obvious. However, Kopecký had good reason to distort the story of the birth of Czechoslovakia in a manner favorable to the Soviet Union. The year was 1948. Though Czechoslovakia was now

[1] Václav Kopecký, *Tridsať rokov Československej Republiky* (Thirty Years of the Czechoslovak Republic), Bratislava, Poverenictvo informacií, 1948, p. 6.

[2] *Ibid.*, p. 7.

under communist rule, he was aware of the devotion of the Czechoslovak people to the idea of national independence, and the preceding thirty years could not be written off by the communist leader as an historical error.

But the truth is that the government and the party which Kopecký now labeled as the cradle of Czechoslovak independence were at the time of its birth convinced that the formation of this republic was exactly that—an historical error. The documents of the Soviet government, the Communist Party of the Soviet Union, and the Third International bear eloquent testimony on the subject. In their opposition to the Versailles Peace Treaty and the policy of the Entente these organs of communist policy repeatedly attacked Czechoslovakia as a state which was created by armed forces, a product of Western imperialism, a pawn of French capitalism, an artificial state which should have never been established. Had a communist leader, immediately after World War I, ascribed the credit for Czechoslovakia's Independence Day to the Soviet Union he would have been branded by Moscow as a deviationist, nay, a bourgeois reactionary.

Indeed, when another communist leader in 1929 had written the history of the Communist Party of Czechoslovakia from a different angle of the "class truth," he did not hesitate to say that the founding of the Republic was of bourgeois, imperialistic character.[3]

Although this particular dalliance with the truth is of no great importance, it does perhaps serve as a symbol of the unashamed deceit practiced by communists and the Communist Party as they maneuvered their way into power and eventually the totalitarian rule in Czechoslovakia.

A Period of Confusion

The beginnings of the radical workers' movement in the years which followed after World War I offer an enlightening insight

[3] P. Reimann, *Geschichte der Kommunistischen Partei der Tschechoslovakei* (History of the Communist Party of Czechoslovakia), Berlin, Carl Hoym, 1929, p. 65.

into the political orientation of a group of politicians who later founded the Communist Party of Czechoslovakia. It explains their ideological confusion; it also accounts, however, for their initial success.

A group of Czech workers, prisoners of war, held a meeting in Moscow on May 27 and 28, 1918 and founded a Communist Party. It issued a proclamation which rejected the idea of a bourgeois Czechoslovak Republic and proclaimed itself for a Czechoslovak Socialist Republic, with the right of self-determination, linking in a strictly Marxist sense "the right of self-determination of the Czech nation to a social revolution."[4]

This was an abortive movement and the eager attempt was quickly forgotten. It was more than three years later that the real Communist Party of Czechoslovakia was founded. In the meantime, Moscow and the communist movement in Europe underwent such experiences as the half-year Soviet Republic in Hungary; a short-lived communist regime in Bavaria; local upheavals in Berlin, Hamburg, and the Ruhr; and the Moscow-made Revolutionary Council in East Poland. By 1921 the high tide of communism in Europe was on the wane. A period of stabilization of capitalism set in, and Marxist theoreticians took time to evaluate the situation.

In Czechoslovakia, communist leaders had failed to exploit the revolutionary mood in Europe and in particular the revolutionary spirit of Czech workers who, as Lenin noted, were ahead of their leaders. The errors of the Communist Party of Czechoslovakia and the Communist International, even in this brief review of their policy, deserve attention, for they facilitate our understanding of the changed strategy of Moscow and of the party during and after World War II.

The political and economic situation in Czechoslovakia in the months following the liberation did not lend itself to dogmatic marxist interpretation. The deep abyss between capitalist monopolists and the exploited laboring masses did not exist nor was it

[4] *Ibid.*, pp. 73-74, 75.

easy to create. Capital to a considerable extent had been concentrated in Vienna and if Czech workers, who indeed had been exposed for several decades to the impact of Marxist teaching, turned their class hatred against capitalists, these feelings were considerably diluted by quite non-Marxist feelings of national ambition and pride. The liberation in 1918 satisfied their national sentiments and in this respect they shared the enthusiasm of all other strata of the Czechoslovak people. In addition, even as the working class identified itself with the rest of the nation in the matter of nationalism and self-determination, the non-socialist parties were themselves decidedly radical in their proposals for social and economic reforms, thereby dulling to a considerable extent the edge of the workers' revolutionary spirit and the effectiveness of their class consciousness. This was an unorthodox situation for a dogmatic Marxist.

There were two left-wing Czech parties in the Viennese Parliament: National Socialists and Social Democrats. The first stood uncompromisingly for the policy of a free Czechoslovakia after the war and was not a Marxist party. The second was split between the more moderate and more powerful group, which also advocated a program of national independence, and a radical left, which did not believe in the possibility of an independent socialist Czechoslovakia, but supported instead the so-called Austro-Marxist solution, i.e., a federation of a socialist Austro-Hungary. The leader of this group was Bohumil Šmeral, a man with whom the history of the communist movement in the first decade of independent Czechoslovakia was closely connected.

After independence, both parties entered the coalition government and scored a considerable success in the first national elections in April 1920. The National Socialists received twenty-four seats in the Chamber of Deputies and were its third strongest party. The Social Democrats were by far the strongest party, with seventy-four deputies.

Šmeral was a lonely figure in the national whirlwind which swept away all his Marxist illusions. The popular leader of prewar days, he now stood isolated in the midst of a national upheaval in which even his followers took part. A Marxist who knew of no national allegiance and thought in categories of materialistic internationalism, first within an Austro-Hungarian framework and later within the realm of a United Socialist Europe, he was now confronted with the imposing strength of Czech nationalism in a small and, to him, provincial, independent Czechoslovakia. However, his mind was keen enough to understand and appreciate the vitality of the national feelings. They should, he reasoned, be capitalized on. Eventually, because of his regard for Czechoslovak nationalism, which was otherwise so foreign to his convictions and inclinations, he came into violent conflict with the dogmatic, revolutionary leadership of the Third International.

The early beginnings of the communist movement in Czechoslovakia were observed in Moscow with suspicion and contempt. At the first postwar Congress of the Social Democratic Party, in December 1918, the left-wing group had only a hazy concept of the meaning of a true, full-blooded revolutionary party. It used such terms as "revolution" and "proletarian dictatorship" at liberty but it also advocated the idea of competition in elections and even cooperation with other socialist parties.

Here, however, was struck the first communist note when a man named Antonín Zápotocký, a delegate of the traditionally radical mining district of Kladno, vigorously criticized the Social Democratic Party policy for its nationalism. Thirty years later this same man was one of the chief strategists in planning the communist putsch in Czechoslovakia, then under the mantle of patriotism and nationalism. The radical left-wing minority lost, however, and the Congress approved the policy of the party's participation in the Czechoslovak government.[5]

The year of 1919 saw the rise of the radical left. The group of communist parties which were already in existence throughout

[5] Ferdinand Peroutka, *Budování státu* (The Making of a State), 4 vols., Prague, Fr. Borový, 1933-1936. Vol. 1, pp. 477-87, 496-524.

the world considered the situation in Czechoslovakia sufficiently significant to justify an invitation, on January 24, 1919, to the first Congress of the Communist International. The Czech party was listed, among others invited, as "The revolutionary elements in the Czech Social-Democratic Party," the membership being "open to those parties which stand completely" on the platform of the Third International.[6]

The trouble was that the "revolutionary elements" continued in not being revolutionary enough and remained within the ranks of the Social Democrats. They did not believe in the strategy of violence. They did not intend to follow Lenin's basic dictum that "it is absolutely required first to demarcate oneself from all. . . ." They still thought in terms of parliamentary procedures. Even the most radical Kladno miners showed some sense of loyalty toward the bourgeois government of Czechoslovakia.[7] When the First Congress of the Comintern met in March 1919 no signature of a Czechoslovak party appeared on its resolutions, manifestos, or proclamations.

The lonely man, Šmeral, first observed this confusing scene of socialist politics in strange isolation. Socialist he was; in the inevitability of a socialist dawn he firmly believed. The idea of a nationally independent Czechoslovakia was anathema to him. "A Czech state," he stated, "as any other small state, has no guarantee for its existence. In world competition, it cannot maintain itself, because of its smallness. Only a world revolution which will change Europe into a united socialist state can save freedom for us."[8] The statement was revolutionary enough, Marxist enough, but there were other forces and considerations at work which qualified the purity of Šmeral's Marxism. He was convinced that communism could not be shoved down the throat of the Czech workers, that their nationalism could not be ignored.

[6] *The Communist International, 1919-1943*, Documents, selected and edited by Jane Degras, London, Oxford University Press, 1956. Vol. I, 1919-1922, pp. 3-4.

[7] Peroutka, *op.cit.*, vol. II, pp. 819-40.

[8] *Ibid.*, vol. III, p. 1,832.

His policy, therefore, took the shape of one that Moscow seemingly acknowledged more than thirty years later, in 1956, as the right of each nation to follow its own path toward socialism.

In the 1920's such a path was socialist treachery. Nevertheless, it would seem that for a short while, when paying his first visit to Moscow in the spring of 1920, Šmeral convinced Lenin and Zinoviev of the special circumstances in Czechoslovakia. He was given a green light to try it his own way. In return he became a convinced follower of Lenin and promised to bring the whole Social Democratic Party into the communist family.

When the Second Congress of the Third International met, however, in the summer of 1920, the Social Democratic Party was far from being ready to join. Its right wing was wholly opposed to the principle; the radical left sent a delegation but one which was instructed by Šmeral to proceed cautiously and in particular to avoid any promises of a revolution in Czechoslovakia.[9]

The Second Congress met in an atmosphere of revolutionary enthusiasm. Once more the leaders, assembled in Moscow, were convinced that the tide of revolution was at its height. The Red Army was on the march in Poland; workers in Germany, Britain, and Czechoslovakia refused to take part in the transportation of war materials for Poland. The resolutions, theses, and proclamations which were carried reflected this revolutionary optimism. The Congress passed a resolution outlining twenty-one conditions for admission to the Communist International. It asked for a relentless class struggle, for violent action against capitalist order, for clear-cut communist propaganda, for a complete break with reformists, the merciless exposure of "social-patriotism" and "social pacifism," absolute obedience to the Executive Committee of the Communist International, and obligatory demarcation of the party as communist. In this spirit "the Communist International has declared war on the entire bourgeois

[9] *Ibid.*, pp. 1,812-44, 1,955-89.

world and on all yellow social-democratic parties," the document boldly stated.[10]

The radical left of the Czech Social Democrats faced a crucial dilemma. It was anxious to join the Comintern and would have no objection to joining in the war against the bourgeois world. But it was itself still "yellow" enough not to accept the other conditions of the resolution. When the party Congress met in September 1920 in Prague, Šmeral continued to advocate caution and avoided putting to a vote the question of the radical left's joining the International. He still thought in terms of parliamentary methods of achieving power and a policy independent of Moscow's dictation.

However, a radical line was in the ascendancy and the radical left mustered a majority in the Congress. The leaders of the Social Democratic Party, as they found themselves in a minority, suspended the session, convened another congress for November 1920, and then expelled the radicals from the party.[11]

Foundation of the Party

Against his will and under pressure from radicals, led by A. Zápotocký, Šmeral was left with no choice than to consider the organization of a communist party.

There were still some obstacles on the road, however. Like the division of the Czech Social Democratic Party, the Social Democrats of the German and of the Hungarian minority were split into moderates and radicals. Moscow wished these factions to unite into one communist party and accordingly sent a series of instructions to Prague. Šmeral vacillated. He was against the fusion with Germans and Hungarians, reluctant to offend the national sentiments of the Czech working class.

The leader of the German radicals, Kreibich, with Moscow's

[10] Degras, *op.cit.*, pp. 166-72.

[11] H. G. Skilling, "The Formation of a Communist Party in Czechoslovakia," *The American Slavic and East European Review*, vol. 14, No. 3, October 1955, pp. 346-58.

support, forced Šmeral's hand. He accused him of provincialism and, rejecting the national aspect of the issue, stated: "Which nations will disappear in this development, which language will maintain itself longest, is to me as a communist an absolutely insignificant question. I am not interested if this world will be German, Slav, or Romanic, if it will be a Caucasian or a Mongolian world; my goal is that it be a communist world."[12]

A leading Czech poet, with a German name, S. K. Neumann, sharing Kreibich's internationalist outlook, published a poem in which he cursed his father for becoming a Czech, a member of this little nation, this rotten country to which the great poet, who wrote in his Czech mother tongue, abhorred belonging.[13]

To the student of communist ideological agility, it will come as no surprise to learn that during World War II Kreibich turned into a great anti-German "Czechoslovak patriot," and that Neumann a few years later publicly voiced, in an "Our Father" intonation, a prayer for the "sacred name" of the country, to make it strong "in its love for Thee. . . ."[14] After the war, communists hailed him as the great Czechoslovak national poet.

In March 1921 the German radicals proclaimed the organization of a German Communist Party. In a proclamation they appealed to their Czech comrades not to damage the cause of proletarian revolution but to put it "above all national interests."

The Czech radicals met in May 1921. The Third International sent them a message which appealed to them to abandon any halfway policy and not to be misled by false feelings of nationalism. It asked the leaders to take steps toward founding a united German-Czechoslovak-Hungarian proletarian party.

Šmeral fought his last battle on this occasion. He was still against a premature revolution, against anything resembling a putsch, and in particular against fusion of the three national elements into one party. But Kreibich denounced him and stated

[12] Peroutka, *op.cit.*, vol. IV, pp. 2,208-09. [13] *Ibid.*, pp. 2,210-11.

[14] S. K. Neumann, "Vstupní modlitba" (The Opening Prayer), *Národní čítanka*, Prague, K. Borecký, 1939, p. 444.

that Moscow had no confidence in him. Allegedly, Zinoviev had said so to Kreibich.[15] The mood was threatening and the meeting finally approved the foundation of the party and the twenty-one conditions of the Third International. It was still, however, only a Czechoslovak section, no minorities being represented.

In June 1921 the Executive Committee of the Third International gave to the newly-formed party three months in which to unite and eliminate all nationalistic tendencies. At the Third Congress in Moscow the Czechoslovak delegation was briskly criticized for anti-Marxist nationalism. Bukharin condemned the party for being less revolutionary than the masses. Šmeral's temperate policy was rejected, his delegation was disunited, and he was subjected to severe criticism from the comrades of his own party. Lenin attempted to compromise. "It is necessary," he stated, "that Šmeral's policy make two steps to the left and that the opposition leftist policy make one step to the right."[16] Šmeral capitulated, and in October 1921 the Communist Party of Czechoslovakia was founded, uniting representatives of all national groups.

A Period of Growth and Failure

Šmeral continued for some time to be the leader of the united party, more as a shadow than a reality. The remnants of the old nationalist, though socially radical, program remained, and many people found certain refuge in following this "shadow." Shortly after its foundation the party had over 400,000 members.[17]

The struggle for party purity had only started. At the May Congress of 1921, the party proclamation had opened with a statement which smacked of bourgeois reactionism: "We stand on the view of the unity of the Czechoslovak Republic." In the light of Lenin's interpretation of the principle of self-determination, this was an outrageous statement. It was a slap in the face

[15] Peroutka, *op.cit.*, vol. IV, p. 2,221.

[16] *Ibid.*, p. 2,232.

[17] Josef Chmelař, *Political Parties in Czechoslovakia*, Prague, Orbis, 1926, p. 45.

to the Communist International's policy that Czechoslovakia was an imperialist state; that Slovaks, Germans, Hungarians, and Subcarpathian Russians were oppressed and exploited by capitalist Czechs; that they had the right, in the name of Lenin's principle of self-determination, to secede from the state.[18]

In addition to Šmeral, even Kreibich now came to the conclusion that there was no favorable climate in Czechoslovakia for a radical Leninist policy on the question of nationalism. At the Fifth Congress of the Communist International, he denounced the program of Slovak autonomy as a bourgeois policy and stated that "only a few adventurers, in the service of Warsaw and Budapest, play with the idea of separation." As to the German minority areas, "there is no irredentist movement there, and no one would understand it if we—as if falling from the moon—came with the proposal to separate this area and join with Germany."[19]

However, under the impact of Zinoviev's criticism the Second Congress of the Party in October 1924 rectified its previous stand on the national question and declared: "The attempts to prove that the right of self-determination in Czechoslovakia for economic, political, or other reasons, up to separation from the state, cannot be at all exploited imply an objective support of Czechoslovak imperialism. The party cannot accept the bourgeois swindle about a Czechoslovak state-nation, through which the Czech bourgeoisie wants to conceal the colonial exploitation and bloody suppression of the Carpathian Ukraine and Slovakia and of the oppressed national minorities."[20]

The resolution was a victory for those opposed to Šmeral. As the party became purer, however, its ranks also became thinner. Its membership dropped from 400,000 in 1921 to 130,000 in 1923 and below 100,000 in 1925.[21] It did succeed, however, in almost mortally weakening the Social Democratic Party. In the national elections in November 1925 the Communist Party carried, all at

[18] Reimann, *op.cit.*, p. 156. [19] *Ibid.*, pp. 207, 217.
[20] *Ibid.*, p. 217. [21] Chmelař, *loc.cit.*

the expense of the Social Democrats, forty-one seats in the Chamber of Deputies. Nevertheless, the more internationalist and violent it was, the more it subsequently lost, not only in membership but also in popularity. In the next elections, in 1929 and 1935, its representation dropped to thirty deputies.

Once more the Third International criticized Šmeral at the session of its enlarged Executive Committee. Zinoviev was joined by Stalin, who in 1928 carried the criticism of the Czechoslovak party leadership, then without Šmeral, to the Sixth Congress of the Communist International.[22]

At the Sixth Congress of the Communist Party of Czechoslovakia, the post-Šmeral leadership, then in the hands of Jílek, was defeated by a new man—Klement Gottwald.

Gottwald entered the party in 1921. Four years later he was elected to its Central Committee and appointed as head of the Agitprop (Agitation and Propaganda Bureau). In 1929 he was elected General Secretary of the Czechoslovak Party.

Gottwald was Stalin's choice. In the preceding year, he had been picked by him to become the first Czechoslovak member of the Executive Committee of the Communist International. Gottwald never forgot the dictum that "for all communists Stalin's words are an immutable law." As Stalin's laws changed he was always flexible enough to follow in his zigzagging footsteps. An exceptionally able opportunist, he survived all purges—against Trotskiists, leftists, rightists, and Titoists.

Elected to the Party's highest office in 1929, he opened a determined campaign for the real bolshevization of the party. At that time, the term implied revolutionary activities, ruthless actions against bourgeois governments, relentless attacks on social-fascists as the former comrades in the Social Democratic Party ranks were called, and complete disregard for national considerations.[23]

[22] Reimann, *op.cit.*, p. 247.

[23] The two writers on the Communist Party of Czechoslovakia, Reimann and Kopecký, while disagreeing on the meaning of almost all other events in the

On a program of an international, class, revolutionary struggle, such people as R. Slánský, A. Zápotocký, V. Široký, J. Dolanský, and V. Kopecký were elected with Gottwald to the Central Committee. We shall find them all after World War II among the ranks of Czechoslovak "patriots," playing the role of ardent nationalists.

In an important speech in the Parliament in December 1929 Gottwald declared a war of violence against the government. When accused of accepting command from Moscow he admitted his going there "to learn—you know what? We go to Moscow to learn from the Russian bolsheviks how to twist your neck. And you know that Russian bolsheviks are masters at it."[24]

In a number of public statements he made his attitude well known. The Czechoslovak foreign policy was one of "hypocrisy and imperialist aggressivity." Czechoslovakia was to him "a nation's jail"; as to nationalism, "as long as the bourgeoisie rules," he stated, "the worker has no homeland, is nowhere at home. Only when there will be here such a situation as in the USSR shall we have a workers' homeland." He spoke against capitalists, promised collectivization, the annulment of debts and taxes, expropriation of banks, factories, businesses, and homes. The patriotic gymnasts' organization, the *Sokol*, was to him a "chauvinistic organization of the bourgeoisie." All progressive measures proposed by socialist parties were "just a game, a farce, treachery."[25]

Another of Gottwald's associates, Kopecký, declared in the Parliament on November 26, 1930, "It is in our program to struggle for the self-determination of nations to the point of secession. We fight against the Versailles Treaty . . . , against

---

history of the party—Reimann's book having been published in 1929, Kopecký's in 1951—are in agreement that Gottwald should have the credit for giving the party a truly bolshevik direction. Reimann, *op.cit.*, p. 156. Václav Kopecký, *30 let KSČ* (Thirty Years of the Communist Party of Czechoslovakia), Prague, Svoboda, 1951, pp. 76-79.

[24] Kopecký, *30 let KSČ*, *op.cit.*, p. 100.

[25] Klement Gottwald, *Spisy* (Works), vol. III, Prague, Svoboda [n.d.], pp. 13, 14, 250, 267.

the peace treaties on which is founded the imperialist domination of the Czechoslovak bourgeoisie and the submission of the oppressed nations of Czechoslovakia." On March 27, 1931 he stated that the "Czech nation cannot be free as long as Czechoslovakia exists," and he promised that communists will fight for "the self-determination . . . of the oppressed [minority] part of the German nation, right up to secession, in the interest of the proletarian revolution . . . for the right of the unification of all parts of the German nation into one entity."

Zápotocký spoke on February 3, 1931 about the "rotten country" of Czechoslovakia and on November 7, 1934 he joined other communist leaders in praising the communist understanding of the principle of self-determination.[26]

Even after such statements as these the democratic government of Czechoslovakia continued to tolerate the Communist Party, permitting it to enjoy the privileges of liberty for the purpose, openly advocated, of destroying it. It was the only communist party in Central and Eastern Europe which was allowed by law to function.

Such statements were, of course, typical of those made by communist leaders in the first half of the 1930's. They are reviewed here only for the purpose of comparison with the speeches Gottwald and others made during and after World War II. Only the names of the speakers were recognizably the same.

However, as early as 1935 the tune had begun to change. The Soviet Union and the communist movement were then threatened by Hitler's Germany and fascism. In May of 1935, Russia signed a treaty of alliance with "bourgeois" Czechoslovakia. Gottwald now approved of the Czechoslovak foreign policy; he appealed to the socialist parties, "the yellow social-fascists" of yesterday, to create a popular front with communists and promised them support even if they remain in the government, as long as it was in the interests of the working class; he offered to defend the

[26] V. Krajina, *Komunismus v praksi* (Communism in Practice), Vancouver, 1950, from a manuscript, pp. 4, 11, 12-13.

country's independence and struck a strange patriotic note by reminding the nation of its great Hussite past.

The party voted in 1938 against the national budget as a whole but rallied its vote behind the budget of the President of the Republic and the Ministry of Foreign Affairs to manifest, as it stated, its support for the Republic, its foreign policy, and defense.

Gottwald spoke against the danger of dismemberment of Czechoslovakia which he had been ready to parcel out only a few years before in the name of Lenin's views on the right of self-determination. On June 24, 1938 he stated in an interview for the American *New Masses*, "We want the whole world to know that the Nazis lie when they assert that Czechoslovakia is an artificial state. We have one of the oldest civilizations in Europe. . . ."[27] With the Soviet Union in danger, Gottwald became a Czechoslovak patriot.

[27] Klement Gottwald, *Deset let*, Sborník statí a projevů, 1936-1946 (Ten Years, A Collection of Articles and Speeches, 1936-1946), Prague, Svoboda, 1948, p. 99.

FROM MUNICH TO SUPER-MUNICH

No study of the communization of Czechoslovakia can ignore the Munich crisis in September 1938.

For twenty years, since its birth, the Czechoslovak Republic had adhered faithfully to the ideals of democracy, to the League of Nations, to the alliance with France, and to her friendship with Great Britain. These were her convictions, her tradition, her way of life. Then, in September 1938 at Munich, all this was destroyed by the hands of her allies and friends. The Czechoslovak people have never recovered from the blow. A wound was opened that would never heal, a wound that was to be a willing host to communist infection.

A Shrewd Maneuver

The Soviet Union and the Communist Party of Czechoslovakia exploited well the tragic events of the Munich crisis. Bound by the treaty of alliance of May 16, 1935 to come to the assistance of Czechoslovakia only in case France would fulfill her obligations, the Soviet Union repeatedly stated its readiness to meet this commitment. It is now known that Moscow repeated her assurances, deeply confident of French inaction.

A conversation which Litvinov had as early as May 11, 1938 in Geneva with Arnošt Heidrich, the closest diplomatic aide to President Beneš, throws a most interesting light on the policy which the Soviet Union pursued at that time and for the following three years. Litvinov told Heidrich that he considered war absolutely inevitable. However, the Soviets knew, he stated, that the West wanted to liquidate Stalin by Hitler and Hitler by Stalin. Such a policy would not succeed because the Soviets had a very good memory about what the West did in the First World War. After the battle of the Marne, instead of launching an offensive action, the Western allies waited until the full strength of the German army could exhaust itself in the struggle against Russia. This would not be repeated; this time the Soviets would wait to see how the Germans fought with the West, and they would intervene only at the end to secure a just peace. "If France goes to your aid, then Russia will go too," said Litvinov to Heidrich, "but Beneš is fundamentally wrong if he thinks that France will come to Czechoslovakia's help."[1]

The calculation proved correct and the Soviet Union reaped a rich harvest; its prestige grew, not only in Czechoslovakia but in almost all countries of Central and East Europe. People believed that the Soviet Union was the only power ready to stand up against an aggressive Nazi Germany. Indeed, it was able to pose as the single champion of the independence of small nations.

The Munich crisis and the position of France and Great Britain also presented the Communist Party of Czechoslovakia with a golden opportunity. For years it had agitated against the independence and democracy of Czechoslovakia, nay, against its existence. Now, in 1938, with the blessing, indeed at the orders, of the Soviet Union, it joined the ranks of the defenders of democracy and of the territorial integrity of Czechoslovakia. On a memorable day in September 1938, when a great Czech patriot of conservative views, L. Rašín, whose father had been assassinated in 1923 by a communist, spoke to a huge crowd from the balcony of the Parliament, Klement Gottwald, the Secretary General of the Party, supported him and declared that the masses wished to fight for the democratic ideals of Thomas Garrigue Masaryk. It would be difficult to assess to what extent the Communist Party of Czechoslovakia gained new adherents for its stand on Munich, but people were undoubtedly impressed.

The Munich calamity threw the whole nation into a maelstrom of political chaos and moral confusion. The grief was too pain-

[1] From an interview with Mr. Heidrich, June 13, 1958.

ful to produce constructive thinking; the impotence was too manifest to produce any action. On October 28, 1938, the twentieth anniversary of the Republic, the Prague populace, in a mass demonstration of its feelings, wore black clothing or black ribbons and laid flowers at the imposing statue of Jan Hus in the center of the ancient Oldtown Square.

The Communist Party, now outlawed by the new government, subservient to Berlin, still rode the wave of national sentiment. As an official source published after the putsch of 1948 described the period, "the Communist Party of Czechoslovakia remained faithful to the 28th of October," and in its proclamation rejected "all the slanders of T. G. Masaryk, Dr. Beneš, and of everything that was democratic and progressive in the first Republic. . . ." It asked its members "to prove that they created the Republic and will create it again."[2]

Two months later, on March 7, 1939, the Czech people again gave a silent and dignified expression of their feelings and convictions. On that day, the anniversary of the birth of Masaryk, they went in great crowds to his simple grave at Lány. Communists ascribed the eloquent manifestation to themselves, saying that "the Communist Party of Czechoslovakia defended Masaryk's bequest," that people demonstrated their adherence "to the great tradition of truth and democracy," that, in fact, it was the party "which organized the mass excursion to the grave at Lány" as "the Communist Party . . . in spite of differences of opinion and his lack of understanding of Marxism valued in Masaryk a great fighter for national freedom."[3]

Lack of understanding it was, indeed. Masaryk had written scholarly works in which he had condemned Marxism as a pseudo-science, and its practices as inhuman, brutal, and antisocial. On the other hand, while he was at this time, in the tragic days of 1938-1939, recognized by the communists as a great

[2] *KSČ v boji za svobodu* (The Communist Party of Czechoslovakia in the Struggle for Freedom), Prague, Svoboda, 1949, pp. 35-36. (Hereafter referred to simply as *KSČ*.)

[3] *Ibid.*, pp. 53, 54.

humanist and a fighter for freedom, only ten years before, in 1929, the official party ideologist, Reimann, had condemned him as a lackey of Western imperialism. Ten years after these tragic days another Party ideologist, Kopecký, did exactly the same.[4]

The Time of Darkness

The ardent patriotism of Czechoslovak communists, which had burst out so suddenly during the Munich crisis, lasted little more than one year. On March 15, 1939 the German army occupied Czechoslovakia and Hitler declared a protectorate over her western provinces, Bohemia and Moravia. Slovakia was compelled by Berlin to declare her independence and she became a German puppet state.

The communist leaders, following what seems a prearranged plan, took refuge abroad. Gottwald, Slánský, Kopecký, and Nejedlý escaped to Moscow; Nosek, Hodinová, and Kreibich to London; Šverma and Clementis to Paris. Some, such as Zápotocký and Dolanský, were caught when trying to cross the border and were sent to concentration camps. The leadership passed into the hands of less known functionaries. On the day of the German occupation of Czechoslovakia, the communist leaders issued a declaration which condemned equally the German fascist invaders and the Czech reactionary bourgeoisie.[5]

In Slovakia a group of Slovak patriots met—the best intellectual and political representatives of the nation—to protest publicly against the violent detachment of the country from Czechoslovakia. "There is no record of communist protest," wrote a prominent Slovak democrat.[6]

Official communist documents, published after the February 1948 putsch, describe in detail the organization of the party as it was adjusted to the new situation and to illegal work. They

[4] Reimann, *op.cit.*, p. 58; Kopecký, *Tridsať rokov*, *op.cit.*, p. 6.

[5] *KSČ*, *op.cit.*, pp. 63-64.

[6] Jozef Lettrich, *History of Modern Slovakia*, New York, F. A. Praeger, 1955, p. 135.

also reproduce several articles which were published in a special issue of *Švetový rozhled* on July 10, 1939, printed in Paris. The issue is full of invectives directed at France and England, of denunciation of the Czech "reactionary bourgeoisie," and of Marxist views on the international situation. The documents point to a united opposition of the Czechoslovak people to the Nazi regime and call for active struggle against it. Their nationalist tone is strongly apparent.[7]

One document offers an enlightening insight into the political attitude of the Communist Party toward the Czechoslovak struggle for independence. Called "Directives about the political work of the Party abroad," it was issued as a secret paper in June 1939 in Paris by the party secretariat for foreign affairs. Stating in the opening paragraph the leading role of the party in the struggle for Czechoslovakia's liberation, the directive then turns its attention to the importance of its members' activities abroad. It points to the advanced state of the organization and activities of the democratic *émigré* groups, led by Dr. Beneš, and is critical of the delay in the ranks of communists. It stresses the necessity of creating a united front of all Czechs and Slovaks abroad and of cooperation with Beneš, "without giving up the party's independent attitude." The directive asks for mobilization of all anti-fascist forces and in particular for close contact with other communist parties. The Czechoslovak cause must become a matter of all progressive elements and must be disconnected from the power interests of the West. The party must remind the world of the great patriotic names in the history of the nation.

"In the question of the leadership of the Czechoslovak liberation movement abroad, the party must have a clear political and tactical attitude, first of all, toward the role of Dr. Beneš. . . ," continues the statement. It is ready to cooperate with him, but it must deny him, in view of his bankrupt policy at the time of

[7] *KSČ*, *op.cit.*, pp. 72-76. *Za svobodu českého a slovenského národa, Sborník dokumentů* (For the Freedom of the Czech and Slovak Nation, A Collection of Documents), Prague, Státní nakladatelství politické literatury, 1956, pp. 44-51, 57-78.

Munich, the place of a leader, which belongs "only to the Communist Party led by Klement Gottwald." "Of course, the party must choose the right tactic" in this question but it must at the same time insist on its leading role and see to it "that from all corners of the world . . . the wish is expressed (by resolutions, telegrams, letters, delegations, etc.) that Klement Gottwald must be in the political leadership of the Czechoslovak liberation movement abroad. . . ."[8]

In contrast to this secret directive, the Czechoslovak Minister to Moscow, Zdeněk Fierlinger, was asked on various occasions by Czech communists in Moscow to convey to Beneš their wish for loyal cooperation and their recognition of his leadership.[9]

The directive continued, "Communists must everywhere be prominent by their devotion to the cause of Czechoslovak independence. . . . They must also join the preparations for the organization of military formations abroad. . . ." Also, they "must defend the view that one must not just wait for the development of the liberation struggle" in which the Czech nation "will receive support from the Soviet Union, the most powerful country in the world."[10]

It will be noted that the directive was issued in June 1939, in the period of "deep peace," of not only the appeasement of Germany by the Western powers but also of the first appeasement feelers from the Soviet Union.

The communists' patriotic zeal and fighting enthusiasm did not last long and the implementation of the directive had to be postponed for two years. Without their knowledge Stalin had been in secret contact with Hitler since April of 1939.

On March 10, 1939, five days before the occupation of Czechoslovakia, Stalin spoke before the Eighteenth Congress of the Communist Party of the Soviet Union. He stressed that the

[8] *Za svobodu českého a slovenského národa, op.cit.*, pp. 84-103.

[9] Z. Fierlinger, *Ve službách ČSR* (In the Service of the Czechoslovak Republic), 2 vols., Prague, Dělnické nakladatelství, 1947, 1948. Vol. 1, pp. 210, 234.

[10] *Za svobodu. . . , loc.cit.*

Soviet Union stood for peace and particularly for "close and friendly relations with all neighboring countries. . . ." He defined the task of the party, among others, "to be cautious and not to allow our country to be drawn into conflicts by warmongers who are accustomed to have others pull the chestnuts out of the fire for them."[11] The "pull the chestnuts" remark was pointedly repeated by Molotov on May 31, 1939.

The dark diplomatic game began. On March 18 Litvinov sent a note of protest to Germany against the occupation of Czechoslovakia, saying that the Soviet Union refused to recognize it. One month later, however, on April 17, the Soviet Ambassador in Berlin, Merekalov, after an eleven-month interval, visited the State Secretary in the German Foreign Office, Baron von Weiszäcker, "to discuss a matter of particular interest to him: namely, the fulfillment of certain contracts for war materiel by the Škoda Works [in Bohemia]."[12]

Then, on May 17, the Soviet Chargé d'Affaires, Astakhov, asked the German Foreign Office to recognize the Soviet Mission in Prague as a section of the Soviet Trade Mission in Berlin, with the inevitable implication of recognizing the occupation of Czechoslovakia *de facto*.[13]

As it turned out, the subject of these Soviet diplomatic calls was only a pretext for opening a series of conversations which ensued in the Nazi-Soviet Pact and in a secret protocol signed on August 23. The first gave to Hitler a free hand against the West, the latter implied the division of Poland and the delimitation of Soviet and German spheres of influence in the Baltic and the Balkans. This was another Munich; it surpassed the first one in magnitude and ultimate consequences. This time, it was administered by the Soviet Union.

Only five days before, the Czechoslovak Minister to Moscow,

[11] Degras, *op.cit.*, vol. III, pp. 321, 322.

[12] *Nazi-Soviet Relations, 1939-1941*, Documents from the Archives of the German Foreign Office, ed. by R. J. Sontag and J. S. Beddie, Washington, Department of State, 1948, p. 1.

[13] *Ibid.*, pp. 4-5.

Fierlinger, reported as he had done before that "the general concept of the [Soviet] foreign policy was, for the foreseeable future, stabilized in every way," that "the Soviet Union would not radically change its policy and return to its former political cooperation with Germany."[14] It must be noted that Fierlinger, a Social Democrat by conviction, developed in fact into a full-fledged fellow traveller and there was no occasion on which he would be critical of Soviet foreign policy.

Among many toasts exchanged on the occasion of the signing of the Soviet-Nazi Pact, Stalin stated, "I know how much the German nation loves its Führer. I should therefore like to drink to his health. . . ." Molotov acknowledged the toast with satisfaction, and raising his glass to Stalin, noted "that it had been Stalin who—through his speech of March of this year, which had been well understood in Germany—had brought about the reversal in political relations" between the two countries.[15] If an interpretation of Stalin's "pulling the chestnuts" statement was needed, Molotov supplied it.

What followed was perhaps the blackest period in the history of Soviet diplomacy. In a few weeks the Soviet Union joined Germany in the invasion and division of Poland. A series of actions led to the annexation of the Baltic States, to a Soviet war with Finland, and to the Soviet occupation of Bessarabia. Germany was declared by Russia to be a peaceful country. The war was, in the Soviet official view, imperialistic and the West was made responsible for its continuation. Even now Fierlinger, as revealed by his numerous messages, found a way to defend the perfidious move of the Soviet government.[16]

As to Czechoslovakia, her dismemberment and occupation were soon recognized *de jure*. In September 1939 the Soviet Union extended full recognition to the Slovak state, and in November a Slovak envoy arrived in Moscow. On December 14 the Czecho-

[14] Fierlinger, *op.cit.*, vol. I, p. 237.

[15] *Nazi-German Relations*, *op.cit.*, pp. 75, 76.

[16] Fierlinger, *op.cit.*, vol. I, pp. 279-84, 286-87, 294-95.

slovak Minister, Z. Fierlinger, was notified by the head of the diplomatic protocol that the Soviet government could no longer recognize his diplomatic character. He was even not received by the Foreign Minister or any other Soviet top diplomat. This was a personal blow to the docile Fierlinger, who had before so firmly declared that "the attitude of the Soviets toward the [Czechoslovak] question was absolutely clear and firm and that the goal of an independent Czechoslovak State will remain once and for all the main requirement of their policy." However, even in this situation Fierlinger found words to defend the Soviet move.[17]

The communist documentary literature related to this period understandably omits publication of those documents which would testify to the position identical with that of the Soviet Union which Czechoslovak communist leadership took on the nature of the war. Instead, in its attempt to create the impression that it stood in the forefront of the national struggle from the beginning, regardless of Soviet-German cooperation, it quotes from various directives which Gottwald purportedly issued from Moscow for the illegal work of the party.[18]

However, other sources tell a different story; some are of communist origin, published in this period of Soviet friendship with Nazi Germany.

Against Their Own Country

In London, soon after the outbreak of the war the exiled President of the Czechoslovak Republic, Dr. E. Beneš, established a National Committee for Free Czechoslovakia. The Chamberlain and Daladier governments refused to recognize the Committee as a government. Nevertheless, although the diplomatic struggle he faced was difficult, Beneš realized that only the victory of the democratic powers could bring independence to his country.

[17] *Ibid.*, pp. 258, 287, 297, 303, 309, 313-15.
[18] *KSČ, op.cit.*, pp. 81-101.

The Czechoslovak communist group in London had met with Beneš in July 1939 and offered him "their cooperation in the common fight. . . ." They had "a number of meetings which took a hopeful turn. But when the German-Soviet treaty was concluded on August 23, 1939, their attitude to the whole of our military and political activities became reserved," remarks Dr. Beneš with diplomatic understatement.[19]

In Paris the communist group established a "foreign affairs bureau" which was led by J. Šverma, who was later called to Moscow. The official communist sources fail to mention the name of one prominent member of the Paris bureau—Vladimir Clementis.[20] He was one of the few communists who publicly denounced the Nazi-Soviet Pact. He was stripped of membership in the Central Committee and when after the outbreak of war the French authorities permitted the formation of a Czechoslovak army, Clementis, whom the French had meanwhile interned, joined the Czechoslovak forces. This was only the beginning of his deviationist crimes; in 1952 he paid for them with his life.

In Prague, three communist leaders who had the temerity to oppose the Soviet-German Pact were promptly denounced by their comrades and turned over to the Gestapo.[21]

After the fall of France, in June 1940, the London *émigré* group was considerably enlarged by arrivals from France, and the Czechoslovak army was evacuated to England. The communists attempted to disintegrate the armed forces by a revolt within its ranks. This time Clementis, trying to mend his fences with the leaders of the party, led the revolt and together with rebels was interned by British authorities. The civilian communists were sent to work in forests, but they managed to issue leaflets agitating against the imperialist war, even accusing Beneš of collaboration with Hitler.[22]

[19] *Memoirs of Dr. Eduard Beneš*, transl. by G. Lias, London, George Allen and Unwin, 1954, pp. 93-94.

[20] *KSČ*, *op.cit.*, p. 72.

[21] *The Curtain Falls*, ed. by Denis Healey, London, Lincolns-Prager, 1951. From the chapter, "Czechoslovakia," by V. Majer, p. 86.

[22] Beneš, *op.cit.*, p. 143.

The Moscow group led by Gottwald was the most important among the exiled communist leaders. As to their attitude toward the war in the period of Nazi-Soviet friendship, the fact that the official party collection of Gottwald's speeches and articles between 1936-1946 does not record a single one in the period between March 15, 1939 and July 29, 1941 is eloquent testimony.[23] He did make a series of broadcasts, but they were devoted to praising the Soviets' peace efforts, the construction of dams, Soviet prosperity, and Soviet nursery schools. It would have been slightly inappropriate to publish such talks in that chapter of the collection titled "V boji za národní svobodu" (In the Fight for National Freedom).

In Czechoslovakia, communist leadership was active in passing resolutions and publishing leaflets. However, those which are characteristic of the communist policy at that time are either not mentioned in the documents published by the party after 1948 or conveniently differ from the original text.

For example, in the fall of 1939, shortly after the Nazi-Soviet Pact had been signed and the war begun, the Communist Party of Czechoslovakia issued a declaration in which it attacked France and England and warned the Czech nation "not to be misled by the words which are being poured upon [them] by Beneš and Masaryk." Attacking those people who believe that "everything that is aimed against Germany can only be to the benefit" of the Czech nation, the declaration condemned this interpretation of war as "thoroughly false . . . ," and continued, "Those who speak in this way have listened too much to Czech broadcasts from Paris and London, which are filled with as many lies as the *Reichssender*." The declaration—blissfully ignoring the party's patriotic statements of a year before—spoke of the Czechoslovak Republic as a country which had been created by peace treaties "for imperialistic and exploitative reasons . . . to guard Germany." "Indeed," ended the declaration, "we cannot wish the victory of Germany, but neither can we wish the victory of England and

[23] *Deset let, op.cit.*, pp. 133, 144.

France because that would mean only to get out of the mud and into the mire."[24]

In January 1940 the communist leadership in Prague published another leaflet in which Beneš was attacked for his friendly co-operation with the Polish government in London.[25] And in yet another leaflet published on October 28, 1940, the national holiday of Czechoslovakia, the Communist Party accused Beneš of supporting "the dirty struggle of the English colonial landlords" and of abusing for such a purpose "the good Czech nation and the blood of its honest sons."[26]

On December 15, 1940 the Executive Committee of the party carried a resolution which states graphically and in detail the party's attitude toward the world situation and the position of Czechoslovakia. The date is significant. Molotov had been in Berlin in November and Soviet-German friendship was at its warmest. France had been defeated in June. Great Britain was determined to continue the war and the United States supported her morally and materially.

In this resolution, the United States and Great Britain were attacked as the chief imperialist powers. The United States was accused of fomenting enmity and war between Germany and the Soviet Union while herself remaining out of the war, so that she might decide the final outcome later in her own favor. However, declared the resolution, it would be the strong Soviet Union, in conjunction with the international working class and all oppressed nations, which would determine the results of the war. The Soviet Union's neutrality was, according to the resolution, making the preponderance of either bloc impossible and thus preventing the danger of an imperialist victory. The resolution continued:

"Soviet-German friendship represents the cornerstone of the international situation against which the imperialist and anti-

[24] V. Krajina, *op.cit.*, from a manuscript, pp. 17-18.

[25] From a copy of the leaflet, dated January 1940.

[26] Krajina, *op.cit.*, from a manuscript, p. 22.

Soviet plans of the Anglo-French bloc have already been dashed to pieces and against which the criminal intentions of the United States of America are now dashing themselves to pieces. The historical importance of the journey of comrade Molotov to Berlin is based on the fact that, on the basis of the continuation of friendly relations between Germany and the Soviet Union, this journey frustrated the plans of the United States to spread the war and turn it toward the East. [The preceding sentence is omitted in the communist documentary source.] The USSR will continue to use the differences between the imperialists to strengthen its own position and will watch for the arrival of the right moment for the final disruption of capitalism. On the basis of its peace policy, the USSR continually earns greater sympathy among all nations, especially among the working people of the great German nation."

Continuing in a strictly Marxist interpretation of the war and the world situation, the resolution, in an equally Marxist vein, then violently attacked Beneš, who "has placed himself still more in the service of British imperialism and is bolstering the disappointed ranks of his followers by inculcating faith in the United States of America." His policy was, the resolution said, aimed at reestablishing "capitalist rule" and was "a new manifestation of total political decrepitude of the political representatives of the Czech bourgeoisie." He was blamed for "chasing Czech citizens into the British imperialist army," for calling the "imperialist war a liberation war"—all these things marking him an agent of the Anglo-Americans, "extremely hostile to the interests of the Czech national liberation fight and most dangerous."

Beneš and his group, the resolution continued, "is a permanent threat that the Czech nation will be fatally misused and led into a tragic collision with the German revolutionary workers and with our chief hope and support, the Socialist Fatherland of all workers, the Soviet Union."

It was the Communist Party of Czechoslovakia, the resolution insisted, that had exposed Beneš, and the people's capacity to resist his chauvinist anti-German activity was growing.[27]

On the occasion of the treaty of friendship which the Soviet Union and Yugoslavia signed on April 5, 1941 the Central Committee rushed into print still another resolution which contained a new directive. Beginning with the old refrain of Beneš' "treacherous" cooperation with the West, it asked for a new solidarity of the Central European nations with the Soviet Union on the basis of the principle of self-determination. Pointedly, however, it stressed "that it is incorrect to use *now* the 'slogan of a Czech or Slovak Soviet Republic.' But it is suitable to apply *now* [author's italics] such slogans as: 'For the freedom of the Czech, Slovak nation under the protection of the power and strength of the Soviet Union.' " Nor was the Slav solidarity appeal to be neglected. Another suggested slogan was, "The future of the small Slav nations, the future of Czechs and Slovaks is defended by the Soviet Union."[28]

Embarrassingly enough, the Soviet-Yugoslav treaty which had generated this new party line was denounced one month later by the Soviet Union in a desperate effort to continue German appeasement. But one part of the directive hammered away at a consistent party line: that the work of the party must be the guarantee that after the collapse of German domination, power "will not pass into the hands of the old Beneš government but that power will be passed in the name of national and social liberation into the hands of the Czech people, Czech workers."[29]

On May 1, the Central Committee of the party issued still another manifesto, in which the plutocrat Beneš was condemned for working "for the England of Lords," and the Czech people were asked to base their struggle "on class solidarity with the German worker."[30]

[27] Beneš, *op.cit.*, pp. 160-62. The full text of the resolution is in the archives of V. Krajina, 20 pp. An adjusted text is in *Za svobodu českého a slovenského národa, op.cit.*, pp. 125-50.

[28] *Za svobodu českého a slovenského národa, op.cit.*, pp. 151-59.

[29] *Ibid.* [30] A copy of the text is in the archive of V. Krajina.

The reasoning of the Czechoslovak communists, as expressed in these continuing manifestos, is beyond comprehension unless it is thoroughly understood as blind ideological subservience to Moscow. Czechoslovakia was occupied by the German armed forces; her truly patriotic leaders were being killed or sent into concentration camps, her economy was being pillaged, her culture Germanized, her universities closed. It is now known that Hitler had planned to exterminate most of the nation and exile the rest to Siberia, and it was the Soviet Union which was actively helping Germany in this policy. To the Czechoslovak people Great Britain was their only hope, and Dr. Beneš was the symbol of their aspiration for eventual freedom. To them, the attitude of the Communist Party of Czechoslovakia made no sense from the standpoint of Czechoslovak national interests. In fact, such utterances, Moscow-controlled, could be thought of only as callously treacherous or incredibly naïve.

Then, seven weeks after the May 1 resolution had been carried, Germany invaded the Soviet Union. The world's military and political situation suddenly shifted, and with it the policy of the Communist Party of Czechoslovakia. It was this change which unhappily but inevitably opened the door to the grand strategy of communist infiltration.

IN THE GUISE OF PATRIOTS

Both the policy of President Beneš during the war and the attitude of the Czechoslovak communists can be understood only in the light of certain relations among the three Big Powers.

Great Britain and the United States, anxious to establish an atmosphere of confidence in their contacts with the Soviet Union, made many military and political decisions that were principally designed to prove to Stalin their continuing good will, not only in their wartime relations but also in an eventual time of peace. The opinion prevailed in the West that after the war Stalin would channel his country's energies into the reconstruction of devastated Russia, would liberalize the Soviet regime, and would abandon the policy of fomenting communist unrest abroad. Certain measures taken by him appeared to support this opinion. In May 1943 the Third International was dissolved, with the explanation that individual communist parties had taken root in their respective national soil. The national anthem of the Soviet Union, the Internationale, which was also the song of international communism, was replaced by a highly nationalistic composition. In September 1943, Stalin received in a solemn audience two dignitaries of the Russian Orthodox Church which had been brutally persecuted since 1917, and thereafter some religious freedom was granted to Church activities. On no occasion did Stalin speak about communism as an issue in the war, but only about democracy and freedom. The imperialist war of yesterday became the great patriotic war.

Aware of the impending attack by Germany on the Soviet Union, in spite of increasing and desperate attempts to appease her, the Third International on May 9, 1941 had issued instructions to the communist parties which remained in many respects valid for the rest of the war. The "Directive for future work" stated, in part:

"1. The time has now come when decisive new steps must be taken along the path to world revolution. The obstacles to be overcome are still formidable and call for a new tactical flexibility which must be carefully worked out and boldly practiced along the following lines:

"(a) The Communist world revolution must be presented as a series of measures to achieve 'true democracy' and all political and military leaders of the Communist Movement must depict their activity in this light. Up to 30 per cent of party members may come out into the open as 'front-line fighters for democracy' in the eyes of the masses.

"(b) The government of the Soviet Union may also find it necessary to make temporary concessions in the same sense in order to further the revolutionary cause in those countries where conditions demand it.

"(c) Until the seizure of power, the Communist Party of the country where revolution is being prepared should be careful to maintain good relations with patriotic and religious circles. No discrimination should be made against the Churches; each should be treated on the same footing in the eyes of the masses. National traditions too should be respected. . . ."[1]

In the Name of Independence and Democracy

Within the new framework of Soviet and Anglo-American relations the policy of the Soviet Union toward Czechoslovakia shifted dramatically on the day of the German invasion. So, too, did the attitude of the Czech communists. The piper in the

[1] Stephen Clissold, *Whirlwind*, London, The Cresset Press, 1949, pp. 238-39. After a prolonged but unsuccessful inquiry about the original source of the Directive of the Third International, the author wrote to Stephen Clissold. He answered that he "got to know of it through the dossiers of the pro-German Serbian police which he had an opportunity of seeing at one time. . . . I think there is little reason to doubt its authenticity," he concluded.

Kremlin still called the dance—but it was a remarkably different tune.

Within two weeks the Soviet Ambassador in London, Ivan Maisky, paid a visit to President Beneš to communicate an official message from Moscow. "The Soviet Union stands for the independence of Czechoslovakia and does not intend to interfere in any way with the internal affairs of the Czechoslovak Republic which solely concern the Czechoslovak people," read the message.[2]

To his friends in the underground in Czechoslovakia Beneš evaluated Maisky's statement in the following way: "The Soviet declaration concerning our internal affairs can be taken seriously. The Soviets, as a state, will actually proceed in this manner. Naturally, the Comintern and the Communist Party will carry on their policy as before. On the other hand, our communists here and at home have no influence, or very little, on the course taken by the Russian government and state. During the entire negotiations with Maisky there was not the slightest indication from the Soviet side that they would request anything in regard to our communists."[3]

Beneš was not taken in by the Soviet government's statement. As a scholar he was acquainted with communist literature; as a statesman he knew more than enough about Soviet and communist tactics. The memory of the preceding two years, from August 1939 to June 1941, was still too fresh for him to accept the Soviet assurance at face value. Equally if not more fresh was the excruciating memory of Munich, of the West's betrayal. The specter haunted Beneš for the rest of his life; indeed, it overshadowed his mistrust of the Soviets. Czechoslovakia must never again be exposed to even a possibility of another Munich—this became the cornerstone of his policy.

From the inception of the war Beneš expected Russia, sooner

[2] Beneš, *op.cit.*, p. 156.

[3] E. Taborsky, "Beneš and the Soviets," *Foreign Affairs*, vol. 27, p. 309. The author was President Beneš' personal secretary during the war and is in possession of many important documents.

or later, to be drawn into the conflict on the side of the West. This calculation proved correct in June 1941. Another historical event, the entry of the United States into the war in December of that year, strengthened still another conviction. This grand alliance, he reasoned, would establish a new balance of power in which both sides would be interested in assuring to the small countries in the heart of Europe an independent life. This was his goal, and the Soviet message was to him the first confirmation that he was on the right path. It became the basic principle of his policy to establish close relations with all major powers in the allied camp, and in particular he wished to demonstrate to Moscow his good will, his determination that Czechoslovakia would always cooperate with the Soviet Union. As time went by, his anxiety to convince Stalin of his sincerity led to decisions which implied a sacrifice of other principles dear to his democratic convictions. However, he believed such steps to be justified by one consideration overriding all dangers: that friendship to Russia would buy respect for Czechoslovakia's independence and for the principle of non-interference in her internal affairs. Once this was guaranteed, Czechoslovakia's democracy would be able to cope with the communists as it had before the war. From Stalin he received the first assurance, and many more were to follow. If in retrospect his hopes and his subsequent actions now seem somewhat reckless or naïve, it can only be said that the total perfidy of the communist mind no civilized man is able to comprehend, no man of good will is able to believe.

Meanwhile, the Czechoslovak communist leaders played their new roles masterfully. Gottwald, the Secretary-General of the party, after more than two years of political silence, appeared before the microphone on July 29, 1941 in Moscow and delivered a fiery patriotic message to the Czech nation. His broadcasts became a regular feature. They were inbued with love of country, devotion to freedom and democracy, with no mention of communism, class struggle, and revolution, the old-time shot and shell of the communist arsenal. He went so far as to quote from

Czech patriotic, conservative poets. On the anniversary of the death of Jan Hus he extolled the greatness of this religious and national leader; on the anniversary of the Czechoslovak day of independence he reminded his listeners of the glorious past of the Republic.[4] Indeed, on one occasion when a social democrat, B. Laušman, went from London to Moscow in the fall of 1942 and in discussions with the communist group there mentioned socialist principles of the future Czechoslovak economy, they opposed the idea energetically and continued to speak about "the interests of the state, the nation, about democracy and freedom."[5]

The patriotic zeal of the Czechoslovak communists in Moscow was accompanied by comparable manifestations of nationalism from other quarters. On August 10, 1941, an All-Slav Congress opened in Moscow. In traditional communist ideology, this was a heresy of unprecedented order: Slav solidarity was an ultra-reactionary idea, based on the racial affinity of the Slav nations, an instrument of Czarist expansionist policy. Now Moscow was to become the center of neo-Panslavism. Alexei Tolstoi, speaking before the Congress, defined the new democratic concept of Slav solidarity as a "process of uniting in order to live as equal people so that there would be no large, no small nations."[6] Such Slav Congresses were held every year during the war in Moscow and in many other cities in the Allied world.

Throughout the war numerous messages were exchanged between Soviet political and cultural centers and the Czechoslovak groups in London. They all stressed the goal of reestablishing a free, independent, democratic Czechoslovakia. Such prominent writers as Ilya Ehrenburg, writing in *Pravda,* spared no superlatives in his praise of Czechoslovak culture and the fame of Czechoslovak history. The Soviet writer V. Litin wrote in *Izvestiia* about Jan Hus and the immortality of Czech culture. A governmental publishing house had time and money to publish

[4] *Deset let, op.cit.,* p. 144ff.

[5] B. Laušman, *Kdo byl vinen?* (Who Was Guilty?), Austria, n.d., p. 29.

[6] *Čechoslovák* (London), vol. 3, no. 33, August 15, 1941.

Comenius' *Orbis Pictus*. General Ignatiev was ordered to commit the complete heresy of reminiscing in a warm way about his contacts with T. G. Masaryk and Beneš during and after the First World War.[7]

There was, of course, a parallel development among the Czechoslovak communists in London. They founded several organizations such as the British-Czechoslovak Friendship Club, the Young Czechoslovakia, the Women's Club, all operating under a patriotic mantle and never mentioning their communist affiliation. The Young Czechoslovakia group had existed since the first days of the war. For almost two years it had sabotaged the efforts of the Czechoslovak officials to organize a Czechoslovak army in England. It had developed a systematic campaign to convince Czechoslovak citizens not to respond to the call to the colors.

Then, on August 9, 1941, the Central Committee of Young Czechoslovakia issued a proclamation calling for the unity of all Czechoslovaks and a united struggle against Nazi Germany. It appealed to everyone to obey the order of the Czechoslovak military authorities in London to join the forces. The declaration stated, "We are proud of our brave Czechoslovak airmen who are not afraid of any sacrifice and who are hitting hard Hitler's war machine. We are proud of hundreds and thousands of our friends who fulfill their patriotic duty. . . ."

The editor of the paper which reprinted this proclamation observed dryly concerning its call to young Czechoslovaks to be in the first row of fighters for freedom: "It may be rather difficult because the first row has been definitely taken by the pilots and soldiers who died on the front in 1939 in Poland and in 1940 in France."[8]

On the Main Front

Although the Czechoslovak democratic leadership was in London during the war and that of the communists in Moscow,

[7] *Ibid.*, vol. 4, no. 20, May 15, 1942.
[8] *Ibid.*, vol. 3, no. 33, August 15, 1941.

the main front was in the country itself, which lay under German occupation. There, opposition to German authorities meant immediate danger to one's life.

It is not the purpose of this study to write a history of the Czechoslovak democratic underground, but a brief look at its organization and a few episodes of its contributions to the war effort serve as a comparison with the communist underground and as evidence of its leadership's attitude toward the democratic movement.

Only a few days after the Munich Conference, plans were created for an underground democratic movement. In October 1938 a group of his close associates made contact with Dr. Beneš, who was in London, through Mr. Drábek. As a result of his second visit to London, in February 1939, the first underground organization was established, called *Politické ústředí* (Political Center). It was later enlarged in ÚVOD, an abbreviation for *Ústřední vedení odboje domácího* (The Central Leadership of the Struggle on the Home Front). The group was composed of intellectuals who were for years closely associated with Dr. Beneš. Another called itself *Věrni zůstaneme* (We Shall Remain Faithful)—reflecting the last words of President Beneš over the coffin of T. G. Masaryk in September 1937. It was led by a few democratic trade union leaders and intellectuals who had been active in the Social Democratic Party educational institute, the Workers' Academy. This group, even before the Soviet Union entered the war, had published a detailed manifesto which combined the principles of democracy and socialism.[9] The third group was composed of officers and called itself *Obrana lidu* (The Defense of the Nation). The groups were in mutual contact, always through one liaison man only, and, as one of the cardinal principles of all underground activity, did not know each other's activities.[10]

[9] *Za svobodu. Do nové Československé Republiky* (For Freedom. In the New Czechoslovak Republic), Prague, Nová svoboda, 1945.

[10] V. Krajina, "La Résistance tchécoslovaque," *Cahiers d'histoire de la guerre.* Paris, February 1950, no. 3, pp. 55-76.

Communists had their own underground organization which was separate from others and was led by relatively unknown men since the leaders of the party were either in Moscow and London or in the concentration camps. A diagram of the communist organization prepared by the German secret police does not list any well-known name and at least in two instances is wrong, listing the names of two communists who were in London.[11]

Soon after the Soviet Union had entered the war the communist group approached ÚVOD with a proposal for cooperation. It was rejected. "The Molotov-Ribbentrop Pact," says Mr. Heidrich, who was at a later period of the war the chairman of ÚVOD, "the attitude of the Soviets toward Poland and toward the defensive war of the western Allies created between democrats and communists such an abyss and provoked between the two camps such distrust that these did not disappear even in the last phase of the war. . . . I want to emphasize that there never was in our country a united, democratic-communist, underground struggle."[12]

Nevertheless, the Central Committee of the party reported on September 16, 1941 that together with the central leadership of the national underground organization it had created a common National Revolutionary Committee of Czechoslovakia and issued a common proclamation. The document appealed to all citizens of Czechoslovakia to form a front of national revolutionary unity, to enter the front "of whatever party [they] may be, to whatever social strata [they] may belong because in the face of death which threatens [them] from Hitler, nothing divides us, everything unites us." A communist source reprints even a photostatic copy of the declaration of the newly-formed united underground organization (copy no. 34).[13] To this Mr. Herben remarks: "We never entered into any agreement with communists, and the name of our organization was put on their proclamation without our

[11] *KSČ*, *op.cit.*, photostatic copy no. 31a.

[12] From a letter of A. Heidrich, April 22, 1958.

[13] *KSČ*, *op.cit.*, p. 109.

knowledge. They were so compromised in the eyes of our people because of their previous policy that they needed a name of a patriotic organization to cover their past."[14]

The underground democratic movement published the newspaper *V boj* (The Fight). Herben was its editor. The design was prepared by Vojtěch Preissig, an American of Czech origin. In 1940 he was arrested and died in the Dachau concentration camp in May 1944. His wife, two daughters and their husbands were likewise detained. The daughter Olga was executed.

The hero of the democratic underground was Professor Vladimír Krajina. The head of the Nazi regime in the so-called Protectorate of Bohemia and Moravia, State Minister K. H. Frank, stated after the war that he had considered Krajina the leader of the Czechoslovak underground.[15] Before the war Krajina had been assistant professor of botany at Charles University and had studied on a scholarship for one year in the Hawaiian Islands. During the war he established a network of intelligence services and was in regular contact with London through secret radio transmitters.

Krajina wrote, "The most important informer to us was Paul Thümel, a German colonel. . . . He was the chief officer of the German intelligence service in Prague, in charge of Eastern Europe and the Balkans." Krajina was thus informed well ahead of time that Germany was planning the invasion of Russia. He passed the information on to London, which was, "including the Prime Minister Churchill," impressed by its detailed and exact nature. After 1940 he was also in contact with the Soviet intelligence service in Prague. "We had the opportunity to see that our information was of great value for the USSR while the information of the Czechoslovak communists was absolutely insignificant," states Krajina.[16]

As to the basic attitude of communists toward the war, there

[14] From an interview, June 10, 1958.

[15] From a letter of J. Drábek, April 14, 1958.

[16] "La Résistance tchécoslovaque," *op.cit.*, pp. 65, 66.

was a marked change following the invasion of Russia by the Nazi armies. Within twenty-four hours the Central Committee of the Communist Party of Czechoslovakia issued a proclamation, calling the German army "the hordes of Fascist beasts," over which the Red Army, "the heroic vanguard of mankind will be victorious." But more interesting was the attitude toward the capitalists and imperialists of a few weeks before: "All nations of the world . . . and their governments . . . especially of the most mature nations, among them America and Great Britain, have realized that the most dangerous common enemy . . . is Hitler's Fascism."[17]

It is also of interest to note, however, that the proclamation spoke about the "Czech" nation and appealed to the "Czech" people, not about the whole of Czechoslovakia. Similarly, the Slovak communist leader, V. Široký, spoke only about Slovakia, praising the Soviet Union, "the country of the happy future of Slovaks." However, he warned against any emphasis on the final goal of "the Soviet Slovakia." Gottwald, in his broadcasts from Moscow, also addressed his words only to Czechs, and avoided mentioning Czechoslovakia by name until 1943. This terminology was not coincidental; it was indicative of possible Soviet intentions to incorporate the two regions within the Soviet Union as a Soviet Czech and Soviet Slovak Republic.[18]

To describe or evaluate the wartime activities of Czechoslovak communists is a difficult task. This is likewise true of such activities in other Central and East European countries. Most of the archival materials is inaccessible and the official publications cannot be fully trusted. One impression they uniformly attempt to create is that Czechoslovak communists were the only active group in the underground movement. One communist source, published in 1949, maintains that the party was actively engaged in the struggle against Germany even during the period of German-Soviet friendship. It claims the credit for national demonstra-

[17] Beneš, *op.cit.*, pp. 162-63.

[18] *Za svobodu českého a slovenského národa*, *op.cit.*, pp. 197, 198.

tions on the historical anniversaries of the Republic, though it is reliably known that these were in fact organized by patriotic groups. Again, it insists the party was responsible for the organization of the boycott of the German-controlled press in Prague in the week between September 14 and 21, 1941.[19] It is known, however, to the author, who during the war was in charge of the broadcasts of the Czechoslovak government in London, that the action was prepared over several weeks by a patriotic organization in Prague and that the London broadcast appealed to Czechoslovak listeners to boycott the press at the request of this group.

It is quite probable that other reports about communist sabotage and guerrilla actions are of equal veracity. Though one publication quotes profusely from Gottwald's messages and instructions, and even from some Gestapo reports on activities of the communist members, no source is referred to for possible verification.[20] The publication does offer photostatic copies of illegal communist newspapers and some leaflets.

The Gruesome Story

A few of the surviving democratic leaders of the underground movement have a different story to tell. The identity of those who relate these events must first be established. They now live in the United States and have made their archives and scripts available to the author, who also questioned them by letter and interview.

Mr. Jaroslav Drábek was a prominent lawyer in Prague before the war. During the war he helped to found the first underground movement and was one of its leaders; later, in December 1942, he was arrested by the Gestapo and spent the rest of the war in Oświęcim and other Nazi prisons. After the war he was appointed as chief prosecutor in the war crimes trials for Czechoslovakia, and was in contact at the Nuremberg trials with Justice Robert H. Jackson.

[19] *KSČ, op.cit.*, p. 109.
[20] *Ibid.*, p. 110ff.

Mr. Ivan Herben belongs to one of the most respected families in Czechoslovakia. His father was an intimate friend and associate of T. G. Masaryk for forty years. He himself, before the war, was a well-known journalist. In the first part of the war he worked closely with Mr. Drábek in the same underground organization and edited the first patriotic illegal newspaper, *V boj*. After his arrest he was in the German concentration camp at Sachsenhausen. After the war he became the editor-in-chief of the daily *Svobodné slovo* and a member of the Executive Committee of the Czechoslovak National Socialists Party.

Mr. Arnošt Heidrich was for thirty years the closest associate of Dr. Beneš. In the interwar period he was his adviser for international conferences and the League of Nations. During the war he managed for a long time to escape the Gestapo and was in regular contact with Beneš through secret radio transmitters. After the war he was appointed Secretary General of the Czechoslovak Ministry for Foreign Affairs.

Professor Vladimír Krajina was, as we have seen, the chief organizer of the democratic underground.

These men are persons of unimpeachable character and what follows is in the main their version of communist underground activities in Czechoslovakia during the war.

The leaders of the wartime democratic movement are deeply convinced that many communists cooperated with the Gestapo. With them they shared undoubtedly one common interest: to liquidate democratic leaders. To this effect the democratic leaders mention several examples.

There was, for example, the incident about which Lord Vansittart spoke in the House of Lords on November 23, 1949. He opened with the sentences: "I shall tell you a story. It is an exciting story, a mixture of nobility and dirt." He then described the glorious deeds of Krajina and the precious information he supplied to the Czechoslovak government in London and to the British government. That was nobility.

Then Lord Vansittart continued:

"Now Kraina [*sic*] was not only anti-Nazi; he was anti-totalitarian. He therefore told President Beneš a great deal about Communist 'goings-on' in Czechoslovakia as well, and for that reason the Communists went about to destroy him. They were mainly responsible for his capture by the Gestapo on January 31, 1943. These dates have some significance. Kraina took poison but the Gestapo pumped him out. I may add that his brother was executed by the Gestapo in 1942, that his son died here in the Air Force in 1941 and that his wife was thrust into the abominable camp of Ravensbruck. I think I have said enough by way of preface to show that this country is greatly in debt to Professor Kraina. . . .

. . . In November 1942, the Czech government in London dropped three parachutists over Czechoslovakia. Their instructions were to link up with Kraina. They also carried letters from President Beneš and General Ingr, the Minister of Defence. But the Czechoslovak Communists intercepted those parachutists; they took away the letters; they deprived the men of their arms and impounded their transmitters—in fact, there was some exceedingly 'dirty work at the crossroads.' Moreover, these Czech Communists were known to the Gestapo, and your Lordships will therefore not be surprised to hear that these letters found their way into the hands of the Gestapo. In consequence, the parachutists were captured on January 16, 1943. Two of them were slaughtered; the third was kept alive and, by means upon which I need not enlarge, he was compelled under the supervision of the Gestapo to transmit false news to this country. But Kraina, who was arrested a fortnight later, found out what was 'in the wind' or 'on the air,' and he warned the London Government."[21]

Happily, K. H. Frank, feeling by this time that the war was going against Germany, had the idea that perhaps he might buy his own life after the war by sparing Krajina's now. He

[21] *Parliamentary Debates*, House of Lords, Official Report, vol. 165, no. 127, November 23, 1949, column 928.

therefore gave Krajina the status of prisoner of war and he miraculously survived. Krajina lives now in Vancouver, Canada.

Before the end of the war, K. H. Frank hid his archives at Štěchovice, a small place near Prague. A German soldier who had been ordered to conceal the archives fell into the hands of the American army and told them about their existence. He informed them also about an "infernal machine" attached to the gate of the cave which was to explode if an uninformed individual tried to open it. One day after the war a group of American soldiers, accompanied by the German informer, drove to the place and took the documents to the American zone of occupation. The incident provoked a diplomatic intervention on the part of the Czechoslovak government and the American authorities returned the archive directly to President Beneš. "The communists were most eager to get hold of the documents," writes Mr. Drábek, "as they assumed that they contained compromising materials." It was decided that the archive would remain in the Hradčany castle, the residence of the President, and that it would be open to one representative of each political party, to one official of the Ministry of the Interior, and to Mr. Drábek, who was the Prosecutor General in charge of the trial of K. H. Frank. "I studied the archive," writes Mr. Drábek, "with my assistant procurators. The documents confirmed to me what we had known before, that the so-called communist underground was no worry to the Germans. In his weekly reports to Berlin, Frank repeatedly stated that communists are no danger to him because he had in their organizations reliable informers." The workers' opposition to the German regime was combatted by giving them various advantages in food and cigarette rations and sending them on vacations. "On the other hand," according to Frank's reports, "the Czech intelligentsia, common people—artisans, railroadmen, mailmen—presented a different problem." It was impossible to Germanize these people and for them Frank requested the permission of *Sonderbehandlung,* special treatment, which meant execution or death in concentration camp. Hitler gave his consent to this policy.

"There is little doubt," continues Mr. Drábek, "that Czech workers were equally opposed to the Nazi regime in Czechoslovakia as was the rest of the populace. But it is true that they liked to smoke more cigarettes, to enjoy German organized vacations, and receive advantageous food rations for extra work; otherwise, however, they hated the Nazis as much as anyone else. They were simply less courageous than the intelligentsia and more materialistic—probably under the influence of the Marxist teaching."[22]

This attitude of the Czech people toward the German occupation authorities is fully supported by a document which is deposited in the Yiddish Scientific Institute—Yivo—in New York. It is a report of the Reich's Chief Security Office, which it is believed was prepared directly for Hitler, concerning the assassination of the German Reichsprotector of the Protectorate of Bohemia and Moravia, R. Heydrich, in May 1942, and concerning German reprisal measures and the reaction of the Czech people.

Reporting the reaction of the Czech people to the act of assassination, the document states that at first they displayed malicious joy but later became aware of the seriousness of the situation. However, "the workers' populace condemned, with few exceptions, the attentate, particularly in view of the personality of the Obergruppenführer. They were grateful to him for many social measures. . . . Contrary to this attitude the Czech intelligentsia and broad masses of the Czech middle class expressed from the beginning satisfaction over the attentate." When trials were held and thousands of people executed or sent to concentration camps, nervousness and fear set in, continues the report. "The attitude of the workers' populace was this time substantially different, too, from that of the intelligentsia. Expressions of sympathy from the circles of workers documented

[22] From a letter of J. Drábek, April 14, 1958.

their generally sweeping loyal behaviour." The execution of the inhabitants of the village of Lidice and its annihilation created general consternation, even among workers. "Only later was an opinion expressed by these circles which recognized the necessity of such a sharp action."

There was a general relief when the conspirators were caught, says the German security office report. "The greatest satisfaction was felt by the workers' populace. These circles expressed many times their determined will to be more active in cooperation with the Germans. . . . However, the Czech intelligentsia remained in opposition and expressed above all its doubts about the correctness of the official policy."[23]

The report is of German origin, and though it maintains that the village of Lidice was always communist it throws a strange light on the political attitude of the class which the Communist Party has claimed to lead. If it is correct, it can possibly be at least partly explained by a compromising situation in the party leadership in the district of Kladno in which the village of Lidice is located. The story is connected with the name of Karel Procházka, well known to the communist leadership though not mentioned in their official sources.

Procházka was a member of the Parliament for the Communist Party of Czechoslovakia before the war. Before the country was occupied by the Germans he had left for Moscow. There, he took special training for work in sabotage and partisan actions. One night in May 1943 he was parachuted close to Kladno, a mining district with traditional communist leanings. Kladno was to become his operational base. He easily found refuge with miners' families who had known him for many years. However, they soon became suspicious of him as one man after another with whom Procházka had come in contact was arrested by the Gestapo. Eventually, after he had served his usefulness, he too was arrested. After the war he moved freely in Kladno, though

[23] *Attentat auf Obergruppenführer R. Heydrich am 27.5.1942 in Prag*, a report submitted by Reichssicherheitshauptamt, Berlin, August 5, 1942. Annex F, pp. 1, 2, 4, 5, 7.

by that time his cooperation with the Gestapo had become publicly known. The Ministry of the Interior, which was in the hands of communists, failed to arrest him. In 1946, however, he was tried before a peoples' court, at the insistence of the Ministry of Justice. A Dr. Z. Marjánko was entrusted with the task of prosecuting such traitors and collaborators. Witnesses testified to Procházka's cooperation with the Gestapo, though the chief witness against him suddenly died under suspicious circumstances before the court could hear him. Procházka had cooperated with Gestapo confidants Fiala and Nachtman, who were at one time themselves among the leadership of the communist illegal organizations. The last two men were secretly sent to East Germany after the war to escape the arm of justice. Procházka was sentenced but released immediately after the communist putsch. His prosecutor, Dr. Marjánko, was arrested and died from torture.[24]

It appears that the case of deputy Procházka was not an isolated one. The name of Julius Fučík was made famous by communists after the war. He was pictured as one of the most courageous leaders of the communist underground, a member of the Central Committee, entrusted with political leadership and press activities. In April 1942 Fučík was caught by the Gestapo because of an "unfortunate accident. Though he was beaten almost to death he did not disclose anything." Then, according to communist reports, while in prison at Pankrác, in Prague, he wrote a manuscript which was smuggled out with the help of the jail guard, Kolinský.[25] After the war, his book *Reportáž psaná na oprátce* became famous and was translated into many languages.[26]

Some persons who saw the German police documents have a different story to tell about Fučík. Before the war Fučík was on the staff of the communist daily *Rudé právo*. He was known for his easy-going life, spending evenings in coffee houses and wine

[24] Ivan Herben, from a manuscript of a book in preparation.

[25] *KSČ*, *op.cit.*, pp. 111-12, 129.

[26] *Notes from the Gallows*, New York, New Century, 1948.

cellars—a playboy.[27] He was arrested, due to his lack of caution, talking and drinking too much. Soon after his arrest he wrote for the Gestapo a sixty-page document giving away the whole system of the communist underground organization, together with many names. Then the chief of the Gestapo anti-communist department, Josef Boehm, would take him out for walks in the Prague streets and for visits in restaurants and wine cellars. Whenever former comrades and acquaintances would greet him or talk to him they were arrested. Finally, having served the Gestapo purpose, Fučík was executed.

The wartime history of Fučík became known from Boehm himself. He was found after the war in the guise of a prisoner of war in the American zone of occupation in Germany and handed to the Czech police in Plzeň. He was investigated by Dr. Josef Mainer and informed him about Fučík. As soon as the Prague communist-controlled Ministry of the Interior heard that Boehm was in Plzeň, it hurriedly despatched its chief investigator, Major Pokorný, who seized the documents and Boehm. Boehm was then removed from the scene and was probably killed, but his investigator, Dr. Mainer, escaped in 1948 and now lives in the United States. Kolinský, the jail guard, though in the service of the Gestapo, was whisked to East Germany after the war. A certain Dr. Johanis, who had warned Fučík's friends about his association with the Gestapo, committed suicide under unexplained circumstances. Fučík's authorship of the much-publicized book is now considered highly unlikely since prisoners at Pankrác were not allowed to have pencil and paper, and the party never published more than a few facsimile pages of the manuscript itself.[28]

Another prominent communist was Jan Vodička, member of

[27] The well-known writer E. Hostovský wrote an excellent study, *The Communist Idol Julius Fucik and His Generation*, New York, National Committee for Free Europe, April 1953.

[28] From a letter of Mr. J. Drábek, April 14, 1958. From an interview with I. Herben, June 10, 1958.

the Czechoslovak Parliament. He spent the war in the concentration camp Sachsenhausen.

In most concentration camps, German communists who had been imprisoned by Hitler in 1933 were in charge of some administrative function of the camps. In some of them one could find "thriving models of ideological cooperation which ignored national boundaries. Czech and other European communists brought into German concentration camps were often saved from the 'death commandos' by fellow German Party members . . . who were in a position to help a foreign comrade by keeping him off the lists or getting him the job of 'blockleiter' for his national group."[29]

The situation was better at the Prague Pankrác prison, where no German communists were interned. One of the most important prisoners in Pankrác, a democrat, writes: "There, there was absolutely no difference between democrats and communists as far as the willingness to help each other was concerned. However, no good news was coming from the concentration camps in Germany. There, communists managed to secure from the Nazi administration various functions which perhaps, in themselves, were not of great significance. However, they were eminently important for the life of individuals in the concentration camps. The communists exploited these functions in order to win for communism many adherents, or at least supporters. As for those who were not ready to submit they made life in the concentration camp unbearable."[30]

It is here that Vodička's story begins. He managed, thanks to his German comrades, to be put in charge of the shoemaker shop, "where he was dreaded by all other prisoners. To gain the confidence of the SS men and to have some personal favors he

[29] I. Duchacek, *The Strategy of Communist Infiltration: The Case of Czechoslovakia*, New Haven, Conn., Yale Institute of International Studies, 1949, p. 25. See also Petr Zenkl, "Jak to dělali" (How They Did It), *Svornost*, March 2, 1952. This is confirmed by Dr. P. Zenkl, who spent the whole war at Buchenwald, and by Professor V. Bušek, who was interned from December 1941 at Mauthausen.

[30] From a letter of Mr. Heidrich, April 22, 1958.

pushed the prisoners into work, tried to increase their working quota, and supervised them thoroughly so that they did not waste materials though the general principle of all other prisoners was to waste as much material as possible. If any of the prisoners did not behave according to his command Vodička denounced him to the SS man. . . . Before the Soviet Union was attacked by Hitler, Vodička would say that nazism will be defeated from within by German communists who will give to the Czechoslovak Republic the place of a new protectorate with complete cultural autonomy within the framework of the Union of Soviet Socialist Republics, the capital of which will be Berlin. When, however, Hitler invaded the Soviet Union, Jan Vodička threatened everyone that the Soviet Union, after the victorious war, will add Czechoslovakia to the Soviets as one of the Union's republics. If someone didn't agree, Vodička denounced him to the Germans. He did so in a refined way. He did not report it directly to the SS men but to German communists who were heading the concentration camp administration. The verdict was clear: a transport of death. Such transports were not put together by SS men but by the camp's administration. On the basis of Vodička's denunciation, one day 48 Czech patriots were included in such a transport of death, as Vodička had branded these people to the German communists as dangerous fascists. These were former deputies, officers, generals. I shall not name any of those who are still at home and on whom Vodička could revenge himself. It is enough, perhaps, to say that I was one of these 48 condemned people. This move created among Czechs in Sachsenhausen such a panic that Zápotocký and Dr. Dolanský [two communist leaders] brought it to the attention of the German communists and in the last minute, instead of these 48 Czech patriots, 48 other prisoners who were mortally ill and about whom it was known that they would die in a few days, were substituted —which was as a rule the case with these transports."[31]

After the war, Vodička was transported from Sachsenhausen

[31] Herben, *op.cit.*, from a manuscript of a book in preparation.

to Moscow and returned to Prague only toward the end of October 1945. The party appointed him the head of its security committee, and he was also elected as chairman of the Security Committee of the National Assembly.

It would be wrong to generalize from a few cases. Undoubtedly the Communist Party had its underground organizations which did not cooperate with the Gestapo or which would not denounce the democratic underground. On the other hand, there were also instances when a democrat would succumb to torture and give away secret information. However, the behavior of some communist leaders is exposed here because after the war the Communist Party, while hiding its own culprits, deliberately accused democrats of treachery and collaboration and claimed exclusive leadership in the underground movement.

A Cloud over the Slovak Uprising

In Slovakia, relations between the communist and democratic underground movement were at first no better than in Bohemia. One of the leading democratic leaders says that "the majority of members of the . . . Czechoslovak resistance at home were recruited from the ranks of democrats and non-Communists. . . ." As to communists, "until the signing of the Nazi-Soviet Pact, they had been in the resistance. From the outbreak of the Second World War until the German attack on the USSR, the Slovak Communists remained entirely passive."[32]

It was only in September 1943 that substantial contacts were established between the democratic and communist underground leaders. In December 1943 they founded together the Slovak National Council, which formulated basic political principles for a liberated Czechoslovakia and the status of Slovakia within the country. These included guarantees for democracy, freedom of religion, and a progressive economic policy.[33]

[32] J. Lettrich, *op.cit.*, p. 195.

[33] Josef Dvořák, *Slovenská politika včera a dnes* (The Slovak Policy Yesterday and Today), Knihovna Národního osvobození, 1947, pp. 20-21; Lettrich, *op.cit.*, pp. 303-05.

In cooperation with officers, the Council prepared a plan for a national uprising. It informed the Czechoslovak government in London and the Soviet commanders. On August 4, 1944 two delegates of the Council, K. Šmidtke, a communist, and Colonel M. Ferjenčik, were flown out to the Soviet front. However, while the democrat Ferjenčik was first interned and then denied the right of open contact with the Czechoslovak Embassy in Moscow, "the delegate of Slovak communists, Karol Šmidtke, was accommodated in a hotel and had from the first day of his stay in Moscow complete freedom of movement."[34]

The communist delegate carried a secret message for Stalin from the Minister of National Defense of the pro-German puppet government of Slovakia, General F. Čatloš. The message said that the Slovak government, under the pressure of German power, had been compelled to declare war on the Soviet Union and its allies. Today, however, the German power was being broken and Slovakia "can give expression to its joy, to its feelings as a Slovak nation, which is of Slav origin, of finding a way through which its Slav brother, the Soviet Union, can become its protector and the guarantor of freedom."

Čatloš further offered to Stalin Slovak armed forces, which were under German orders, "for the common cause with the Soviet Union." The army would remain nationally independent but, after a coup, would become part of the Soviet armed forces. It would also cooperate with Czech units but on the basis of mutual independence. Slovak communists would provide contacts with the Soviet Union. The state relations would be settled after the war in the sense that they "would be decided in harmony with the interests of the Soviet Union. . . ."[35]

The proposal was, of course, disastrous to the Czechoslovak cause. To accept it would not only mean cooperation with a traitor but it would also imply a new dismemberment of Czecho-

[34] From a letter of General Ferjenčik to I. Herben, January 18, 1954.

[35] I. Herben, *Jak tomu opravdu bylo* (How It Really Was), no. 124, September 25, 1953.

slovakia, this time by the Soviet Union, and the sovietization of Slovakia.

The Czechoslovak government in London had been informed through its own secret channels of the Čatloš proposal. Beneš warned against it in a strongly-worded telegram to Fierlinger, the Czechoslovak Ambassador to Russia, and asked him to convey his feelings to the Soviet government. The proposal was handed by Šmidtke "to the Soviet authorities with the comment that it was naïve."[36]

It seems that the Deputy Foreign Minister Vyshinsky had some interest in Čatloš' message. In a conversation with Fierlinger, August 26, he "confirmed that the Soviet government had no intention to protect traitors. Vyshinsky admits at the most that even Quislings can be used for a little while for certain purposes."[37]

Fierlinger trusted the Soviet assurance. He and the Czech communists were resolutely indignant at the suspicion that the Soviet intended to exploit the Slovak traitor for political purposes. However, Šmidtke's own view about the naïveté of Čatloš' proposal was clarified at a meeting with the Czechoslovak political group, held August 27, when he stated "that it was a question of unifying all anti-German forces in Slovakia, that it would not be correct to reject his [Čatloš'] offer, stating however that it is a Moor's role, and after he fulfills it, the Moor can go."[38] It is difficult to imagine that Šmidtke would have presented such views without proper instruction from the Soviet government.

The Soviet Ambassador to the Czechoslovak government in London whom Beneš questioned on Čatloš first pleaded ignorance and then, after having received instructions from Moscow, said to Beneš, "The negotiations were conducted by the Communist Party; the Soviet government had nothing to do with it." At any rate, after Beneš' energetic protest the idea was abandoned.[39]

[36] Fierlinger, *op.cit.*, vol. II, p. 329. [37] *Ibid.*, p. 326.

[38] From a memorandum written about the meeting by one participant; it is in the possession of I. Herben.

[39] E. Táborský, "Benešovy moskevské cesty" (Beneš' Moscow Trips), *Svědectví* (New York), vol. I, nos. 3-4, p. 203.

On August 29, 1944 the Slovak national uprising was proclaimed. In a few days a good part of Slovakia was in the hands of the insurgents. The German high command sent reinforcements to close in on the revolutionaries. The Czechoslovak government in London immediately requested the Allies for help and greeted the uprising as one of the most glorious events in Czechoslovak history.

The Moscow radio was strangely silent for one full week. Apparently it could not be sure that the uprising was led by the "right" people. Nor did it wish any Central or East European nation to contribute to its liberation without a simultaneous action on the part of the Red Army. The Red Army was only eighty to one hundred miles from the liberated territory but it did not move. It did help some partisan units which were led by military and political officers who had been parachuted into Slovakia by the command of the Fourth Ukrainian Front. Urgent requests from the Czechoslovak government for assistance for the national insurgents were answered with repeated promises, but bad weather, it was alleged, prevented air operations. When it arrived it was "too late, and in an insignificant volume, and even this came only for the partisans and not for the army of the insurgents. Throughout the entire uprising, the Soviet Union sent no more than 150 anti-tank rifles, 350 infantry rifles, a few thousand mines, and a few aircraft, for which the insurgents had no fuel. Soviet reluctance to help the uprising was even more marked in the matter of flying in the Czechoslovak brigade [which was part of the Czechoslovak forces organized in the Soviet Union]. Although the weather in September 1944 was generally favorable, the Soviet Air Force took a full six weeks to fly in 2,800 men. . . . Instead of troops, the Soviet aircraft were flying in Soviet partisan officers and political commissars, as well as Czech and Slovak Communist agitators and politicians. . . ."[40]

The Allied High Command tried to help the Slovak uprising.

[40] Lettrich, *op.cit.*, pp. 210-11.

However, the assistance was militarily of little significance because political considerations prevented any major operation. Three aircraft with arms, ammunition, and drugs landed in the liberated territory on September 17. The weather, according to Soviet information, did not permit flights at that time. Then on "October 7," says Major O. H. Jakes, who served in the OSS in Bari, Italy, "we undertook the greatest operation of the kind ever organized in Bari. We loaded into the planes eighteen tons of arms, ammunition, chemicals, and other materials. . . . The Flying Fortresses were accompanied by sixty-four fighters. The plan worked perfectly."

Other attempts worked less perfectly. Major Jakes explains that the American Command in Bari had to negotiate with the Soviet Command about each planned flight. First, it would not answer; when it did, it gave such a short time for the operation that it was not possible to prepare and implement it. Or it would answer that it needed the airstrip in Slovakia for its own operations on specific days, but it was later established that the Soviet flights did not take place.[41]

A British officer, Colonel Threlfall, who also landed in Slovakia, provided an explanation by admitting "that the Western Allies were not permitted to make any military commitments to the Slovak insurgents, because Slovakia was in the sphere of Soviet military operations and there could be no Western interference in this sphere without Soviet permission."[42]

Left alone, the Slovak national uprising and its army were liquidated in about two months by the overwhelming German forces.

The first few days of jubilation over the uprising were accompanied by some confusion. A democratic paper, *Čas*, which was published in the liberated territory, commented on a meeting that "it was moving to look at the platform in the solemn hall of the Slovak National Council and to hear the words which

[41] *New Yorské Listy* (New York), April 29, 1949.
[42] Lettrich, *op.cit.*, p. 213.

confirmed that it was a brotherhood of peace and love when a priest sat next to a communist leader and cooperates."[43]

This, of course, was exactly the impression that the communists wished to create. Meanwhile, behind the scenes, not quite well-informed about the Moscow line, G. Husák, one of the communist leaders, recommended for consideration a declaration of Slovakia as one of the Soviet Republics. But when J. Šverma, a Politburo member, had been parachuted from Russia with fresh instructions the idea was quickly abandoned.[44] Nor did another communist, L. Novomeský, who was sent during the uprising from Slovakia to London, "conceal his doubts as to whether it was wise for Slovakia to remain within the small Czechoslovakia when it could join the Great Soviet Union."[45]

The Slovak uprising was a deed of the combined forces of democratic and communist leaders and officers. Nevertheless, a communist official publication states it was "the work of the Communist Party of Slovakia. . . . The Communist Party in Slovakia was the only organized force in the national liberation struggle." The document then proceeds to describe the extensive help which the revolutionaries received from the Soviet Union: "Stalin even changed the original strategic plan of the Red Army. . . ."[46] If, however, the Slovak uprising was crushed by the German Army it was due, according to another communist source, *Rudé právo*, to the refusal "of the Western Powers to give serious aid to the Slovaks."[47]

If the preparation of the Slovak uprising had brought the democratic and communist leadership together by the end of 1943 and if the cooperation, as tenuous as it was, then continued

[43] B. Laušman, *Pravda a lož o slovenskom národnom povstaní* (Truth and Lies about the Slovak National Uprising), Petrovec, Yugoslavia, Bratrstvo-Jednota, 1951, p. 34.

[44] *Ibid.*, p. 35.

[45] J. Stránský, *Personal Résumé*, No. 2 of *Recollections and Reconstruction of the Czechoslovak February 1948 Crisis by a Group of Democratic Leaders*. See Chapter 7, footnote 24.

[46] *KSČ*, *op.cit.*, pp. 190, 192.

[47] *The New York Times*, February 2, 1948, p. 4.

in the Slovak National Council, in Bohemia the two factions never created a common organ, nor did they cooperate. Mistrust toward communists continued and in the last phase of the war it was motivated, in addition to the critical attitude of democrats for the communists' behavior in the first period, by "the clear and constantly increasing attempts of communists to present their underground activities as the only struggle against Nazi Germany. It was to us, the democrats, an indication of things to come."[48]

Without a Mask

The "indication of things to come" was revealed in a unique document. It was not an indication; it was a proof.

In July 1943 the Central Committee of the Communist Party of Czechoslovakia issued a brochure, directed to "tested comrades." It was an analysis of the nature of the war, a set of instructions for the continuing struggle of the proletariat, and a definition of its wartime goal. The language and the contents of the brochure point unmistakably to Marxist views, motivated by class consciousness and class hatred, highly reminiscent of the innumerable statements of the Third International in the 1920's and patently irreconcilable with everything the Soviet leaders and communists elsewhere were stating publicly.

In the first chapter, concerning the nature of the war, the document defines it as "a swindle—a bloody swindle—which capitalism places on the backs of the toiling masses." The Western capitalists are, it states, equally as guilty as Nazi Germany.

The second chapter, "The Development of the War," warns against the illusion that the capitalist world wages the war for the liberation of European nations. Though the Second Front is important as a help to the Red Army, the danger of a long-term occupation of Europe, which would result from such an invasion by the Anglo-American armies, must be combatted by preparation of a revolutionary situation. For the capitalists "this war does

[48] From a letter of A. Heidrich, April 22, 1958.

not only mean the defeat of Nazism but above all a new, bigger, more thorough version of capitalist peacetime deception of the proletariat, of the working masses of the whole world and, therefore, also of our laboring people. [Communists] *must defeat Nazism in such a manner that the fruit of the victory be not harvested by social fascists and in the end devoured by the bourgeoisie. . . .* The proletariat must, therefore, fight openly and in the underground, alternately and simultaneously, in the name of its own class struggle *for the defeat of nazism, for an armed revolutionary uprising of the Czech laboring people, for a victorious revolution, for the destruction of the political power of the bourgeoisie and social fascists, for the placing of this power in the hands of the workers and thereby preventing the materialization of a peace in the Czech lands dictated by the capitalists abroad.*" (Italics in the text.)[49]

The third chapter of the brochure analyzes the situation in the Czech lands, denouncing the subservience of the bourgeoisie to the German occupation authorities. It warns against President Beneš whom, it admits, "not only the bourgeoisie and landlords but even a considerable part of [the] proletariat" see as the central figure in the liberation struggle.[50] This is all wrong and dangerous, for this popularity in the broad masses may "unite and pacify the bourgeoisie and landlords with the proletariat in a new state system of compromise."[51] To prevent such a development, an active, organized struggle by the laboring masses is absolutely necessary. How to organize the fight is described in chapter four, and the objectives of such a struggle are developed in chapter five of the document.

Chapter six is entitled, "Revolution and the New State." It states that "the supreme revolutionary goal is the *establishment of a Czech Soviet Republic* and its attachment to the *Union of the Soviet Socialist Republics*."[52] The statement is stressed re-

[49] The document is signed Central Committee of CPC and dated Prague, July 1943; 31 pages single spaced. Chapter II, p. 7, of a typewritten copy.

[50] *Ibid.*, Chapter III, p. 3. [51] *Ibid.*, p. 4.

[52] *Ibid.*, Chapter VI, pp. 19-20.

peatedly. As "the revolution must break and destroy to the last molecule the whole bourgeois, capitalist system," every enemy of this aim will be liquidated. "No matter if after the war we must deport one hundred, two hundred, or eight hundred thousand tainted individuals to the forced labor camps outside the boundary of our new state."[53] There is only one way, the way *"of revolution. Revolution—and to the East. To the East to our Slav tree-trunk. To the East to our proletarian Union. To the East, the best that the toiling people of the whole world have created and which the Russian proletariat has strengthened by its present struggle. To the East. To the East. To the East."* (Italics in the text.)[54]

This, then, was the real face of Czech communism which lay behind the smiling mask of patriotism and nationalism.

Cooperation Abroad

In a strange contrast to the profound abyss between democrats and communists on the home front, the representatives in London established regular contacts which led to close cooperation. President Beneš anticipated the decisive position of power which the Soviet Union was to have in European affairs after the war. He desired sincerely and honestly a close alliance with the Soviet Union; he wanted Czechoslovakia to be its loyal friend, without sacrificing friendship with the West.

The Soviet government and Czechoslovak communists had their own ideas and plans and found it opportune to play the game seemingly according to Beneš' rules.

In London, in addition to the government, there existed the Czechoslovak State Council. Composed of politicians and a few prominent people, the Council was a representative body which discussed Czechoslovak politics and advised the President on administrative, political, and economic matters. In November 1941 the State Council was enlarged by four members of the Communist Party, Nosek, Hodinová, Való, and Kreibich. Kreibich,

[53] *Ibid.*, p. 21. [54] *Ibid.*, p. 23.

it will be remembered, had been the most ferocious agitator against the existence of the Republic in the 1920's. Later, another communist, Dr. Bedřich Vrbenský, who lived in the Soviet Union, was added. No other communist leaders in Russia joined the State Council. They were willing to cooperate with Dr. Beneš but did not wish to be associated with his administration.

In the State Council the communist members on various occasions manifested their democratic convictions and their great respect for President Beneš. They never mentioned communism. It was difficult to match their patriotism. The former representative of the German minority in the party, Kreibich, was second to none in his condemnation of his fellow nationals and asked for their severe punishment. All were full of praise, not only for the Soviet Union, but also for the United States and Great Britain.

There were also communists in the governmental service. This was not the result of subversive, clandestine infiltration, but was instead an open policy of the Czechoslovak government. They appeared to work loyally and frequently discussed future plans for the liberated country. In the Council of Ministers there were no communists; this body represented different political opinions from democratic right to democratic left. But communists served willingly and eagerly in governmental offices entrusted even to conservative ministers. "In London the communists approved with applause my budgets," writes Dr. L. Feierabend, who had been prominent in the conservative Agrarian Party in the interwar period and who was Minister of Finances in the London government, "and they frequently expressed thanks for my work."[55]

The London communists often appeared on the radio broadcasts beamed to Czechoslovakia. From time to time there were difficulties in editing their scripts when they were too radical in appealing to the nation to sabotage the German war machine. However, their speeches always struck a highly nationalistic tone, reminding listeners of the glory of Czechoslovak history and invoking the memory of the names which have been dear to

[55] From a letter of L. Feierabend, April 15, 1958.

every Czech and Slovak. President Masaryk was their favorite theme. President Beneš was praised for his work.

Of special political significance was a formal request of the London communists in July 1942 to include in the Czechoslovak government's broadcasting program regular talks for the people in Subcarpathian Russia. In the same period a group of Czechoslovak soldiers from Subcarpathian Russia issued a proclamation saying that they were proud to fight in the ranks of the Czechoslovak army and that they knew of no sacrifice too great to contribute to the renewal of a democratic Czechoslovakia.[56]

Both the request and the proclamation were considered justified and natural at that time. In contrast to these utterances, however, and, more importantly, in contrast to the official declarations of the Soviet government, Subcarpathian Russia was never returned to Czechoslovakia but was attached by violent means to the Soviet Union.

Contacts between Dr. Beneš and the Moscow group of Czechoslovak communists were opened through a mediary, Z. Fierlinger. A strange mediary he was. Politically he was a member of the Social Democratic Party, but it soon became clear that he was more a fellow-traveler than a social democrat and more a representative of Soviet interests than those of Czechoslovakia. Together with a small group of the London social democrats, he was instrumental in splitting his party and led his wing into complete communist subservience.[57]

In his messages to Beneš he was critical of the "western spirit" of the London government and stressed the necessity of developing and maintaining the closest and friendliest relations possible with the Soviet Union.[58] When the London government, on January 19, 1942, after many months of preparatory work, signed an agreement with the Polish government in exile—an agreement

[56] *Čechoslovák* (London), vol. 4, no. 28, July 10, 1942; no. 20, May 15, 1942.

[57] J. Horák, "Českoslovenští socialní demokraté v druhém odboji" (Czechoslovak Social Democrats in the Second Liberation Struggle), *Svědectví*, vol. II, no. 1, Spring 1958, pp. 38-54.

[58] Z. Fierlinger, *op.cit.*, vol. II, pp. 38, 39-41.

which envisaged a Polish-Czechoslovak confederation after the war—Fierlinger not only was quick to communicate to Beneš the Soviets' displeasure, which was indeed his duty, but also expressed his own critical attitude toward the agreement, which was far beyond the realm of his diplomatic duties.[59]

Fierlinger, though himself not only a social democrat but also a member of the diplomatic corps, participated in many of the meetings of the Moscow communists. In May 1942 he reported to Beneš that "as far as the future is concerned they accept in principle the idea of constitutional procedure and a democratic coalition, they emphasize, however, that the coalition be led by firm and honest people. . . . In the question of religion they are for complete freedom of all denominations; they even do not exclude political cooperation with Catholics."[60] The report sounded reassuring, indeed.

Relations with the Soviet Government

Even during the dark period of the Nazi-Soviet Pack Dr. Beneš maintained contact with I. Maisky, the Soviet Ambassador in London. On July 18, 1941 the prewar alliance was renewed and an agreement was signed by Maisky and Jan Masaryk, the Minister of Foreign Affairs, which stipulated mutual assistance between the two countries during the war and the organization of a Czechoslovak army in the Soviet Union from citizens who until that time had been interned there. The ceremony took place at the Soviet Embassy; the author was among the officials who accompanied Jan Masaryk. After the two representatives had put their signatures to the agreement and as they were shaking hands Masaryk said to Maisky, in his typical informal way, "And Subcarpathian Russia is ours." Maisky jovially replied, "Yes, the Subcarpathian Ukraine is yours." (The Soviets and Czechoslovak communists used the term, the Subcarpathian Ukraine, for political reasons.)

59 *Ibid.*, pp. 46-56. 60 *Ibid.*, p. 73.

The same day, the British government granted full recognition to the London government, and the American government recognized it as a provisional government. A Czech communist publication later stated that "the Soviet Union was the first big power to recognize [the Czechoslovak] government abroad" and was critical of England, France, and the United States, which "left open the question of the boundaries of our state."[61]

This statement at least is correct. The British government did grant full recognition as a direct consequence of the speedy Soviet move. It was Masaryk who related a telephone call from Eden. "So you achieved agreement with the Russians," he said ruefully, "and once again we shall be late." "As usual," answered Masaryk.[62]

The same was true concerning the question of Czechoslovak boundaries. In both cases Beneš reacted strongly to the quick, decisive statements of the Soviet Union on the one hand and to the tardiness of the West on the other. He was pleased to have repeated assurances from the Soviet government on Czechoslovakia's territorial integrity, particularly as it included Subcarpathian Russia. Moreover, he was repeatedly assured about the Soviet Union's attitude toward Czechoslovakia and her national affairs.

When Beneš met with Molotov in London on June 9, 1942, he received from him a declaration "that the Soviet Union had recognized the Republic in its pre-Munich frontiers" and obtained his consent to announce it publicly "as a binding obligation."[63] In a telegram to Fierlinger, Beneš added that "Molotov further stated that in nothing will they intervene in our affairs."[64]

In return Fierlinger reported to Beneš, October 15, 1942, that Soviet officials had told him that "they wish Czechoslovakia to be a fully free and independent state . . . , [and] expect that we shall ourselves solve our internal problems with the assistance of a

[61] *KSČ*, *op.cit.*, p. 103.
[62] L. Feierabend, *Memoirs*, in manuscript, vol. v, p. 672.
[63] Beneš, *op.cit.*, p. 204.
[64] Fierlinger, *op.cit.*, vol. II, p. 75.

people's democratic coalition. . . ." They considered "any ideological and personal struggles superfluous and damaging."[65]

One cannot consider every message of Fierlinger as authentic. Insofar as they correspond to identical information from reliable sources, they can be taken as a correct interpretation of events; on other matters they must be read with reservations. He pursued in Moscow his own personal aims and was in agreement with the communists there; in addition, his book was published in 1948 when he, former social democrat though he was, was rewarded by the party for his wartime service by membership in the Politburo.

He was, however, undoubtedly correct when he reported Soviet opposition to Czechoslovak-Polish cooperation. Beneš explained in lengthy telegrams the Czechoslovak position and in one emphasized: "We shall never ally ourselves with anyone against the interests of the USSR. This has been the case so far. However, we do not want ever to be its vassal, nor its instrument, nor its card in its diplomatic or other games. On the other side, we always want to be its grateful and reliable ally and true friend."[66]

Beneš meant every word of it. On January 17, 1943 he received an answer from Fierlinger. It seemed encouraging to read: "Here they want Czechoslovakia to be internally firm and strong because they respect her democratic tradition."[67]

Beneš' assurances were of no avail. Under Soviet pressure the negotiations with the Polish government were suspended. Its international position, already exposed to heavy Soviet attacks, deteriorated further.

From the ruins of the Czechoslovak-Polish friendship grew a new idea, and Fierlinger claims to be its author: a treaty of alliance with the Soviet Union.[68] Beneš welcomed and supported the idea, for he expected that such a treaty would clarify all questions between Russia and Czechoslovakia. It would also, he reasoned, be a document of assurance to the Russians of the best

[65] Fierlinger, *op.cit.*, vol. II, p. 92. [66] *Ibid.*, pp. 99-100.
[67] *Ibid.*, p. 101. [68] *Ibid.*, p. 116.

Czechoslovak intentions toward her, and for Czechoslovakia a guarantee of Russia's respect for Czechoslovak internal affairs.[69] In March 1943 Beneš asked Moscow if the Soviet government was ready to "conclude with Czechoslovakia a treaty similar to the Anglo-Soviet Pact and adapted to Czechoslovak conditions. Would Moscow consider it possible," was another question, "to stress in the treaty the mutual obligation of both partners not to interfere in the internal affairs of the other partner?" On April 23, the answer came and it was positive on every point.[70]

During the preparatory work for the treaty the British Foreign Office tried to dissuade Beneš from signing it, at least during the war. It did not wish the settlement of postwar problems to be predetermined by a wartime agreement, and particularly wanted to prevent Poland's isolation. Suddenly, on July 1, 1943, Anthony Eden "showed a protocol to Beneš which was signed during Molotov's visit in London, as well as some other documents from which it was obvious that Great Britain and the Soviet Union had reached an agreement not to sign during the war any bilateral treaty with small nations," writes Beneš' former personal secretary.[71]

The Soviet government never told Beneš about this agreement. When asked about it, Bogomolov, the Soviet Ambassador to the Czechoslovak government in London, insisted that such an agreement did not exist. Later he conceded that the idea was informally accepted, with the expectation that the British government would prepare a formal draft. When they did not, the Soviet government thought that the whole thing was abandoned.[72]

Beneš, once pleased that an agreement with Russia was being negotiated along the lines of the Soviet-British treaty of alliance of May 1942, now found with displeasure that his policy was to become a matter of diplomatic controversy between Moscow and London.

[69] *Ibid.*, p. 121. [70] Beneš, *op.cit.*, p. 242.

[71] Táborský, "Benešovy moskevské cesty," *op.cit.*, p. 194.

[72] From an interview with Mr. L. Feierabend, June 16, 1958. Mr. Feierabend was Minister of Finances in the Beneš government in London.

The British officials intervened diplomatically through all channels opened to them. Knowing Mr. Feierabend's anti-Soviet views and, at the same time, his close relations with Beneš, Sir Philip Nicols, the British Ambassador to the Czechoslovak government, conveyed to him in forceful terms the position of the Foreign Office. Feierabend went to see Beneš immediately. Beneš retorted in a slightly angry manner, "Nicols didn't tell you that I had offered the British the same treaty and to sign it even before I go to Moscow."[73]

Whether Beneš' offer was meant seriously or only as a diplomatic maneuver, it is difficult to tell. There is no confirmation of this offer from another source. However, the British refusal would be only another indication of the absence of a positive policy toward Central Europe on the part of the British government—a fault which had tragic consequences.

Whatever may have happened in the matter, it was decided that the question would be discussed at the Moscow Conference of the Foreign Ministers of the three Big Powers. At the conference held in October 1943 Molotov opened the discussion of the question and presented the text of the envisaged treaty. "Eden and Hull took note of our actions and expressed their satisfaction at the wording and the aim of the treaty," writes Beneš.[74]

The road to Moscow was open. Dr. Beneš was soon to go on a trip which proved to be fateful for him and for his country.

[73] From an interview with Mr. Feierabend, June 16, 1958.
[74] Beneš, *op.cit.*, p. 245.

A FATEFUL JOURNEY

Toward the end of November 1943 President Beneš left London by plane to embark upon his long-contemplated mission to Moscow. Beneš was at once an experienced and skillful statesman and a dedicated democrat. As a statesman he was thoroughly aware of the future balance of power in Europe: the Soviet Union's powerful influence in Central Europe on the one side and on the other the absence of any planned and determined policy by Great Britain and the United States toward the area. It was a different picture from what he had envisaged in the first two years of the war, but it was a fact and Beneš, the statesman, recognized that fact. Nor, on the other hand, could he overlook the evil augury from Poland and Yugoslavia, two allied countries which like Czechoslovakia had governments in exile but for which Soviet-supported communist National Committees were claiming exclusive rights of representation. Obviously, any return to Czechoslovakia, which was to be liberated mainly by the Red Army, required Stalin's consent. To achieve this Dr. Beneš was willing to go a long way to convince the Soviet government of his sincerity in the matter of Czechoslovak cooperation with the Soviet Union.

As a convinced democrat he insisted on reestablishing a policy of complete political freedom in his country immediately after its liberation. Indeed, as a part of this policy, he sought the cooperation of communists, hopeful that their radicalism would be tempered through their experiences in a coalition government. At the same time he would thus be offering to the Soviet Union still another proof that no Czechoslovak government would even consider pursuing an anti-Soviet policy, the presence of communists in the government to be a guarantee, if one was needed.

Negotiations with Stalin

On his way to Moscow President Beneš stopped at the Habbanyiah airport in Iraq, where he was welcomed on behalf of the Soviet government by Alexander Korneichuk, the Deputy Foreign Minister and well-known Ukrainian writer. Bad weather kept the party there for ten days. Korneichuk was a most affable person. He spoke freely to Beneš about the mistakes the Soviets had committed in the past and was particularly emphatic in his condemnation of the "old ideology of leftist trends and deviations which were often abstractly international and had nothing in common with the tradition of the Russian and Ukrainian people." He had nothing but contempt for "the old extremist Bolshevistic type."[1]

Dr. Beneš was only too eager to listen to such views. He was a subtle diplomat and in his discussions with Korneichuk he developed his own ideas about the postwar world, stressing particularly the principle of equality among the Slav nations and criticizing the old Czarist concept of Slav solidarity which had been an instrument of the Russian policy of expansion. Korneichuk assured him that the Russia of today was different from that of old times, that it was progressive, altogether democratic, that it rejected both the old Slav expansionism and international communism. It has become nationalist.[2]

Beneš was highly pleased by what he heard from Korneichuk; he was anxious to hear more of the same from Stalin himself. In this he was not disappointed.

Beneš was received with honors and had several conversations with Stalin and Molotov. He had prepared and now presented to them several memoranda concerning diverse questions. One of them concerned Subcarpathian Russia, an area of particular interest in the light of subsequent developments. It stated, "Czechoslovakia will be recognized internationally as the Czechoslovak

[1] E. Taborsky, "Beneš and Stalin—Moscow, 1943-1945," *Journal of Central European Affairs*, vol. XIII, p. 159, quoting from Beneš' personal notes.

[2] Fierlinger, *op.cit.*, vol. II, pp. 182-89.

national state, i.e., a state of Czechs and Slovaks to which there will be attached the Subcarpathian Ukraine with the special autonomous statute."[3]

In a conversation on this subject Stalin "cut him short and said 'Subcarpathian Russia will be returned to Czechoslovakia. We have recognized the pre-Munich frontiers of Czechoslovakia and that settles it once and for all.' "[4]

Beneš was deeply impressed by his conversation with Stalin and by what he saw in the Soviet Union. On December 12, 1943, the Treaty of Friendship, Mutual Aid, and Postwar Cooperation was solemnly signed. Article 4 was of particular significance. It stipulated: "The High Contracting Parties having regard to the interests of their mutual security, have agreed to maintain close and friendly cooperation after the reestablishment of peace and to regulate their actions according to the principles of mutual respect of their independence and sovereignty and non-interference in the internal affairs of the other signatory. . . ."

In private conversations Stalin and Molotov repeatedly assured Dr. Beneš of their firm intent to respect the principle of non-interference toward Czechoslovakia. They "went so far in their wiles that they almost refused to listen whenever Beneš tried to explain how he imagined the future development of things in Czechoslovakia after the war. They wanted to show him how unjust were the accusations of those in the West who suspected them of secret intentions."[5]

Beneš himself summed up his Moscow conversations in a cablegram to the Foreign Minister, Jan Masaryk, stating: "The political discussions and negotiations have taken place up to this point in the utmost harmony, friendship, and cordiality. . . . I consider all our negotiations as wholly successful. It can be stated that personally I did not expect that the problems would be posed

[3] Taborsky, "Beneš and Stalin," *op.cit.*, p. 166, quoting from Beneš' personal papers. It is of interest to note that no mention of a memorandum which would deal with Subcarpathian Russia is made in Beneš' *Memoirs*.

[4] *Ibid.*, p. 167; from Taborsky's diary on the Moscow trip.

[5] *Ibid.*, p. 162. See also Fierlinger, *op.cit.*, vol. II, p. 190.

so clearly, so definitely and with such a prospect of cordial and harmonious cooperation for the future. . . . Progress here in the development of ideas since 1935 and especially since the war is great, real, and definite. To imagine that the present outlook towards the Internationale, religion, *cooperation with the West*, Slav policy, etc., is merely tactical would be a fundamental error. The growth of a new Soviet empire, a decentralized one, with a firm place for the other Soviet Nations in the spirit of a new popular democracy, is undeniably and definitely on the march. . . . I think it can be regarded as certain that all treaties and agreements not only with us but also with the British and with America will be kept. . . . Throughout our discussions there was not a single occasion on which our partners did not stress that whatever question might arise they are not concerned with our internal affairs and that they would not interfere in them."[6]

President Beneš returned triumphantly to London. He sent a secret message to the underground leaders in Czechoslovakia in which he assured his friends of Stalin's guarantee of the integrity of Czechoslovak territory. "The Soviet Union believes," the message continued, "that the Republic will remain democratic and progressive. . . . The Soviet Union does not request anything special from us. Our policy will simply be the policy of our democratic majority."[7]

After the war, recalling his Moscow experience and struggling with the reality which had so soon obscured his optimism of that period, he tried to answer for himself the historic and crucial question: What was and is the place of Czechoslovakia in Europe? He answered that the Western, centuries-old orientation of his nation "is not a value which can be put off and on like a coat, or according to some momentary change of political regime." Then he added, sincerely but in an obviously diplomatic attempt to find a compromise: "*We have always taken deliberately a general*

[6] Beneš, *op.cit.*, pp. 261-62.

[7] Taborsky, "Beneš and Stalin," *op.cit.*, p. 168, quoting from Beneš' personal papers.

and universal line. That is to say, a line which includes not only the development and progress of the West, but also the progress and development of the East. . . . And so our answer to the question: West or East? is to say deliberately and plainly: *West and East.* In this sense—*and in this sense only*—did I sign and approve the treaty with the Soviet Union of December 1943, *intentionally and consciously linking it with the Anglo-Soviet treaty of May 26, 1942.* At the time I firmly believed that this treaty would continue in operation after the war ended. Was I right or wrong?"[8]

In 1947, when writing his memoirs, Hamlet-like he put to himself the agonizing question, "Was I right or wrong?" One year later, a few days before his death, he answered the question himself: "My greatest mistake was that I refused to believe to the very last that even Stalin lied to me cynically both in 1935 and later, and that his assurances to me and to Masaryk were an intentional deceit."[9]

Negotiations with Communists

The second part of Dr. Beneš' visit to Moscow was devoted to negotiations with Czechoslovak communists. These contacts were almost as gratifying as were his conversations with Stalin. Beneš invited the communists to enter the government in exile; they politely refused but offered to continue support of his policy. They were against the government in exile's return to Czechoslovakia, insisting that a new government should be constituted before that time. Then they discussed future political developments in Czechoslovakia. Beneš tested them on the question of a possible fusion of the three socialist parties, the Czechoslovak National Socialists, the Social Democrats, and the Communist Party. He also wanted a party of conservative convictions to be in the government. On the first question the communist answer

[8] Beneš, *op.cit.*, p. 282.

[9] Taborsky, "Beneš and Stalin," *op.cit.*, p. 162n, quoting from Beneš' message to the author.

was evasive; on the latter they agreed without advocating the abolition of the right-wing Agrarian Party, some leaders of which had been compromised in the period of the Munich and post-Munich crisis. The conversations resulted in an agreement, based on the premise that inasmuch as the country would need complete unity of all political elements to recover quickly from the ravages of war, a National Front government would be formed to maintain this unity. The communists proposed that during the process of liberation National Committees take over the local administration with wide powers. For a long time over the Moscow radio they had appealed to people in Czechoslovakia to form such committees. Beneš agreed in principle but left open the question of their powers. He wanted free elections to be held within six months after the war; to this they did not object.

On one basic problem Beneš and the communists disagreed: Munich. The President continued to maintain the conviction that he had been right in submitting to the Munich dictate. The communists attacked him relentlessly and by implication threatened to bring the matter up at any time they might choose.[10]

Gottwald wanted to be sure that the London group of Czechoslovak communists were informed about the conversations with President Beneš as he understood them. He sent, through Beneš' good offices, a letter to their leader, V. Nosek. In the letter he urged the London government to appeal to the nation to intensify the war efforts. This meant more sabotage, more active armed struggle. This, he insisted, was the government's responsibility and it was not discharging it in a satisfactory manner. He also asked for a law punishing any kind of active collaboration with Germans. The Slovaks, he insisted, must be assured of a proper autonomous position in Czechoslovakia.

As to the postwar development, Gottwald proposed to return to the old Constitution and old laws until a newly-elected Constitutional Assembly could provide new laws. There was to be

10 Beneš, *op.cit.*, pp. 268-75. E. Táborský, "Benešovy moskevské cesty," *op.cit.*, pp. 201-02. Fierlinger, *op.cit.*, vol. II, pp. 196-201.

one exception to the rule: a Provisional National Assembly would be elected by the Provinces' National Committees, these by the District National Committees, and these in turn by the Local National Committees, which would be elected by the people themselves. A future provisional government would be composed of the three socialist parties (Communists, Social Democrats, and National Socialists) and of representatives of conservatives, Catholics, and agrarians. The socialist parties, though in the leading position, however, must not appear, nor feel themselves to be, a "bloc of the Left," but as representatives of the overwhelming majority of the nation. This was an obvious attempt on Gottwald's part to continue to play the game of an all-national patriotic movement and to conceal the communist, class-struggle nature of their policy—a policy which was secretly confided only to "the tested comrades." (See pages 73-75.)

Since in all probability the communists would be the strongest party after the war, continued Gottwald, they should have the right to the Prime Ministership: "For the time being they do not claim this right without, however, giving it up in the future. On the other side, we consider it quite obvious that communists must have the opportunity to play a truly effective role in the new government, which, besides other things, means that, for instance, the portfolios of Interior and National Defense must be held by communists. The new Prime Minister, of course, must be a man of the bloc."[11]

Another message which Dr. Beneš took to London came from Zdeněk Fierlinger. This Ambassador of the Czechoslovak government, though never before a prominent member of the Social Democratic Party, now posed as a self-appointed leader of the party and revealed himself once more as an ever-anxious servant of the communists. His letter was addressed to the left wing of the Social Democratic leaders in London and expressed complete agreement with Gottwald. Facing the problem of a split in the London group—the democratic led by V. Majer and the radical left led

[11] The letter is dated Moscow, December 21, 1943.

by B. Laušman—he appealed for another attempt at unification on the basis, of course, of close cooperation with the communists. "It is not necessary," stated Fierlinger, "to speak about a new socialist program" since the future policy would be "truly national and patriotic" and only "later at home could [there be] prepared a fusion of socialists and communists as there will be no longer any reason for major differences in their programs."[12]

Out of courtesy or perhaps for political reasons, both letters were given to President Beneš in an open envelope. They remained secret for five years. But Beneš could no longer have been in doubt as to the goals of the Communist Party or of his Ambassador in Moscow.

In spite of this illuminating experience Beneš described his conversations with the communists as a "good and successful work. I realized at once," he continued, "that in spite of some very important differences it would be possible for our national camp to reach agreement at critical moments about the fundamental problems of our postwar policy. . . . So I was full of hope that what happened a year later to the Poles and Yugoslavs would not happen to our movement."[13]

He shared his hopes publicly with the nation and the government after he returned to London. He reported to his closest friends on the home front in Czechoslovakia, in a secret message: "In all details I negotiated with representatives of our communists in Moscow and I am, of course, in constant contact and cooperation with our communists here in England. They all stand on the soil of the Republic, they go along with the president and the government and cooperate patriotically. At the moment of the defeat of Germany it will be possible to nominate a new government in agreement with our people at home in the Republic. The communists will enter it. . . . I am urging, therefore, communists in Slovakia and in the Czech lands that they, in the same spirit, take part in the liberation activities at home together

[12] The letter is dated Moscow, December 21, 1943.
[13] Beneš, *op.cit.*, p. 275.

with other groups and that they prepare together with them a united revolution. It is important to prepare a harmonious concentration of all sections of the nation for the most difficult period of the last struggle, for the transitory period after the war and for the foundation of the new Republic. For these difficult and complicated tasks, a unity is absolutely necessary because only in this way shall we overcome them to the benefit of all citizens of the Republic."[14]

To Sir Robert Bruce Lockhart, the noted British diplomat and a devoted and long-standing friend of Czechoslovakia, Beneš, and Masaryk, he expressed the belief "that Czechoslovak Communists were not as other Communists. . . ."[15]

Yet, after his return from Moscow, in strange contrast to his public optimism, Beneš scribbled some notes recording his impressions of his conversations with the communists. These read as follows: "(1) The Communist Party will also stay after the war (lack of agreement about one unified party). (2) National Committees in the communist understanding are in fact soviets. (3) The totalitarian tendencies of communists remain—under the guise of the National Front in fact one party only should govern. (4) The participation of communists in the government has one aim: to get hold of positions and have the decisive influence in preparation for the seizing of all power in the state."[16] The professional optimist was troubled by the nagging voice of his analytical mind.

As to the Moscow communists they let it be known to Beneš, through their fellow-travelling Fierlinger, that they "had agreed that [the] conferences had taken a satisfactory course and that

[14] Táborský, "Benešovy moskevské cesty," *op.cit.*, p. 202.

[15] Sir R. B. Lockhart, "The Czechoslovak Revolution," *Foreign Affairs*, vol. 26, July 1948, p. 634.

[16] From a letter of Professor Jaroslav Stránský to the author, April 16, 1958. Mr. Stránský was Minister of Justice in the London government and the leading member of the Czechoslovak National Socialist Party which had been for many years the party of Dr. Beneš. Mr. Stránský received the information about the note "from a source which is reliable above and beyond any doubts."

results had been reached which they themselves had not expected."[17]

The statement was deceptive and framed to permit a diabolic interpretation, one which a few years later when they came to power the communists were free to make. A member of the Politburo stated that Beneš was oriented on London, Gottwald on Moscow: "Our line in the liberation struggle was fundamentally different from the line of the London faction. . . . We led the national liberation movement from the point of view of the aims of the working class, they from the point of view of the aims of the bourgeoisie. We never cultivated national unity in the sense of doing away with class differences and in the sense of solidarity with the bourgeoisie." The communist policy was to hold only a "formal loyalty" to the Czechoslovak government.[18]

Another communist source, describing the Moscow negotiations, alleges that "Dr. Beneš arrived in Moscow with his own concept of a new settlement of affairs in the liberated Republic; it was entirely different from the concept of comrade Gottwald. According to Dr. Beneš' original plan, the administration of the Republic, for instance, was to be taken over by officers specially trained for the purpose."[19]

To put such an idea into Beneš' mouth is fantastic. But once it was done it was easy to state that Dr. Beneš soon saw the futility of such a plan and that further negotiations were then "conducted on the basis of comrade Gottwald's concept."[20]

At the end of the conversations, as described by an official communist publication, Gottwald stated that in spite of some differences in principle "the communists [would] most loyally cooperate toward the best interests of the liberated Republic. It is their wish to see the transition from the provisional Czechoslovak regime abroad to the new regime at home to proceed organically

[17] Beneš, *op.cit.*, p. 275.

[18] Kopecký, *Tridsať rokov ČSR*, *op.cit.*, p. 24.

[19] *KSČ*, *op.cit.*, p. 172.

[20] *Loc.cit.*

and in harmony. The only thing they require is a 'clean game,' 'fair play'; they ask frankness and honesty in further cooperation with the party of the laboring class and working people."[21]

The statement is worthy of Iago.

[21] *Ibid.*, p. 174.

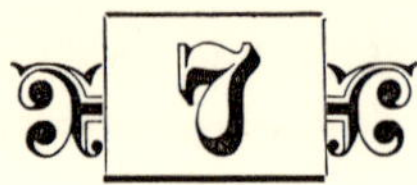

THE STRUGGLE BEGINS

SINCE June of 1941 the communists had established themselves as Czechoslovak patriots and nationalists. Through 1942 and 1943 they had played the role of loyal partnership with other political parties and their members were accepted in governmental service. The time had now arrived to capitalize on the positions they had thus gained.

At the same time the Soviet Union had convinced the statesmen of the West of the sincerity of its pronouncements that after the war it would direct its energy toward the reconstruction of its devastated country and would allow all other European nations to have governments of their choice, provided only that they pursue a friendly policy toward Russia. Most important, by the end of 1943, military developments pointed clearly to the fact that most of Central Europe would be liberated by the Red Army. To the Soviet government the year of 1944 was the time for exploiting the results of its policies and its military achievements.

From Rose to Gray

For sometime after his return from Moscow, Dr. Beneš and some of his associates continued to picture the prospects for the future in rosy colors. When the Moscow conversations on the nature and extent of power of the National Committees left some doubt in his mind he thought to set them aside by a speech he made on February 3, 1944. It is suggested, he stated with deliberate ambiguity, to found National Committees in every community, district, and province, which would be of "temporary" duration, first for the purpose of organizing the struggle against the Germans and then to administer the areas provisionally until conditions permit free elections. He emphasized the necessity "to come in time to an exact agreement about their jurisdiction."[1]

Only a handful of people, initiated in the happenings behind the scene or skilled in the language of diplomacy, could read in Beneš' cautious lines an indication of his disagreement with the communists on this issue of utmost importance. It took Gottwald less than one week to place his own interpretation on Beneš' statement, confident that the President would not disavow him publicly. On February 9, 1944, he appeared on the Czech radio program in Moscow and reminded the listeners of "the President's summons to create National Committees ... which will be elected publicly." He also appealed for an all-out struggle, for organization of partisan units without delay. If some still waited for a "signal, that signal was now being given by the Head of the State and the Supreme Commander of the Czechoslovak armed forces."[2] Again, Gottwald knew that Beneš did not agree with such a radical form of propaganda.

April 8, 1944 was an historic date in the annals of the war insofar as Czechoslovakia was concerned. The Soviet army reached the Czechoslovak boundary. Six months later, on October 18, the border was crossed.

While in Moscow Beneš had discussed with Stalin the problem of the relations between the Czechoslovak administration of the liberated territory and the Red Army. He had received full assurance "that the occupation of the [Czechoslovak] territory should always be left to [Czechoslovak forces] . . . that the [Czechoslovak] internal order should be respected. . . ." The two statesmen had agreed to clarify all questions connected with the expected entry of the Soviet troops onto Czechoslovak territory "in good time."[3]

Accordingly, on May 8, 1944 an "Agreement about relations between the Soviet Commander in Chief and the Czechoslovak

[1] P. Korbel, *National Committees in Czechoslovakia*, New York, Free Europe Committee, February 1954, p. 1.

[2] Gottwald, *Deset let*, *op.cit.*, p. 234.

[3] Beneš, *op.cit.*, p. 263.

administration after the entry of the Soviet armies into the territory of Czechoslovakia" was made public. The agreement divided the territory into an area of war operations, in which the sole responsibility for the conduct of war rested with the Soviet Commander in Chief, and into liberated territory, which would be under the exclusive responsibility of a Delegate of the Czechoslovak government who was to administer the territory according to Czechoslovak laws and who was to restore the Czechoslovak armed forces. The implementation of the agreement was eagerly awaited, but when the moment arrived the Czechoslovak people, Dr. Beneš, and with them all the Western allies experienced a profound shock.

Meanwhile the Moscow communists continued their line of highly nationalistic propaganda. As partisan groups started to spread in Czechoslovakia, calling themselves by such patriotic names as *Jan Žižka, Prokop Holý, Jan Hus, Miroslav Tyrš*, and *Generál Štefánik*, the Moscow radio acclaimed their actions and later even alleged that these units were composed of or at least led by communists.[4]

Now, however, with the Soviet army on the border of Czechoslovakia, the statements of the Moscow communists took on a new tone. Gottwald began to praise the working class for its resistance to German oppression, but he also began to suggest to his worker listeners that they would have as much power in the liberated country as they chose to take by their own struggle. At the same time, attacks on the bourgeoisie began to reappear. Gottwald's favorite theme, the National Committees, began to take on new meaning. He asserted that they would have vast powers and that whether they would be elected by acclamation or secretly would depend on the local situation.[5] Such and similar statements were an open invitation to communists in the country to try their hand.

In spite of these signs, or perhaps because of them, the London

[4] *KSČ*, *op.cit.*, pp. 167-68, 209, 241.
[5] Gottwald, *Deset let*, *op.cit.*, pp. 242-56.

government in exile continued its systematic preparation for an orderly renewal of the country's life in a framework of freedom and legality. The President enacted a constitutional decree legalizing National Committees, but at the same time defining their transitory character, and setting up a Provisional National Assembly. The Ministry of Justice drafted a law for the punishment of traitors and collaborators; the Ministry of the Interior a law for the administration of the country; the Ministry of Finances prepared new currency; the Ministry of Reconstruction negotiated assistance with UNRRA and elaborated a program for the rehabilitation of the country. These were democratic measures. In addition, all members of the government were in agreement on a plan for the nationalization of mines and heavy industry, for land reform, and for a new system of social insurance. These were far-reaching economic measures of a progressive, socializing nature; they were all to be put before the electorate for a final decision.

In the summer of 1944 Dr. Beneš, impressed as he was by the closeness of American-British and Soviet cooperation and friendship, still believed that this friendship would be a safe foundation for Czechoslovakia's independence. On July 16 he sent a message to his friends in Prague stating: "[Russia] will need their help in many ways. The devastation and the sufferings of Russia are beyond imagination and the Soviet Government's main aspiration is the speediest possible reconstruction of the country. *That is also the guarantee which makes our treaty of alliance with the Soviet Union so real and so vitally valuable for us.* That is why the Soviets will not interfere in our internal conditions any more than in those of other countries."[6]

Nevertheless, clouds were gathering on the bright horizon of Dr. Beneš' analyses and calculations. In April, during negotiations with the Soviet government concerning the relations between the Red Army and the Czechoslovak administration in

[6] Taborsky, "Beneš and Stalin," *op.cit.*, p. 156n.

liberated territory, the Czechoslovak government in London suggested to the American and British governments that an identical agreement be signed with them. The two Western governments declined.

When the Ministry of Finances prepared invasion money, the Soviet government accepted it, while the Allied High Command declined to do so, stating that the question of the Allied Army crossing the Czechoslovak boundary was not under consideration.[7] The meaning of such a position was apparent: the Western powers had no military plans for Central Europe, nor had they any affirmative policy toward the area. By default it was to be left to the Soviet Union.

In August and September of 1944 the clouds darkened. This was the period of the Slovak uprising. Not only did the Soviets give little help to the insurgents; they also prevented the Americans from sending arms to them (see pp. 70-72). The meaning of this policy became all too clear: Czechoslovakia was within the Soviet sphere of military operations, to the exclusion of Anglo-American actions. Though this agreement had probably been reached at the Teheran Conference in November 1943, the Czechoslovak government was never informed about it, vital as it was to the national interests and the future of the country.

Slowly the political structure that President Beneš had envisaged began to crumble. One of the three pillars which supported his concept was the balance of Soviet-Western interests in Central Europe—and this pillar tottered when the American and British governments by their inaction manifested their lack of active interest in the area. The second pillar, a central one, was Soviet non-interference in Czechoslovak national affairs. Here a serious flaw appeared when the Soviet government contemplated negotiations with the traitor General Čatloš. The third pillar—the ability of Czechoslovak democrats to temper communist radicalism through cooperation—was beginning to sway.

To say that events proved President Beneš' concept wrong is

[7] From an interview with Mr. L. Feierabend, June 12, 1958.

to oversimplify both the problem and its solution. No other alternative seemed available unless he chose to follow the path of the Polish and Yugoslav governments which led to permanent exile, to action from which there was no return. His final defeat stemmed rather from the fact that he could not guess the measure of improbity of either the Czechslovak communists or his wartime ally, the Soviet Union. Nor could the West. Trust, good will, loyalty—these were the qualities which betrayed him, the quicksand upon which his political structure was built.

From Gray to Dark

The government in London nominated F. Němec its Delegate for administration of the liberated territory. He was a leader in the Social Democratic Party but not of Fierlinger's left-wing group. Immediately the Moscow communists protested both the procedure of the appointment and the choice. Fierlinger, as an Ambassador, surely owed some allegiance to his government; instead, he associated himself with the protest. Instances of insubordination on his part were piling up. For a long time he had established a record of siding with the Soviet government and the Czechoslovak communists on all political, personal, and administrative matters. He was obviously an agent; even his own memoirs, published after the communist putsch, proudly point to his service to the communist cause during the war years.[8]

When evidences of Fierlinger's disloyalty accumulated, the Czechoslovak government in exile, the group of men so completely devoted to Beneš, unanimously voted to propose to the President that he be recalled from Moscow. The President declined. Though critical of his Ambassador, he saw in the move an anti-Soviet and anti-communist demonstration, and he did not wish to endanger the confidence which he thought he had gained with them.

On August 25, 1944 F. Němec, the governmental Delegate, reached Moscow, accompanied by a group of political, economic,

[8] Fierlinger, *op.cit.*, vol. II, p. 294ff.

and military advisers. A few days later, when the Slovak revolutionaries seized an area in central Slovakia, the governmental delegation flew in to greet them. A certain Turjanica, Němec's political adviser and a member of the Communist Party for Subcarpathian Russia, wrote an article a few weeks later for the Slovak communist daily, *Pravda*, in which he said: "What is the future Carpatho-Ukraine to be like? The Carpatho-Ukrainian nation must have equal rights with their Slovak and Czech brothers within the Czechoslovak Republic. . . . In the Carpatho-Ukraine, the Carpatho-Ukrainians should be masters, living in brotherly union with the heroic Czech and Slovak people."[9] The statement seemed to augur well for future developments.

On October 18 the Soviet army crossed the Czechoslovak boundary. Ten days later, on the anniversary of Czechoslovak national independence, the governmental Delegate, F. Němec, established his headquarters on Subcarpathian soil, in Czechoslovakia, in the town of Chust. His first official act was to issue a declaration by which he made known to the populace the establishment of his office. The next day, a Sunday, a mass meeting was held in the town square; all speakers, Turjanica among them, proclaimed glory to President Beneš and Stalin, to the Czechoslovak Republic and the Soviet Union.

The following day, the governmental Delegate ordered a bulletin printed, calling all Czechoslovak citizens of military age to the colors. Then came the first jolt. The printer of the proclamation was arrested by the Soviet military and the Delegate was forbidden to post it. The Soviet military authorities then issued an appeal to the population to join the Red Army. Protests that these were Czechoslovak citizens were of no avail.

The Sunday mass meeting now emerged as a staged demonstration to cover this move. The existing local National Committee was dissolved at the order of the town's Soviet military commander with the explanation that it was a self-appointed body

[9] F. Němec and V. Moudry, *The Soviet Seizure of Subcarpathian Ruthenia*, Toronto, W. B. Anderson, 1955, p. 275.

and was replaced by another National Committee, the list of which had been prepared by the Soviet political police of NKVD and Turjanica, the same man who only a few hours before had pledged allegiance to the Czechoslovak government. The committee immediately "voted" a resolution asking for the inclusion of Subcarpathian Russia in the Soviet Union. A chain reaction followed. In one town or village after another, local communists led by Turjanica, who was—the irony of it—political adviser to the government's Delegate but taking his orders from the Soviet commanders, formed National Committees and voted the same resolution. Those who were ready to serve on a pro-Czechoslovak Committee were promptly arrested by the Soviet authorities. The Czechoslovak Delegate himself was under surveillance in his headquarters, virtually a prisoner of the Red Army. He was not allowed to exercise any influence in the zone of military operations either. That was in consonance with the Soviet-Czechoslovak agreement of May 8. However, National Committees were being formed in the zone, and when the Soviet commander handed over an area, as the Red Army advanced, to the Delegate's nominal administration, communist-controlled Committees had already been in existence adopting the now familiar resolutions. Communist agitators were allowed to cross freely from the Delegate's zone to the area of military operations. The whole political movement was under the direction of General Mekhlis, the political commissar of the Fourth Ukrainian Front.

On November 19 the Communist Party of Subcarpathian Russia, which had so suddenly appeared out of nowhere, passed a resolution asking for the separation of the country from Czechoslovakia and for its incorporation into the Soviet Union. One week later, a conference of National Committees delegates was convened in Mukačevo, one of the few larger cities. Six hundred and sixty people attended the meeting, which voted unanimously to accept the party resolution. A National Council for the Carpathian Ukraine was formed. It gave the Delegate an ultimatum to leave the territory within three days; in case of non-compliance with this "categorical decision and demand," the Council was ready to "take necessary steps with all resulting consequences."[10] The Delegate refused, pointing out that his position allowed him to take orders only from the Czechoslovak government.

The Delegate had been assured of free contact with his government in London. However, this was interpreted by the Soviet authorities, with the eager approval of Ambassador Fierlinger, to mean communication through Red Army channels and through Fierlinger's "good offices." The Soviets thereby knew the text of every message. Němec is convinced that Fierlinger deliberately neglected to send many of his reports.

At last one of the members of the Delegate's staff established secret contact with London, a move which was illegal, according to the Soviet understanding of Czechoslovak freedom, and punishable by death. Here was a melancholy situation indeed—a Delegate of the Czechoslovak government forbidden, from the "liberated" territory of his own country, to communicate with his superiors.

The first report, received in London on November 28, stated: "It is necessary to act now. The Czechoslovak government's authority cannot be exercised. Where is the Treaty? Czechoslovak property is being stolen in front of our eyes. The Red Army even carries the telephone wires away. Nobody seems to have the courage to oppose them. The NKVD is here and operates. The people see it and cannot feel respect for the Czechoslovak Administrative Delegation. The people are puzzled. The officers of the political service of the Ukrainian Front Command direct the propaganda for the Communist Party. The destiny of the Delegation is in your hands. If you do not intervene at Moscow, we cannot master the situation. It is forbidden to communicate with you. I am calling you in secret. Your answer must be worded cautiously. Signed: Krucky."[11]

The next day the Ministry of Foreign Affairs in London received another call: "The risk of calling you directly is mount-

[10] *Ibid.*, p. 120. [11] Duchacek, *op.cit.*, pp. 11-12.

ing. I am perhaps calling you for the last time. We are under pressure. Only your demarche in Moscow can save us. Whoever refuses to volunteer for the Red Army is in danger and has to take refuge in the mountains. Many do. The same happens to those who refuse to vote Communist when local or district Committees are being formed. The terror is directed by the political service of the Red Army. Try to send a courier plane and bring me to London. You should know everything. Signed: Krucky."[12]

On November 30 the chairman of the district National Committee at Chust ordered all Czechoslovak flags removed. The whole country was in a turmoil of confusion and helplessness, completely under the control of the Red Army secret police. In desperation and to escape isolation, the governmental Delegate left December 8 for Moscow. He hoped to be able to establish direct and unhampered contact with President Beneš and to clarify the situation in conversations with Soviet officials. Within a few days he was to feel the full blast of invective, plot, and counterplot against him and against the Republic.

He reported in detail to the President about his experience. Beneš in his answer, always hopeful, expressed the opinion that the separatist movement was fomented by Ukrainian communists, without any agreement with Moscow and perhaps even against its wishes. He insisted on the pre-Munich boundaries.

In a long conversation with the Moscow Czechoslovak communists the Delegate maintained that one-third of the population was for separation, another third unmistakably pro-Czechoslovak, and the last third either uncommitted or indifferent but willing to join the winning party.

The attitude of the communist group underwent an eloquent change. In the 1920's, it must be remembered, they had called Subcarpathian Russia a colony of Czech imperialism. Then, in 1938, they declared themselves ready to fight for the integrity of Czechoslovak territory. During the war, they first avoided any mention of Subcarpathian Russia and spoke about Czechoslovakia

[12] *Ibid.*

as a country of Czechs and Slovaks. Then, later, when the Soviet government recognized the pre-Munich Czechoslovakia, their appeals were also addressed to Subcarpathians. A photostatic copy of the "Oath of Allegiance of the Czechoslovak Partisans," drafted probably as late as in May 1944 by the second official of the Party, R. Slánský, includes all three nationalities of Czechoslovakia.[13]

Now, however, in December 1944, the situation was different. The time of diplomacy, pledges, and pretending had passed. Hard-headed politics, backed up by the Red Army's weapons, produced another party line. Gottwald, who had not visited the liberated territory (if it still deserved such a terminology) but made his estimates from and in Moscow, rejected the Delegate's evaluation of the situation and expressed the conviction that ninety per cent of the populace was for separation and the remaining ten per cent were fascists, collaborators with the enemy, and the wealthy. He stressed, seconded by Ambassador Fierlinger, that it was impossible to dampen the enthusiastic longing of the population for union with the USSR. Moreover, they were equally emphatic in their declarations that the Soviet government was not behind the movement, that it was entirely spontaneous.[14]

The Soviet diplomat in charge of East European Affairs, V. Zorin, gave Fierlinger repeated assurances that the Soviet government would continue to respect the Czechoslovak-Soviet treaty and that it would maintain a policy of non-interference in the affairs of Subcarpathian Russia. The recruitment of soldiers into the Soviet forces was, he insisted, the result of the enthusiastic reception they had received in the country.[15]

After a delay of three weeks, on December 26 and 27 respectively, the Delegate was received by Vyshinsky and Molotov. They insisted that they held to the letter of the Czechoslovak-Soviet treaty but that of course they could neither hamper a spontaneous movement nor ignore the wishes of the Subcar-

[13] *KSČ*, *op.cit.*, pictures 69-70.

[14] Fierlinger, *op.cit.*, vol. II, p. 409.

[15] *Ibid.*, p. 426.

pathian people. The Moscow Czechoslovak communists and Fierlinger, supposedly acting independently from the Soviet government, asked for immediate cession of the territory to Russia. The Delegate, now near to nervous collapse, associated himself with the idea. He was sharply rebuked by Beneš, who refused to abandon the position inherent in the pledges made by their ally and friend, the Soviet Union.

During the conversation between the Delegate and the communist group a political bomb exploded. A Slovak communist, L. Novomesky, who during the time of the Slovak uprising had been in London and who was now participating in the Moscow discussions, alleged that the President had told him that he had offered Subcarpathian Russia to the Soviet Union in December 1943 when he had been in Moscow.[16] This was an extremely serious statement; to this day the issue has not been entirely clarified, inasmuch as Beneš' diplomatic language permitted broad interpretation.

On January 23, 1945 Stalin intervened personally in the Subcarpathian crisis and wrote to President Beneš a letter which offers a clue to the moot question. In his letter Stalin ascribed to a "misunderstanding" the Czechoslovak government's worries "that the Soviet government [intended] unilaterally to solve the question of Subcarpathian Ukraine." However, he stated, the Soviet government could not forbid the population "to express their national will." He reminded Beneš of the conversation he allegedly had had with him in Moscow in December 1943 in which Beneš was "prepared to cede the Subcarpathian Ruthenia to the Soviet Union. As you will certainly remember," continued Stalin, "at that time I did not give my consent to it." He assured Beneš that the Soviet government had no intention of breaking the agreement with Czechoslovakia or of harming her. However, the question must be solved, he added, either before or after the end of war by an agreement between the two governments.

[16] Němec, *op.cit.*, p. 129.

Facing a *fait accompli,* Beneš now retreated and answered Stalin's letter in a spirit which surely—after the crushing experience with Moscow—was contrary to his inner convictions. He attributed the happenings in Subcarpathian Russia to "purely local factors," thus absolving the Soviet government from any responsibility. Expressing full trust in the principles of the Soviet policy he excluded the thought that the Soviet government would want to solve the question unilaterally. He would wish to have it settled after the war. Without reacting to Stalin's remark about the conversation in Moscow, Beneš assured him, however, that his standpoint on the question had not changed since he had discussed it with the Soviet Ambassador in London in September 1939. At the end of the letter Beneš assured Stalin of the Czechoslovak people's sentiments of unparalleled friendship toward the Soviet Union and thanked him for all the support.[17]

President Beneš' answer was in the same spirit of good will and concession which had characterized his policy toward the Soviet Union and for which he hoped to be repaid by Stalin's understanding.

Dr. Beneš' letter clearly reveals his silence to Stalin's statement about his "willingness," expressed in December 1943, to give up Subcarpathian Russia in favor of the Soviet Union. However, it does confirm that in the past he had expressed himself about the desirability of seeking an agreement with Moscow on the area. In diplomacy, desirability may easily be understood as an offer. On the other hand, it will be remembered that Beneš handed Stalin in December 1943 a memorandum which clearly included Subcarpathian Russia within the Republic. Did Stalin's pledge of returning the area to Czechoslovakia and his statement recognizing the pre-Munich frontiers of Czechoslovakia—which "settles it once and for all"—did that pledge and that statement pass into oblivion? (See pp. 84-85.)

[17] For the text of the letters see E. Taborsky, "Beneš and Stalin," *op.cit.*, pp. 173-75.

As his former secretary admits, Beneš did speak with Soviet diplomats in the years of 1939-1941 in the sense ". . . that Subcarpathian Russia cannot remain in Hungarian hands but must belong either to Czechoslovakia or to the Soviet Union. . . . He used this statement deliberately to sound out the Russians as to whether or not they intended some day to raise demands for Subcarpathian Russia. And as much as he wished Subcarpathian Russia to be Czechoslovak again, he was by no means ready to insist on it at the price of Soviet friendship."[18]

As it turned out, his "sounding out" policy was seized upon in January 1945 as an offer, the question was not settled once and for all, and, above all, the highly-prized Soviet friendship proved unobtainable.

Whatever the truth may be, the staged campaign to bring Subcarpathian Russia into the Soviet Union, conducted as it was by the Soviet military and political officers, was a blatant violation of the Czechoslovak-Soviet treaty, particularly the stipulation on non-interference in the internal affairs of Czechoslovakia.

The final secret message to London about the situation in Subcarpathian Russia was pathetically futile, emphasizing only the tragedy of the situation. It was sent on January 26, one day after Stalin's letter to Beneš, by Monsignor F. Hála, one member of the Delegate's political advisers staff who remained behind in Subcarpathian Russia. The message read: "The people are becoming more and more pro-Czechoslovak. Their feeling is now being expressed aloud. With no effort on our part, the Ruthenians come to our former recruiting office and express their desire to join the Czechoslovak Army and *go with it* farther West. The average is sixty recruits daily. They are mostly students, teachers, and enthusiasts. The intelligentsia first considered it their duty to work for incorporation into the Ukraine. Now, they come to our offices and beg: 'Give us a plebiscite. We want to vote.'"[19]

It was too late. The "spontaneity" of the first days would not

[18] Táborský, "Benešovy moskevské cesty," *op.cit.*, p. 207.

[19] Duchacek, *op.cit.*, p. 14.

be ignored by the Soviet government. It was a spontaneity similar to that experienced by the Baltic States in 1940.[20]

The eastern area of Czechoslovakia now being lost—that loss to be confirmed later by a formal agreement, signed June 29, 1945, to maintain *decorum*—Dr. Beneš and the government in exile were gravely worried that the experience would be repeated in Slovakia. Their worries were not unjustified. On January 13 Beneš received another secret radio report from Chust: "The educational officers of the First Corps of the Czechoslovak Army fighting on the Soviet front, all of them Communists, are being sent to Slovakia with instructions to start a movement advocating the *incorporation of Slovakia* into the Soviet Union. The Czechoslovak Administrative Delegation feels stranded on a desert island. There are signs of demoralization. Some of our officials believe that all Czechoslovakia may become part of the Soviet Union. They act accordingly. Signed: K. Zavadil."[21]

Then, another message, dated January 21: "In Michalovce, Slovakia, the Communist Party has just published the first issue of their newspaper, *Pravda*, under the auspices of General Mekhlis, chief of the Red Army's political service. The Communists have instructions to concentrate on gaining complete control of the National Committees."[22]

And another warning one month later: "From parts of Slovakia which are still under the complete jurisdiction of the Red Army, there is a daily arrival of several members of the Communist Party, mostly educated persons and students. When they reach the Rear Zone, Communist Headquarters immediately sends them all over the area. Thus, the Communists do not lack agitators. They organize National Committees wherever they had not already been formed, or change their composition if it does not correspond to the Communist pattern. *The presence of the NKVD increases the self-confidence of these agitators and backs up their*

[20] The account on Subcarpathian Russia is based, unless otherwise stated, on the documentary book by the governmental Delegate, F. Němec, *op.cit.*, pp. 89-156.

[21] Duchacek, *op.cit.*, pp. 9, 13.

[22] *Ibid.*, p. 8.

threats, which are plentiful. *The people are confused.* The Slovak Democratic Party has no such aid coming in from the Operational Zone. They have so far been unable to issue a newspaper of their own. Communist activity plus the great number of Communist agitators concentrated in one area creates an impression of strength *which does not exist*." (Italics in the text.)[23]

The author of the message was certainly correct—and subsequent events in Slovakia confirmed his opinion—in stating that communist agitators created an impression of strength "which does not exist." It is most difficult to imagine the pious Slovak peasants welcoming communists and the Red Army. But the Soviet hordes, grinding unceasingly ahead like a bulldozer, accompanied by political officers and by highly vocal communist campaigners, made them bewildered, speechless, submissive.

Home via Moscow

It was high time for Dr. Beneš to return home to Czechoslovakia if he wished it to be a free home. The country was being liberated from the east by the Red Army, not by the American and British Armies from the west, and the only way to return from the six-year exile led through Moscow.

President Beneš inquired of Moscow, in January, about the transfer of his government to Slovakia. He wished also to enter into negotiations with the representatives of the political parties about the composition and establishment of a new government to enter the liberated territory. The Moscow communists agreed and suggested the Soviet capital as a suitable place for such negotiations.[24]

On February 14 London telegraphed to Moscow that the President would be ready to leave about February 23. He intended, the message continued, to stay in Moscow about one week and divide his time between conversations with the Soviet government and the political parties. He wished to keep these activities

[23] *Ibid.*, p. 9. [24] Fierlinger, *op.cit.*, p. 574.

separate. As to the new government, he envisaged that it would consist of communists, social democrats, national socialists, the Catholic Party, and agrarians. Beneš' telegram further stated: "According to the discussions up to the present, there would be in the government two Czechoslovak national socialists, two Catholics, two Czech agrarians (if there are such), four Slovaks (two left and two right), and one neutral (Masaryk). The discussion about the chief of the government is being left to the end, the number of communists and social democrats will be agreed upon in Moscow. The distribution of portfolios, with the exception of three or four cases, will probably create no major difficulties. I will consider the government as entirely provisional till the liberated Moravia and Bohemia express themselves in full freedom."[25]

In another telegram London informed the Soviet government that a group of about two hundred persons, politicians and officials, would leave by boat. It would include about fifty members of the diplomatic corps, accredited to the government of Czechoslovakia, a request which was received by the Soviet government "with no small embarrassment."[26]

Two members of the government, Feierabend and Majer, warned President Beneš against the trip to Moscow. For the former the warning was a culmination of his critical attitude toward Beneš' policy of friendship toward the Soviet government and the Czechoslovak communists. Feierabend told the President that he would be virtually their prisoner and suggested that only a delegation of political leaders be sent. Feierabend knew, too, that Moscow would never permit him to go there; he belonged to the hated Agrarian Party and had had several *rencontres* with Bogomolov, the Soviet Ambassador to the Czechoslovak government in London. However, Beneš was firm in his decision to go to Moscow; but equally firm were his assurances to Feierabend that under no circumstances would he agree to permitting the

[25] *Ibid.*, pp. 580-82.
[26] *Ibid.*, p. 586.

Ministry of the Interior and the Ministry of National Defense to be concentrated in the hands of one political party.[27]

As for Mr. Majer, he had specific reasons for advising Beneš against the trip. His political group, the social democrats, was divided into the left and right wings. The political position of social democrats was and proved to continue to be of key importance. As long as Majer could protect his right wing against the pressures and attacks from the left wing, led by Fierlinger, he could hope to maintain his party's independence from the communist encroachment. The President's answer to Majer's objection revealed the sad reality: "Moscow was the only road because otherwise he would have to give up everything to the communists without a struggle and [Czechoslovakia] would be in an even worse situation than Poland was. I recognized that he was right," remarks Mr. Majer.[28]

It appears that there was no other opposition to the decision to return to Czechoslovakia via Moscow. The government in exile agreed to hand over its resignation to the Prime Minister, Monsignor Šrámek, who was empowered to make it officially known whenever he considered it to be a suitable time. Political leaders were to go to Moscow as members of the individual parties' delegations.

[27] From an interview with Mr. Feierabend, June 12, 1958.

[28] *Recollections and Reconstruction of the Czechoslovak February 1948 Crisis by a Group of Democratic Leaders*, stenographic report, meeting, November 12, 1949. Little has been known so far about the developments preceding Beneš' trip to Moscow, even less about the crucial negotiations there. After the communist putsch in February 1948 a group of prominent democratic *émigré* leaders met regularly during 1949 and the first part of 1950 to attempt a detailed reconstruction of the events which led to the communization of the country. They were: Professor Jaroslav Stránský, the leading member of the National Socialist Party, Minister of Justice during the war and Minister of Education after the war; Václav Majer, the leader of the right wing Social Democratic Party, Minister of Reconstruction during the war and Minister of Food afterward, and Blažej Vilím, the postwar Secretary General of the same party; Jaromír Smutný, the Chancellor of the Republic, the chief officer to President Beneš; and Lev Sychrava, a prominent journalist and intimate friend of Dr. Beneš. Their discussions were stenographed and kindly made available to the author. They are hereafter cited as *Recollections and Reconstruction*. J. Stránský summed up the discussions in a *Personal Résumé*, Nos. 1, 2, and 3.

After some delays the departure from London was arranged for March 9, 1945. However, it was postponed for another two days when President Beneš suddenly became ill—an illness which later incapacitated him physically in the fateful period of national affairs. On March 17, 1945 the President and the political delegations reached Moscow. He was welcomed with the same ceremony as in December 1943 but in a political atmosphere that was obviously reserved. When he was received by Stalin, the conversation was rather general—Stalin by now had lost interest in pretending cordiality; he had already acquired what he wanted. Individual questions were left to negotiations with Molotov, who extracted from Beneš a written statement on Subcarpathian Russia.[29]

On one occasion only, a witness states, was the grimness of the scene dissipated. Stalin gave a dinner in Beneš' honor and in one toast he asked that the Red Army which was not "an army of angels" be forgiven for misbehavior in Czechoslovakia. In another toast he spoke about Slav solidarity and formulated the new communist concept of the idea by saying: "We wish that all will be allied irrespective of small or large, but that every nation will preserve its independence and regulate its internal life according to its ideology and tradition, be they good or bad. It rests with each state individually how it arranges it. . . . The Soviet Union will not interfere in the internal affairs of its allies. I know that even among you there are such who doubt it. Perhaps even you are a little dubious [said Stalin turning to Beneš in a weaker voice] but I give assurance that we will never interfere in the internal affairs of our allies. Such is Lenin's neo-Slavism which we bolshevik communists are following. There can be no talk of a 'hegemony of the Soviet Union.'"[30] This feeble ray of hope which for a moment relieved the grimness of the Moscow scene did not last for long. The crux of the matter was in negotia-

[29] Táborský, "Benešovy moskevské cesty," *op.cit.*, pp. 210-12.
[30] Taborsky, "Beneš and Stalin," *op.cit.*, pp. 179-80.

tions concerning the program and composition of the future government.

At the opening session Gottwald proposed that meetings be chaired alternately by him, Fierlinger, and J. David. This was the first successful tactical move. The role of Gottwald and Fierlinger in the chair does not require amplification. As to David, he was one of the oldest members of the National Socialist Party—a good man but a weakling, inclined to side with the communists. Though Stránský was the leader of the National Socialists delegation, in the interests of maintaining the good will which prevailed in every controversial matter over many considerations he did not insist on sharing in the chairmanship.

The next thing which occurred was that, as Majer had feared, his followers were eliminated from the social democratic delegation which was reshuffled according to Fierlinger's wishes.

The Catholic Party delegation was paralyzed by Šrámek's illness and Monsignor Hála's psychological shock which he had suffered as a result of his excruciating experience in Subcarpathian Russia. From the beginning of the negotiations the communists were in a position of leadership, acting on the assumption that they would undoubtedly be the strongest party in the country, an assumption which other delegates apparently failed to contest.

The problem of Slovak representation worked in the communists' favor too. The delegates of the Slovak National Council which had been constituted in 1943 introduced themselves as exclusive representatives of the Slovak nation. They were composed of an equal number of communists and democrats. The latter sided with the communists on all decisive questions in the tragically happy conviction that they had struck a good bargain in matters of Slovak autonomy. In addition, the Slovak branch of the Social Democratic Party fused with the Communist Party during the Slovak uprising in August 1944, an event which had a discouraging effect upon the rest of the social democrats.

The position of President Beneš was of crucial importance. Not only did he live separately from the delegations but he also abstained from their meetings. In retrospect it is most difficult to comprehend his attitude, but he obviously withdrew into the role of the strictly constitutional head of state whom the individual delegations kept informed but who deliberately abstained from any intervention and influence in the negotiations. He had indicated previously his wish to leave the initiative and responsibility in national affairs to party leaders, but since he had for five years of the war exercised almost supreme power and decisive influence, his new role in Moscow not only was a surprise to the democratic delegates but was also welcomed by the communists. So it was that this man of unparalleled prestige, the indisputable leader of the nation, made the decision to remain above party politics in this crucial hour. The fact is, of course, that this was not party politics from which he withdrew; it was a moment of decision between freedom and totalitarianism. The cause of Czechoslovak democracy suffered an irreparable loss at this fateful hour of its history.

"At the Moscow conference," states one of its chief democratic participants, "there came into conflict not two political emigrations—from London and from Moscow—but here for the first time there was joined the battle of two political worlds."[31] The London government had conscientiously prepared many legislative proposals designed to effect a smooth transition from the war to a peaceful political life, adequate economic reconstruction, and social progress. However, it was not prepared to face the solid front of the Moscow communists. It had no plan for a common strategy; indeed, so sincere was its intent to cooperate with the communists in full loyalty that it had deliberately discarded any idea of a common procedure for fear of creating suspicion on the part of the communists.

The communists proceeded differently. They presented the democratic delegates with a thirty-two-page document, outlining a program of radical action in all spheres of life. On one point, the nationalization of key industries, they were hypocritically

[31] J. Stránský, *Personal Résumé*, No. 1.

timid. "There was nothing in their proposal about the nationalization of industry, and the section which spoke about the state control of key industries was inserted in the program only during the negotiations, and this did not happen at the insistence of communists,"[32] stated Mr. Majer, who represented the view of the London democratic group which wished to be honest with the Czechoslovak people.

The original communist draft omitted specific mention of a constitutional guarantee of human and political rights. When the communist negotiators were requested to amend it "they smiled and immediately inserted the clause on constitutional freedom," remarked Professor Stránský.[33] There was some further argument but basically the communist proposal was accepted.[34]

The composition of the government was of even greater importance than the program. When Fierlinger went to Tehcran to welcome the President on his way to Moscow, he informed him that the communists proposed him (Fierlinger) as Prime Minister. Beneš advised him in a friendly manner that he should first bring to an end his diplomatic mission in Russia and then enter politics later. The democratic delegates, including the social democrat Majer, would have preferred naming Gottwald Prime Minister rather than to follow the subterfuge of naming such a fellow-traveller as Fierlinger. However, at communist insistence, Fierlinger won, and President Beneš, who by now disliked him thoroughly, nevertheless expressed some relief as he had feared the West's reaction in case of Gottwald's appointment. The communists did not wish the Premiership at this time for tactical reasons; Fierlinger was their man anyhow.

The composition of the twenty-five-member government and the distribution of the portfolios likewise demonstrated communist domination. On the surface the representation of the political parties was equal: the four Czech parties—Communists,

[32] *Recollections and Reconstruction*, *op.cit.*, meeting of November 12, 1949.
[33] *Ibid.*, meeting of December 20, 1949.
[34] *Ibid.*, meeting May 9, 1950.

Social Democrats, National Socialists, and Catholics—each had three members in the government; the two Slovak parties—Communists and Democrats—also had three members each. Six members entered the government as "personalities of national repute and experts without regard to their political membership," as the official explanation read. When, however, the parties' allegiance was counted *in toto* the communists had eight representatives in the government: three from the Czech and three from the Slovak branches of the same party plus two "experts," Z. Nejedlý and V. Clementis. In addition, two of the three social democrats were eager fellow-travellers, Z. Fierlinger and B. Laušman, and the "expert" in the Ministry of National Defense, General L. Svoboda, had during the war frequently manifested his subservience to the communists. When the distribution of the portfolios was analyzed in the light of political power it became apparent that almost all positions of importance were in the hands of this group; the Premiership, two of the five Deputy Premierships, the Deputy Foreign Ministership, the Ministry of National Defense, the Ministry of the Interior, the Ministry of Education, the Ministry of Information, the Ministry of Industry, the Ministry of Agriculture, and the Ministry of Social Welfare.[35]

Two men deserve special mention—L. Svoboda, the Minister of National Defense, and Jan Masaryk, the Minister of Foreign Affairs—each for different, mutually exclusive reasons. Svoboda, a relatively insignificant officer in the Czechoslovak Army, was chosen during the war at the insistence of the communists and with the backing of the Soviet military as the commander of the Czechoslovak units which fought on the Russian front. He conceded to all Soviet requests, worked closely with Fierlinger and with him sabotaged the military policy of the London government. Svoboda was an obvious fellow-traveller. It will be remembered

[35] Unless otherwise stated, the factual information about the negotiations in Moscow is based on the following sources: *Recollections and Reconstruction*, *op.cit.*, meetings of November 12, 1949, December 20, 1949; *Personal Résumé*, No. 1, *op.cit.*; Interview of Mr. V. Majer, June 14, 1958.

that President Beneš while still in London was resolved that the Ministry of Defense and the Ministry of the Interior must not be in the hands of one party. Nominally, the resolution was maintained; politically, it was not.

Jan Masaryk was the great son of a greater father, a Westerner in heart and mind. He was strictly non-partisan; he belonged to no party but to his country. As Beneš had faithfully served T. G. Masaryk, now Jan Masaryk wished to serve with equal devotion Edvard Beneš. When he accompanied the President to Moscow in March 1945 Masaryk met Gottwald for the first time in his life. Gottwald, in their first visit on March 20, treated him to a display of brutality and vulgarity, perhaps hoping to intimidate this openly democratic statesman. They met for two and a half hours. Gottwald opened with a belligerent remark that communists were not interested in individuals except as they were able to perform certain functions. Then he accused Masaryk of "a public anti-Soviet demonstration" by failing to accompany President Beneš on his previous trip to Moscow in December 1943. Masaryk's explanation to Gottwald that he had attended an UNRRA conference in the United States was brushed aside. He had, Gottwald insisted, spoken with contempt about Moscow on various occasions.

Gottwald then criticized the foreign policy of the London government for which Masaryk, as its Minister of Foreign Affairs, was responsible. It was not conducted, he alleged, in the spirit of uncompromising friendship with the Soviet Union; it was too cautious and considerate in its attitude toward the West; it was late in recognizing the new situation in Poland and Yugoslavia.

Gottwald then emphasized his full support of Fierlinger whom Masaryk, it was well known, despised. Masaryk, though he expressed the desire to avoid any controversy about Fierlinger, could not abstain from observing ". . . that from the day he became the envoy of the London government to Moscow, in all his reports there was not a single word even mildly critical of the Soviet Union, and that therefore, not quite unnaturally, the impression had been created in the London government that he was more papal than the Pope himself."

The two men then discussed the question of Subcarpathian Russia. Gottwald wanted its immediate settlement. Masaryk retorted that he could recognize no other boundary for Czechoslovakia than that of 1938, and further expressed the view that this would also be in the Soviet interest. Gottwald then lashed out with even greater bitterness into a personal attack. He told Masaryk that in him he saw only a representative of one class. Masaryk protested. Gottwald answered with a lecture on communist philosophy. "He also very openly condemned parliamentary democracy which gives to the people an opportunity to vote once in five years but then they have very little to say about public affairs. . . ." Masaryk argued about this too. Gottwald then stated in a dictatorial fashion that from now on the foreign policy of Czechoslovakia must be adjusted without reservation to a policy of complete cooperation with the Soviet Union. He was not quite sure if Masaryk understood this new situation. Masaryk said that he did.

The day following the conversation Masaryk wrote a memorandum about it. The last words read, "At the end, only one sentence. During the First Republic [1918-1938] when the political parties had no courage to attack the President [T. G. Masaryk], they attacked his Foreign Minister [Beneš]. Today, the President is Dr. Beneš and the Foreign Minister is Jan Masaryk. That's all."[36]

Shortly after this unpleasant and foreboding experience Masaryk left Moscow to participate in the United Nations Conference in San Francisco. The conference was plagued by the vexatious question of the representation of Poland. At the opening session of the Steering Committee, Molotov asked Masaryk to propose that the invitation be directed to the Lublin Polish provisional government:

[36] Jan Masaryk, *Memorandum*, Moscow, March 21, 1945.

"Masaryk declined with the comment that he would do so when the matter appears on the agenda. A few minutes later Gromyko sought Masaryk out with a message from Molotov that the proposal must be made immediately. Masaryk refused. A while later, Pavlov, Molotov's interpreter, came to Masaryk with a written message from Molotov threatening that the alliance between the Czechoslovak Republic and the Soviet Union made no sense if he was not willing to make the proposal.

"Masaryk almost collapsed under this threat. Almost the whole of Czechoslovakia was then occupied by the Red Army and President Beneš was under its control, more or less a prisoner. Jan Masaryk, therefore, made the proposal. The Steering Committee rejected it, of course. Masaryk then passed Molotov's threatening note to me with the remark, 'Keep it well, you will need it.' "[37]

Thus writes Dr. Ján Papánek, one of Masaryk's closest friends and former Permanent Delegate of Czechoslovakia to the United Nations.

The San Francisco experience was the first demonstration of the meaning of Gottwald's dictum that the Czechoslovak foreign policy must be adjusted to that of the Soviet Union "without reservation." This dictum, the whole conversation with Masaryk, the negotiations in Moscow about the program and composition of the government—these were all the product of the political and military developments in Europe. The Red Army was advancing by leaps and bounds in Czechoslovakia. The Allied Army was still far away. The Soviet Union had a preconceived, determined policy; the West had little or none. The Czechoslovak communists were aggressively pushing ahead with their well-prepared plan and strategy; the Czechoslovak democrats, beaten down by their experiences in Moscow, had no common strategical plan, save that of maintaining good will at all costs. The cost of such good will was frequent and unwarranted concessions.

If Munich, the betrayal of Czechoslovakia by the West, was the pathogenesis of Czech communism, if wartime political and mili-

[37] From a letter of J. Papánek, May 16, 1958.

tary developments encouraged the spread of the infection, the Moscow conference can be described in retrospect only as the deathbed of Czechoslovak democracy. From that day on the disease was epidemic; there was no stopping it. The communists and the Soviet Union were, of course, largely responsible for the tragedy, but the more painful truth is that all democrats and all democracies share in that responsibility.

By this time the Czechoslovak democrats could cling to one forlorn hope, that Beneš' overwhelming authority and popularity and the Czechoslovak people's devotion to democratic ways of life might eventually triumph over the wrongs wrenched out of them during this Moscow conference, if only the Czechoslovak government, so long in exile, could be transplanted to its native soil. Undoubtedly a despairing wish was parent to this thought, but what other road was open? The country already overrun by Russia, the choice that now remained was that of the best of all bad choices. If anything was to be saved, the government must return. Even that was subject to full cooperation.

Indeed, one of the closest associates of Dr. Beneš notes that the communists in Moscow went so far as to threaten that "if the program is not accepted the London government will not be permitted to return to Czechoslovakia." Fierlinger, who later came to be referred to derisively as "Quislinger," stated "that had not these claims of the Moscow group been accepted, there would have been no train to take the delegation home."[38]

However, the communist demands were met and a train was made available. On March 31, 1945 the President and the politicians left Moscow. Beneš was accompanied on the journey by the recently-appointed Ambassador to Czechoslovakia, V. Zorin, who later was to play a key role in the final downfall of the Republic. At that time, however, he was not appreciated by such

[38] *Desať rokov. Československá otázka v Spojených národoch*, S úvodom Jána Papánka (Ten Years, The Czechoslovak Question before the United Nations, with an introduction by J. Papánek), Chicago, Československá Národná Rada Americká, 1958, p. 18.

figures as Fierlinger, who, on one occasion when questioned about Zorin's ability, characterized him as a "complete dumbbell."[39] Unfortunately, this time he was wrong.

On April 3 the President reached the second largest city in Slovakia, Košice. This was the city that was to become identified with the newly-formed government, out of which came the program that was to haunt the Czechoslovak people on their dismal three-year regression into the night.

[39] *Recollections and Reconstruction*, *op.cit.*, meeting February 7, 1950.

IN THE "LIBERATED" HOMELAND

It is important to grasp the chaos and the complications within Czechoslovakia to which Beneš returned: a country suddenly freed from six years of military and political occupation by a foreign power.

The prewar democratic administration, Czechoslovakia's economic system, her cultural and political institutions had all been abolished by the German authorities and replaced by nazi or nazi-controlled institutions and a wartime economy. With the liberation these German institutions disappeared, and in every village, town, and district people connected with the German administration were immediately replaced. The master of yesterday was declared the traitor of today. The pent-up bitterness of the oppressed burst out into sentiments of hatred and vengeance. Totalitarian organizations of the youth, of farmers, and of workers were dissolved to give place to new supposedly democratic institutions. Major factories, some under direct German control, others managed by collaborators, were to return to former owners or be put under new management. Universities were to be opened; other schools, poisoned for six years by the nazi spirit, were to be free educational centers once again. Old established cultural institutions, theaters, academies of science, desecrated and abused during the war, were to be revived. A free press was to be reestablished. Numerous tasks of reconstruction and rehabilitation were to be initiated without delay. It was, in fact, a revolution. Its successful accomplishment under the best of conditions would be an enormous task, but, under the threat of the Red Army and harassed by an aggressive communism, it became all but impossible.

To meet such a situation, such an atmosphere, required unity of spirit and purpose in the nation. But the nation was far from such a unity. Indeed, the yawning breaches in its national unity were probably the most tragic heritage of the six years of enemy occupation. Czechoslovakia was divided on the one hand between those who had fought for years with the underground or who had huddled out their lives in concentration camps, whose wounds would never heal, and those who had collaborated, willingly or forcibly, with the enemy. It was divided between the London emigration and the Moscow emigration, between the Western front Czechoslovak soldiers and the Russian front Czechoslovak soldiers. The gulfs between these groups were deep, always emotional, sometimes rational, rarely bridgeable.

The government which presided over such a situation called itself a government of national unity; its political parties formed a National Front.

Košice, the Temporary Capital

On April 4, 1945, the President of the Republic, as it had been agreed in Moscow, nominated a new government. Košice became its temporary seat. In receiving the government, Dr. Beneš considered it important to mention that he would be "a constitutional president," a statement which confirmed his previous decision to respect the limitations imposed upon the head of state by the basic law of the country. He was to proceed on a strictly constitutional basis—in a revolutionary situation.

The following day the governmental program, as was also agreed in Moscow, was made public at a solemn ceremony. The President attended the opening session and then withdrew when the program was presented. He wished to demonstrate the government's sole responsibility for the program and to its implementation.[1] Beneš' action may have been important to a political analyst but it was probably hardly noticed by the general public.

The first chapter of the governmental program mentioned the temporary character of the government and stipulated that a

[1] Stránský, *Personal Résumé*, No. 1, *op.cit.*

Provisional National Assembly would be replaced by a Constitutional Assembly on the basis of free elections which "will take place in the shortest possible time."[2] Actually, it took thirteen months before the elections were held.

The government further promised to speed up the organization of the armed forces and to shape it after the unexcelled example of the Red Army. Ominously enough, the nucleus was to be the corps which had fought on the Russian front. The army was also to be subjected to political education led by "educational officers." Command posts could be taken only by "officers of sincerely democratic and truly anti-fascist convictions." The statement was subsequently interpreted in such a way by General Svoboda, the fellow-travelling Minister of National Defense, and by the chief of staff, General Boček, as to exclude or threaten those officers who, remaining faithful to the Republic, did not join the Communist Party.

A chapter on foreign policy promulgated the closest alliance with the Soviet Union and paid ungrateful lip service to friendly relations with the United States and Great Britain but "particularly close friendship with France," where communists were strongly represented in the government.

In internal affairs, the program placed all local power in the hands of the National Committees. It guaranteed the right to vote to all citizens of eighteen years of age and above except for traitors and collaborators—an exception which was widely used for communist purposes. It stated, however, that "constitutional liberties will be fully guaranteed, particularly freedom of the individual, of assembly, association, expression of opinion by word [of mouth], press and letter, the privacy of home and mail, freedom of learning and conscience and religion." No sooner were the constitutional freedoms declared than they were violated.

[2] For the text see *Program prvé domácí vlády republiky, vlády národní fronty Čechů a Slováků, Sbírka dokumentů* (The Program of the First Government of the Republic of the National Front of Czechs and Slovaks), Prague, Ministerstvo informací, 1945.

In a chapter on the relations between Czechs and Slovaks the program of the government carved out of Czechoslovak unity a far-reaching autonomy for Slovakia.

All members of the German and Hungarian minority who were unable to prove their active opposition to fascism were to be deprived of Czechoslovak citizenship. All traitors and collaborators were to be punished. All fascist organizations were to be uprooted; the government was "not to allow renewal, in any form, of the political parties which transgressed so gravely against the interests of the nation and the Republic. . . ." This prohibition was directed particularly against the Agrarian Party, which had been the strongest party in Czechoslovakia before the war and which held conservative views. This undemocratic decision had been accepted, after some resistance, by the non-communist parties in the hope that former voters of the Agrarian Party would join their ranks or at any rate would not vote for the Communist Party. A shock awaited them in that respect in 1946.

The property of all enemies of the state and of all traitors was to be confiscated, the program stated, and managed by organs of the National Administration. It promised a new land reform.

In the economic sphere the program called for a speedy reconstruction of the country, offering support to private initiative and private enterprise and general commerce. The currency and credit system, the key industries, insurance and mines were to be "under a general state control," a term which was a thin disguise for "socialization," a word which the communists for the moment wished to avoid for tactical reasons.

Such was the program which the new government presented to the nation. With a few exceptions, it had the ring of a democratic, economically progressive spirit. It reflected the experiences and consequences of the war. If faithfully implemented, it offered some avenues for a free life within a socialized economic system.

Meanwhile, the group in London was getting ready to leave by ship, to reach Slovakia by way of Rumania. The communists, whether politicians or officials in the administration, were most eager to be included. London was no longer of interest to them. There were many things to be done in Czechoslovakia. Under pressure, ten communists above the number originally decided upon by the government managed to be included.

These days were charged with emotion. After six years, the exiles were on their way home. "The members of the so-called first line," relates Hugo Skala, who was the head of a department in the Ministry of Finances, "came to our office for money for the trip. Everybody felt friendly and bade us warmly, 'Goodby. We'll see you at home.' Only Nosek [the leading London communist] felt somewhat uncomfortable to come for money to the Ministry headed by Feierabend, for whom they had once had high praise but whom they were now ready to denounce as a traitor."[3]

Mr. Skala was in the so-called "first line." He writes:

"On the boat the communist group kept to themselves and spoke very little to us, non-communists. Then, suddenly everything changed when we heard, somewhere on the Mediterranean Sea, the news about the new Czechoslovak government and its program. The communists were jubilant and started to be aggressive, particularly the journalist Nový. They began to campaign for the party, and I think gained a few people—social democrats.

"When we reached Košice, my first experience in my own homeland was to be arrested. There were five of us. We were told the curfew was at 2 a.m. It was about 11 p.m. when we went back to our hotel and a Soviet guard stopped us. He argued that Košice was on Moscow time, and so I spent my first night at home in prison."[4]

If Košice was not on Moscow time, it did appear to be on Moscow policy. The President was under constant surveillance of the newly-appointed Soviet Ambassador, V. Zorin, and the Soviet military. He was never able to establish direct contact with those officials who remained in London, headed by his close

[3] From a letter of Professor H. Skala, April 29, 1958.
[4] *Ibid.*

associate, Hubert Ripka, though he had been promised such a service.

Nor was the President able to establish contact with Prague, where in the last days of the war a communist-controlled National Committee came into being. When his political friends who had just returned from prisons and concentration camps—Krajina, Heidrich, Jína, Jílovský, Němeček, and Drábek—visited its headquarters to ask for facilities to establish communications with Beneš, the communist deputy chairman, Smrkovský, refused even to receive them.[5]

Mr. Majer, the Minister of Food in the new government, relates that he "had to pass through three cordons of Russian soldiers" to see Beneš. To characterize the position of the government in the liberated town of Košice he further says: "I broadcast a speech one day. After I had finished and left the building one of the technicians rushed to see me and said, 'I want to tell you, but don't give me away, that the speech you just made was heard, at the furthest, forty kilometers [25 miles] from Košice.' I asked him if this was true also in case of the President's broadcast. He said it was."[6]

In such a situation, with the government under the control of the Red Army and the communists behind the scene calling every move, Gottwald had the arrogant courage to appeal to Beneš at Košice to "remain President of the Republic till his death."[7] At this moment, at least, Gottwald was probably honest. Nothing could have suited the communists better than to have as head of the state, fronting their policies, a person of national popularity and world prestige, but one who was in most respects their prisoner.

At one moment—but not for long—a flickering spark of hope appeared. On April 18, 1945, the American Army crossed the Czechoslovak boundary from the west. Hastily an agreement was

[5] From an interview with Mr. Drábek, June 15, 1958.

[6] *Recollections and Reconstruction*, *op.cit.*, meeting November 12, 1949.

[7] Smutný, *Únorový převrat 1948*, *op.cit.*, vol. v, p. 43.

signed to govern relations between the Allied commander and the Czechoslovak authorities. "I shall never forget the deep emotion with which Beneš, who always hated to bare his feelings, received the news, . . ." reminisces his former secretary. "'Thank God, thank God,' he said. . . . Unable to control his excitement he began to pace his study, and to judge by the expression in his eyes he was already visualizing the beneficial political consequences of this event. Then he rushed into the adjoining room to share the good news with his beloved wife. 'Haničko, Haničko, the Americans have just entered Czechoslovakia,' I heard him say to Madame Beneš in a voice still quivering with emotion. 'Patton is across the border!' In a few minutes he was back, instructing me to send Patton a telegram of congratulations and welcome."[8]

The possible consequences of Patton's thrust failed to materialize. Though the road to Prague was open, with little if any German resistance, his army did not advance. On higher orders they stopped when they reached the point already agreed upon with the Soviet High Command. The shadow of Teheran blotted out Czechoslovakia's last hope.

The shock was overpowering. When, in 1944, the American and British governments had declined to sign an agreement with the Czechoslovak government covering their armies' entry onto Czechoslovak soil, when again in the summer of 1944 they had not given substantial support to the Slovak uprising, a few individuals in the government in London had guessed the reason. But now millions of Czechoslovak people witnessed, horror-stricken, a military decision which they immediately knew would have the most drastic political consequences. To them there was only one possible interpretation: the West was not interested in Czechoslovakia, in her democracy. She belonged in the Soviet sphere. The psychological impact was devastating.

Other events were to follow which confirmed their fears. In

[8] E. Taborsky, "The Triumph and Disaster of Eduard Beneš," *Foreign Affairs*, vol. 36, no. 4 (July 1958), p. 680.

the author's opinion they contributed more than anything else to the downfall of Czechoslovak independence and freedom. On May 5, 1945 a revolution broke out in Prague. There were two untouched German armored divisions in the vicinity of the capital. The revolutionaries seized the radio station and appealed continuously for help, both publicly and secretly. The American advance forces were some sixty miles from Prague; the Soviet forces, one hundred twenty. Hubert Ripka, representing the Czechoslovak government in London, intervened immediately with the British government to send the Royal Air Force to bomb German concentrations. On May 7 the Czechoslovak pilots serving with the British Air Force were given an order to be in readiness for take-off. Suddenly, however, at the order of the Allied High Command the operation was cancelled.[9] On May 8, when the armistice was signed, fighting in barricaded Prague went on unaided. On May 9 Soviet tanks entered the ancient capital. History will now forever record that it was the Soviet Union who was the liberator of Prague. Once again, military decisions made political history.

Ironically, the communists tell a very different version as to why American forces came to a halt. Soon after the communist putsch, in February 1948, their newspapers published the statement that the American Army deliberately stopped its advance because they wanted the Czechoslovak people to be massacred by the Germans; and when the American Air Force bombed industrial objectives in Czechoslovakia it was only to eliminate Czechoslovak industry from competition in world markets.

Although this falsification of wartime history is one of the communists' more breathtaking efforts it is by no means the only one. For example, the six years of strenuous, at times exasperating, work of Dr. Beneš and his government in London, which, we have seen, was first denounced and then exploited for communist purposes, was after the putsch roundly condemned as highly damaging to Czechoslovak interest. "The truth is," one of its

[9] Ripka, *Le coup de Prague*, Paris, Plon, 1949, p. 29.

foremost spokesmen, Kopecký, says, "that at the beginning [of the war] they did not even dare to present themselves to the West as representatives of the Czechoslovak Republic. . . . The truth is that the Western powers did not recognize Czechoslovakia and her government abroad till 1941, when the Soviet Union entered the war." If Czechoslovakia was renewed, stated this communist leader, it was only thanks to the Soviet Union. Beneš was oriented on London, Gottwald on Moscow.[10] In the first phase of the war, in the period of Soviet-German friendship, the Czech "bourgeoisie cooperated with Germans," wrote Kopecký, and ". . . Beneš agreed with this slavish subjection."[11] He stated that the Communist Party leadership followed an entirely different line from Beneš; it made no concession to him; "it worked toward the goal of the victory of the program of the Communist Party of Czechoslovakia in the liberation struggle . . . to follow Gottwald," not Beneš. Kopecký admitted that "with the victory of the Soviet Army there was also the victory of the program of the CPC" and alleged that "the Beneš clique only tried to vegetate on the successful march of communists in the Czechoslovak liberation movement."[12]

This statement was made in 1951. But in 1945, after the war had ended in Europe, the communist policy of infiltration was to be concealed under the cloak of nationalism for another three years.

In the Countryside

In the last days of the war the Red Army's advance into Czechoslovakia was spectacular in every way. It rolled on, wave after wave, seemingly without number, without end. They were "no angels," as Stalin frankly admitted. Pillage and rape were the order of the day. The people were dumbfounded. So these were the Russian liberators, the great Slav brothers, they would whisper in astonishment.

[10] Kopecký, *Tridsať rokov*, *op.cit.*, p. 23.

[11] Kopecký, *30 let KSČ*, *op.cit.*, pp. 136, 138. [12] *Ibid.*, pp. 145, 146, 147.

Before the populace was able to shake off the paralysis of shock, local communists, until then in hiding or known secretly as patriots, came into the open, taking over the administration of the village or town. They founded National Committees. These were quickly joined by other local people. It was an act of courage to manifest at that time one's democratic convictions or to risk controversy or conflict with a communist.

Immediately after the Red Army's advance, the local communist organizations were quickly supported by the political commissars and the NKVD, the Soviet secret service. To organize administration and to campaign they needed paper, typewriters, money, printing machines, etc. These were quickly supplied to the communists by their Soviet comrades. The democratic local organizations had to struggle for them.

Communists called for the arrest of collaborators, and many persons whose only crime was that they did not join the party were sent to prison on the charge of cooperation with the enemy. Their property was sequestrated, to be administered by a group of people appointed by local National Committees. It is not difficult to imagine to whom most of these appointees owed their allegiance. To help these administrators in safeguarding the property, communists called for the organization of a workers' militia. The Red Army was quick to supply them with rifles.

From mountains and forests partisans descended on villages and towns, supposedly to help in the maintaining of public order. In some areas the population had never heard about the existence of partisan units in their vicinity. They were obviously formed at the last moment and were equipped with arms by the Red Army to terrorize the local populace.

In the boundary regions, where the Sudeten German minority had lived, the opportunity was ripe for mass seizure of power. The Germans either withdrew with the retreating German Army or were quickly expelled. Czechs moved in. The chaotic situation allowed communist functionairies and their hordes of followers to seize both power and property.

There was an apparent pattern in these developments. A village, or town, or region was liberated. The Red Army commissars brought in a group of communists; other political persons were forbidden to enter because officially the area was still in the theater of war. A National Committee, the key unit of the communist technique of infiltration and power, was "elected" on the street—and the rest followed with an almost inevitable dreariness.[13]

Those who listened to the radio in these days could hear the frequently-repeated proclamations of the party; they followed an almost immutable pattern. A few days after the government had been formed at Košice, for example, the party issued a proclamation which made an appeal for the organizing of National Committees, for the organization of a workers' militia, for taking over the administration of the enterprises of collaborators and of Germans. It emphasized at the end that the Communist Party of Czechoslovakia had entered the government to guarantee the fulfillment of this new people's democracy program. National unity was still its chief slogan. The performance was repeated in Bratislava, the capital of Slovakia, when the government members stopped there on their way to Prague.[14]

Many people, of course, fully understood the meaning of these happenings. They saw that the Communist Party obviously had a prearranged plan, prepared in all details; that under the surface of national unity, communist forces were really operating to establish a communist dictatorship.

The democrats fought back. There were many people, on the national and local level, who had the courage to oppose the avalanche. Some positions were gained or regained. But they were caught unprepared, unorganized, without physical means

[13] The brief description of the situation in the liberated parts of Czechoslovakia is based on: a long letter from Mr. H. Skala, April 29, 1958, who made the trip from Košice to Prague by car between May 2 and 9, 1945; Duchacek, *The Strategy of Communist Infiltration*, *op.cit.*; Jan Stransky, *East Wind Over Prague*, New York, Random House, 1951.

[14] *Deset let*, *op.cit.*, pp. 259-62, 263-64.

of power, equipped principally with the weapons of decency and good will—poor equipment in the face of sheer force. Their voices were like a whisper in the thunderstorm of vulgarity, violence, terror, and fear.

Many observers believe that the communists could have completely taken over the power in those desperate days of May 1945, the days which were called liberation. They held the key positions in the national and local government, they were organized, they had arms, and the Soviet Army stood behind them. Since they did not assume complete power, it is probably because the Soviet government, because of the international situation, did not give the signal—not yet. Later, after they did take over, in February 1948, Gottwald had to do some explaining to the party leaders as to why they had to wait three years.

On May 10, 1945 President Beneš returned to Prague. It was a triumphal entry into the capital, a city which is filled with many a monument of past glory. He was not a leader of a government or of a political party; he was the embodiment of the nation's longing, its truly national hero.

Before the year came to a close the Red Army withdrew. Perhaps Beneš began to breathe again. Perhaps he had been right. Perhaps there was still a hope. Perhaps the tradition of freedom, the devotion to constructive, cooperative work was still to prevail. For a time it seemed so.

INFILTRATION IN WIDTH AND DEPTH

A BASIC question must be asked at this juncture. Can cooperation between democrats and communists ever be a workable avenue for the solution of national problems, serving the national interests?

In Czechoslovakia the democratic parties and the head of state, Dr. Edvard Beneš, were convinced of the possible values of such cooperation. It may well be that it was the absence of any other alternative that made necessary the formation of a coalition government with its strange combination of two irreconcilable ideologies. However, the point is that the democrats were ready to take it, because it appeared not only necessary but possible. Their hope was that through daily contacts in matters of practical politics the two irreconcilable extremes would work out a mutual adjustment, a living and workable synthesis; that communism would advance toward democracy, and indeed, necessarily, liberalism toward socialism.

The democratic leaders had worked in this direction during the war. The communist leaders had given the appearance of following the same goal. When the first disillusionment occurred in the spring of 1945 it was already too late to change: the communists were firmly established in key positions of power. Any attempt to make a change would have been met with certain revolution, directed by the Communist Party from these positions of power. Only one hope remained: that the Soviet Union, for reasons of international politics, and the Communist Party of Czechoslovakia, for reasons of its own position, would in their own interests consider a peaceful cooperation with the democratic parties; that meanwhile democracy would find the strength to face with confidence the communist competition.

For two and a half years, from the spring of 1945 until the autumn of 1947, there were signs which appeared to give support to this way of thinking. The Communist Party was outwardly anxious to encourage this trend. However, behind the relatively tranquil scene, it methodically followed the policy of deepening and widening its position of power.

At the beginning of 1948 the democratic parties were resolved to stop the violent growth of communist influence and to test their own strength by democratic methods. Again, it was too late. By that time the communists were firmly in control of almost all factors of force. Also, the democratic method proved to be ineffective against the method of violence.

On July 9, 1945 Gottwald, not only the chairman of the Communist Party of Czechoslovakia, but now also one of the Deputy Prime Ministers, made an important speech before the functionaries of the party. It contained an analysis of the situation, a deliberately vague statement of the party goals, and a less vague directive for future action.

First, Gottwald claimed for the party a great patriotic rôle during the war. Second, he insisted that the party still followed the Marx-Lenin-Stalin line. Third, he stated that the Communist Party marched "along the pathway of national and democratic revolution, not along the line of socialist revolution." The struggle between the working class and the bourgeoisie had only started, with the advantage currently in the hands of the working class, which had already gained the decisive power in the country, while the bourgeoisie had been compromised. In this situation, fourth, the party had some specific tasks: it must realize the importance of National Committees, "an instrument to rebuild from the very foundations the political structure of the whole state." It must, further, see to it that the security organs, the police, be transfused with a new "people's" blood. The army, too, must be "truly democratic," since it, as well as the security forces, was the instrument of power. The party must secure its place in the national economy by way of a system of national administration over the confiscated properties of the enemy and of collaborators. It must gain the peasants' support and strengthen its position in the trade unions, cooperatives, and agricultural associations.[1]

The directive was clear enough to be understood by Gottwald's followers, and they set out to implement it.

Capturing the Mind

Pressure and violence may compel people to work or to make public statements against their convictions, but they cannot compel them to a specific way of thinking. Communists are aware of their powerlessness to force entry into the domain of inner thoughts. In Czechoslovakia, therefore, they tried to penetrate the secret depths of people's minds by another method, through pretense and lure.

Aware of the ever-present power of nationalism, they continued, as they had during the war, to present themselves as true patriots and to appeal to the national sentiments of the nation. The glorious history of Czechoslovakia was interpreted in Marxist dialectics. "Even the ascetic Hus was [to them] a socialist fighter against the squires' exploitation, and they gave to that great miracle of the Czech national awakening [at the beginning of the 19th century], though priests took the lion's share in it, a vulgarly materialistic interpretation." The nationally and religiously imbued Hussites were to them peasant rebels.[2]

In Slovakia, where the farce of independence during the war left behind widespread sentiment for autonomy among the conservative elements of Catholic peasantry, they played intensively upon this chord of Slovak nationalism. Patriotic Slovak leaders found themselves caught in this communist web of provincialism

[1] *Deset let*, *op.cit.*, pp. 278-89.

[2] Petr Zenkl, "Jak to dělali" (How They Did It), *Svornost*, January 20, 27, 1952.

and could not afford, for the sake of popularity, to be less radical, less nationalistic than the communists. This policy did not, of course, prevent them from shifting to a policy of centralism at a later period when Slovakia, in spite of all this chauvinistic agitation, turned against them in the elections.

The respectful attitude of the communists toward T. G. Masaryk, a sacred name in the hearts of the Czechoslovak people, has been noted before (see p. 34). Claiming themselves "to be the sole heirs of all the finest and best in the national tradition from the Czech kings in the Middle Ages to the distinguished life of Masaryk" they pretended to be his true followers and eulogized him as "the most prominent defender of social progress, justice, and liberty."[3]

A few days after they had seized power, in February 1948, they had the arrogance to claim that Masaryk, the philosopher of humanitarian democracy, would have approved of their victory. A few years later, however, in one of their more dazzling acrobatic displays, they opened a campaign against him, even publishing a tome on Masaryk's "anti-people and anti-national policy."[4]

In an address to young communists Gottwald asked them "to love their homeland."[5] In a letter which he sent to the physical-culture organization *Sokol*, which had since the second half of the nineteenth century stood in the forefront of the nation's patriotic and democratic aspirations, he saluted them as "Brothers and Sisters" and, praising their great tradition, reminded them of the nationalist, old-time slogan, "Every Czech—a Sokol."[6] At the May Day celebration of the party in 1947, prominently dis-

[3] Richard Hunt, "The Denigration of Masaryk," *Yale Review*, vol. 43, no. 3, p. 419.

[4] *Dokumenty o protilidové a protinárodní politice T. G. Masaryka* (Documents about the Anti-People and Anti-National Policy of T. G. Masaryk), Prague, Orbis, 1953.

[5] Klement Gottwald, *Spisy* (Works), three volumes, 1946-1948, 1931-1932, Prague, Svoboda, [n.d.], vol. 1, p. 167.

[6] *Ibid.*, pp. 249-51.

played placards appealed to communists to participate at the forthcoming *Sokol* Congress.[7]

When a UP correspondent once asked Gottwald whether a communist can also be a good patriot, he pointed eloquently to the party's work for the welfare of the working people, for freedom and peace and democracy; hence "it is not only possible but also necessary that good communists be also good patriots."[8]

After the war, passions were running high among the Czechoslovak people, as they were elsewhere in the world. Years of privation, oppression, and wholesale massacres had produced great bitterness. The Big Three agreed that the German minority, which before and during the war had proved its treacherous attitude toward Czechoslovakia, should be transferred to Germany. Although this decision was historically and politically justified, the communist-held Ministry of the Interior, which was in charge of the transfer, permitted its execution to be sometimes accompanied by excesses of brutality which no decent man can condone. The most irresponsible elements of the party were given a free hand, in the process, to satisfy the baser sentiments of some sections of the populace and thus gain popularity in this self-proclaimed contest in patriotism.

In another field, in culture, the communists followed a less violent but equally vulgar policy. With the state-controlled radio stations in their hands, it was many months before they permitted any German music to be played. Ironically, and indicative of how far from the cultural temper of the nation these patriots were, people tuned their sets to the midnight concerts of the Berlin symphony orchestra to hear Beethoven, Bach, and Mozart. Communist poets, and there were many, struggled to surpass each other in nationalistic apotheoses.

Communist leaders played not only at the role of patriots but also at the role of democrats. They repeatedly expressed their respect for the political programs of the other parties, excluding

[7] *Svobodné slovo*, May 15, 1947.

[8] Gottwald, *Spisy*, *op.cit.*, vol. 1, p. 292.

only fascist reactionaries—a term which, however, they were always ready to apply to any effective opposition. Gottwald stated to a foreign correspondent that the coalition of the party with the democratic parties in the government was not "opportunistic, temporary," but an expression of the nation's unity, that parliamentary democracy would remain in Czechoslovakia and that the communists would "be the most vigilant guardian of the new Constitution" which was then being debated in the Parliament.[9]

In matters of religion the party was extremely flexible. It required tolerance toward this "opium of mankind." During the war the Czech communist leader in London, V. Nosek, had made reassuring statements in private conversations that communists would maintain their views on religion but "will never stand up against it actively."[10]

When Monsignor Šrámek, an old statesman and the Prime Minister during the war, came to Moscow in March 1945 the Soviet government and the Czechoslovak communists there were anxious to show him particular honors. After the war, the Monsignor sat in the meetings of the Ministerial Council next to Gottwald as one of the Deputy Prime Ministers. Perhaps with the naïve hope of winning Gottwald's good will, or more probably with a touch of sardonic humor, Šrámek gave a beautifully executed crèche one Christmas to Gottwald's little granddaughter.

One communist leader, later President of Czechoslovakia, A. Zápotocký, spoke on Christmas eve 1945 about "the beautiful, unforgettable and mystical poetry of Christmas"; about "the enchanted star over the lighted Christmas tree, speaking to all people of good will, promising that the dark night will one day change into the light of day"; about "the midnight Mass in the church from which resounds the rejoicing carol, proclaiming 'the

[9] *Ibid.*, p. 127.

[10] From an interview with J. Slávik, June 12, 1958. Mr. Slávik was Minister of the Interior in the government in exile and, after the war, Ambassador to Washington.

birth of the new man—the Savior' "; about "the religious education, the mystical magic, the secrets and miracles, ennobling the whole Christian mind."[11]

On Christmas Day in 1945, when all Czechoslovak newspapers according to an old tradition observed the day with special solemn issues, the Communist Party daily, *Rudé právo*, published on its front page a drawing of Bethlehem and a poem by a well-known communist poet, adoring Christ the Creator. Local communist functionaries and party rank and file attended church services.

When the Vatican asked the Czechoslovak government to approve of Joseph Beran's appointment as Archbishop of Prague, the communist Deputy Foreign Minister, V. Clementis, attached so little political importance to the act that, as Professor Stránský wrote, "he didn't even put it on the agenda of the Ministerial Council but presented it *per rollam* to the Deputy Prime Ministers during its session." Stránský described it thus: "I sat in the Ministerial Council opposite Gottwald. When Clementis submitted the document to him for signature he read it quickly and signed it, adding the remark, 'I don't know anything about this bloke.' Before Beran was consecrated [in the fall of 1946] Gottwald asked me—as I was serving as Minister of Education responsible in the matter—if he should attend the consecration. I told him that I highly recommended it."[12]

Another witness, A. Heidrich, the Secretary General of the Ministry of Foreign Affairs after the war, who, in the absence of Jan Masaryk and V. Clementis, was the highest officer in the Ministry, adds that Gottwald telephoned him on the eve of the solemn act to be sure of Heidrich's attendance. He himself, he stated, was in bed with a bad case of the flu, but nevertheless he said he would make a special effort to come. This he did, together with some five or six communist members of the govern-

[11] A. Zápotocký, *Po staru se žít nedá* (One Can't Live the Old Way), Prague, Práce, 1949, pp. 134-35.

[12] From a letter of Professor J. Stránský, April 22, 1958.

ment. He was obviously ill, but he remained in the chilly Cathedral through the whole ceremony, which lasted more than four hours. He was the first to congratulate the new Archbishop.[13]

Gottwald's presence at a *Te Deum*, held by the Archbishop after the communist putsch, was interpreted by the press as a proof of continuing religious freedom.[14] Shortly thereafter, however, Gottwald opened an all-out struggle against the Church and religion and went so far as to intern "that bloke" Archbishop Beran indefinitely.

To please the pious Slovaks, Gottwald on July 5, 1947 attended a special celebration for two saints, Constantine and Methodius, who in the second half of the ninth century had converted inhabitants of the Great-Moravian Empire to Christianity.

The party carefully abstained from any attack on parochial schools. Though secularization of education was a part of the governmental program, the democratic Minister of Education, Stránský, was allowed to establish a new Catholic secondary school. He planned to save parochial institutions from "nationalization" by putting them under the administration of the Theological College of Charles University in Prague, which, in turn, was responsible to the Ministry of Education.[15]

In the field of economy the communists avoided mentioning their goal. In dozens of public statements which Gottwald made in the period of the coalition government he spoke about "the specific Czechoslovak road toward socialism," which was not "through the dictatorship of the proletariat and the soviets"; about a "regime of a peculiar, quite Czechoslovak type," about "quiet development toward socialism without further revolutions" which he described as Marxism "under new conditions"; about "the national and democratic nature of the revolution, not a socialist revolution."[16] In these views, which were a patent

[13] From a letter of Mr. A. Heidrich, April 22, 1958.

[14] *Svobodné slovo*, June 23, 1948.

[15] From a letter of J. Stránský, April 22, 1958.

[16] Gottwald, *Spisy*, *op.cit.*, vol. 1, pp. 117, 233. *Deset let*, *op.cit.*, p. 284. See also H. F. Skilling, "People's Democracy, The Proletarian Dictatorship and the

denial of Marxism and Leninism, Gottwald was faithfully and loudly followed by his chief lieutenants, Slánský, Švermová, and Clementis. Little did they realize that a few years later they would be accused of treachery to socialism by trying to prove "the peculiarity of the situation in Czechoslovakia and devise a theory about an independent, specific, Czechoslovak road to socialism, different from the bolshevik road in the Soviet Union."[17] Little did they imagine in that period from 1945 to 1948 that they would be executed in 1952 for statements which only echoed the speeches of their leader, Klement Gottwald. He, the ablest opportunist of them all, survived the purges.

Small wonder that this carefully-prepared program for winning the minds of the Czechoslovak people succeeded to a considerable extent. It is human nature to hear and accept as true what one wishes to hear. The idea that Czechoslovak communists were first of all Czechoslovaks, and only secondarily communist, gained credence. Some people began to say that these people were not really communists at all. Among such optimists were even some democratic leaders. So it was that "operation grand deceit," a carefully-prepared plan to capture the minds of the great masses, produced at least in the first two years after the war remarkable results.

Instruments of Persuasion

The press and the radio were the most powerful weapons in the hands of the Communist Party, and the Minister of Information, V. Kopecký, exercised a ruthless control over all mass media. With the broadcasting stations the system of control was simple: since they were state-owned (as in many other European countries) nothing could go on the air which would contradict the directives of the Minister of Information. Numerous measures were employed, however, to control the press in a

---

Czechoslovak Path to Socialism," *American Slavic and East European Review*, vol. 10 (April 1951), pp. 100-16.

[17] Kopecký, *30 let KSČ*, *op.cit.*, p. 173.

country for which freedom of expression had been solemnly promised in the Košice program.

The Ministry of Information immediately after the war suppressed three conservative dailies of long standing (*Národní politika, Národní listy, Venkov*) with the explanation that they had served fascists. Others, because of the same accusation, were ordered to change their names and thus lost their valuable identity. No newspaper or periodical could appear without the Ministry's license; nor could one be owned by a private person, but only by political parties or public institutions. Such antidemocratic measures were justified by such excuses as "postwar conditions" or "the spirit of modern democracy."

The distribution of paper was one of the most effective instruments of control. According to even a communist source, five dailies in Prague, communist or under communist control, were given enough paper in 1946 to publish 1,030,000 copies, while the dailies of the four democratic parties together printed no more than 743,000 copies.[18] When, for instance, the newspaper of the largest democratic party, the Czechoslovak National Socialists, *Svobodné Slovo*, wished to print a Sunday edition for its 540,000 subscribers, it had to buy the newsprint on the black market.[19]

The same pressure was extended to the publication of books. If the name of the author suggested a point of view which would displease the communists, the answer to the publisher was not political but economic: no paper.

A special committee of journalists was appointed to guard with great vigilance the integrity of Czechoslovak journalism and to purge all collaborators from its ranks. But the committee included, among others, several persons who had found protective refuge in the Communist Party to cover their own wartime collaborationist activities.

[18] K. F. Zieris, *The New Organization of the Czech Press*, Prague, Orbis, 1947, pp. 23-24.

[19] I. Herben, "L'Asservissement de la presse en Tchécoslovaquie," *La Presse derrière le rideau de fer*, Paris, November 1948, pp. 23-30.

Explicitly there was neither formal nor factual censorship of the press. Yet the general feeling that the tenuous relations among the parties of the coalition, or as it was called the government of National Front, must be maintained, imposed upon editors extreme caution and self-restraint. The name of the Soviet Union was sacred; to touch upon it critically meant to run the grave risk of confiscation and arrest on the basis of the prewar law for the defense of the Republic, a law which the communists now used for their own purposes.[20]

Then, too, there was frequent pressure from the communist-controlled trade unions, a pressure which was in fact censorship. Several times, as the result of an article critical of the Soviet Union or the policy of the Communist Party, workers in paper mills refused to deliver paper to democratic newspapers in Prague and Bratislava or to load or unload it, and linotypists refused to set up the newspaper.[21]

In a similar fashion the Ministry of Information supervised state-owned theaters and film companies. In gratitude to the Red Army for the liberation of the country, and in response to the spirit of Czechoslovak-Soviet friendship, wartime Soviet plays and pictures, frequently of mediocre value, inundated this area of culture. Traditional contacts with Western culture were neglected. In the field of motion pictures, for instance, the Ministry of Information committed the country to import 60 per cent of all foreign films from Russia in 1946, 70 per cent in 1947, and to raise the percentage to 80 in 1948 and to remain on that level.[22]

The democratic parties tried to fight back against this communist encroachment upon the people's minds. Members of the government protested against the Ministry of Information's biased policy and many journalists fought valiantly for a mean-

[20] From an interview with Mr. Paul Tigrid, June 8, 1958. He was editor of the Catholic Party weekly, *Obzory*.

[21] Herben, "L'Asservissement de la presse en Tchécoslovaquie," *op.cit.*, pp. 28-29. See also *The New York Times*, March 12, 1946, p. 12; June 2, 1946, p. 35; September 1, 1946, p. 12; March 7, 1947, p. 7; August 9, 1947, p. 14.

[22] Gracchus, "Memorandum on Czechoslovakia," *The Nineteenth Century and After*, vol. 140, p. 176.

ingful freedom of the press. There was freedom of religion, of assembly, of education, but it was a freedom fraught with fear and subject to risks. No "rights" were denied, but to arouse displeasure was to run the risk that a license might be curtailed or withdrawn, for ostensibly good and valid reasons. Such was the powerful position of the Communist Party, controlling as it did the Ministry of Information.

If such pressures were not always effective in the communist policy of influencing the public mind, still other pressures were available through another key Ministry which was in communist hands, the Ministry of the Interior.

As an aftermath of war, no accusation was more damning than to brand a person as a fascist or a reactionary. Communists used the term at liberty to frighten democrats in important positions if they were opposed to party practices or were even mildly critical of Soviet foreign policy or certain aspects of Soviet relations to Czechoslovakia. To spread fear among even the noncommitted masses, denunciations were encouraged. The communist daily *Rudé právo* invited its readers "to write down these treasonable activities [of making anti-Russian remarks] and file complaints with the police. This is not a dishonorable act but a patriotic one."[23] When a high-school student at Jablonec removed Stalin's picture from a school room, he was arrested.[24]

"Do good to the devil, he will repay with damnation," says an old Czech proverb. Czechoslovak democrats were beginning to learn its truth as a result of their experiment of cooperation with communists. Their good will was answered with communist terror.

The process of pressure and infiltration was likewise applied in public administration, both on the local and the national level.

On the Local Level

The Presidential Decree of December 4, 1944 laid down certain legal foundations for local administration. National Committees,

[23] *The New York Times*, December 14, 1947, p. 62.
[24] *Ibid.*, December 6, 1947, p. 2.

as they were called, were to take charge of community affairs without any governmental interference.

It has been noted that the National Committees came into being under conditions of chaos and terror in the presence of the Red Army. From the beginning democrats were in the minority: the people were either too frightened to vote for them in the disorderly, usually non-secret elections or were taken in by communist promises and persuaded to vote elsewise. Many persons who had collaborated with the German occupation authorities during the war joined communist ranks to seek protection from punishment. Democrats did not offer them a similar service: it was not their policy nor were they in a position to do so.

Courage is a rare virtue, not too often found among the large and politically disinterested masses, whose principal protection has frequently been to join the "winning side." They sense with unmistakable instinct the elements and place of power. They know, too, that power yields some practical results, distributing favors to followers and discriminating against the opposition. The communists were adept at both. In a country where, as a result of the war, both land and industrial property underwent a process of drastic change, the opportunity for both favor and discrimination was clear. Small wonder, then, that the membership of the party swelled to the figure of 1,172,000 in September 1947 and even to 1,354,601 in February 1948.[25] Before the war membership was 100,000. The National Committees were controlled by communists. Gottwald proudly informed the party functionaries on January 16, 1948 that the party had channelled 60,000 members into the National Committees.[26]

The Secretary General of the Party, R. Slánský, giving an account before the first session of the Cominform in September 1947 about party activities, reported that all three chairmen of the Provinces' National Committees were communists, that out

[25] *Zasedání devíti komunistických stran* (The Session of Nine Communist Parties), Prague, Svoboda, n.d., p. 103.

[26] Gottwald, *Spisy*, *op.cit.*, vol. 1, p. 26.

of 163 district National Committees 128 (80 per cent) and out of 11,512 local Committees 6,350 (57 per cent) were chaired by communists. Almost 140,000 party members worked in various National Committees and their commissions.[27]

On the National Level

The measure of the Communist Party's power on the national level and the potentialities of its infiltration were determined by the number of offices it held in the government and by their political and economic importance. Since there were no communists, or possibly only a few, employed by the prewar Czechoslovak governments, the party now claimed the right to bring its adherents into the governmental service. Before long the Ministries of the Interior, Information, Education, Social Welfare, and Agriculture were flooded. The process was slower but still substantial in the Ministries of Industry and of National Defense, where the fellow travellers Laušman and Svoboda respectively were eager to admit adherents. In the Ministry of Foreign Affairs a group of seasoned diplomats managed for the most part to hold their positions, but with the help of the Deputy Foreign Minister Clementis many important political appointments were made from party membership. The Ministry of Finances succumbed with the nomination of Jaromír Dolanský in 1946. Among important offices only the Ministry of Justice remained free from communist infiltration. It was administered by Dr. Prokop Drtina, one of the most courageous fighters for the integrity of the Czechoslovak judiciary during this most troublesome period of its history.

With the mass arrival of communists in governmental offices, the number of civil servants inevitably rose to the uneconomic figure of 700,000. After they were well entrenched, the Ministry of Finances made the proposal that the number of employees be reduced—a measure which, of course, was meant to affect principally non-communists.

[27] *Zasedání devíti komunistických stran*, *op.cit.*, p. 105.

The governmental offices became hot-beds of infiltration, subversion, and denunciation. No confidential work could be performed, since loyalty to government was superseded by loyalty to the party. The party secretariat gave directives to state employees concerning their official activities, and they in turn reported back on the decisions taken in the Ministries and about the actions of non-communist public servants. If a democratic Minister intended to pursue a policy which was not in accordance with the party line, it was immediately reported to the secretariat and the communist leaders moved vigorously to try to prevent the Minister's move through every channel of political pressure.

The situation was aggravated by another though by now familiar device. Some communists, acting undoubtedly on party orders, gave the impression that they were independent of its control. Vocally critical from time to time of the Soviet Union, particularly of its methods in foreign-trade negotiations, they invited criticism from their colleagues only to denounce them to the secretariat. Others were not known to be communists, posing only as experts. It was not until the decisive days of the national crisis in February 1948 that they stripped off their disguises and emerged as full party members.

Innumerable illustrations of these methods could be cited; perhaps a few will suffice. There was the case of Mr. E. Loebl. A communist with some experience in business, he was in charge of the negotiation of trade agreements in the Ministry of Foreign Trade, administered by Hubert Ripka, the staunch anti-communist liberal. Loebl gave the impression of an easygoing, jovial fellow who well understood the importance to the Czechoslovak economy of trade with the West. British and American representatives liked to negotiate with him. He frequently expressed his contempt for Soviet foreign trade practices and in other ways exhibited his independence from Russian or communist control. When, however, in the critical week of February 1948, the communists organized Action National Committees and took over administrative offices, Loebl's character was transformed. He became the leader of one such committee in the Ministry of Foreign Trade, denied his superiors the right to enter their own offices, and purged the Ministry of all anti-communists.

Or, there is the story told by Mr. Hugo Skala, once chief of one of the largest departments in the Ministry of Finances and now a teacher at the University of Georgia. In addition to being a financial expert, he was a devoted democrat. There had been only sixteen communists, out of some thousand employees, in the Ministry before it came under the control of the communist Minister Dolanský in the summer of 1946. The new head of the Ministry immediately established an enormous cabinet of eighty members, all communists. "This was not an infiltration," writes Professor Skala, "this was an occupation. From that time on, the Minister's cabinet decided almost everything without non-communist employees' participation. Since the summer of 1946 until the communist putsch I saw my own Minister twice." He continues: "Some time before the communists had taken over the Ministry a certain Mr. Dub was recommended to me by one of my colleague friends. He came from a rich family, and I had no reason to suspect his political leanings. I gave him a job on a temporary basis. After he reported to me in January 1948 that he had finished his assignment, I advised him to enter the service of the nationalized industry. He asked time to think it over and to inquire—with the party. Only later I found that he had been a member of the party all that time and possibly longer, that he had denounced me to Slánský, the Secretary General of the party, and had even taken official files to its secretariat."[28]

I can also cite my own experience. In the Ministry of Foreign Affairs in which I served for fourteen years and which, due to the nature of its work, requires absolute reliability and loyalty, communists were not numerous, but they occupied some key positions. Before I assumed my duties in Belgrade in September 1945, President Beneš instructed me to return to Prague frequently and to report to him orally. "Don't write down anything of a

[28] From a letter of Mr. H. Skala, April 29, 1958.

confidential character; the Soviet Embassy would have it the day after your report arrives in the Ministry of Foreign Affairs."

The counsellor of the Embassy in Belgrade, a Mr. Horvát, was a communist who gave more energy to spying on me than to official work. No sooner had I succeeded in getting rid of him, when I caught him smuggling money out of Yugoslavia, than his place was taken by the first secretary, Karpíšek. He belonged to the Fierlinger wing of fellow-travellers in the Social Democratic Party and was even more anxious than his predecessor had been to denounce his colleagues. Soon after the putsch, the party rewarded him with an ambassadorial assignment in Egypt. Another member of the Embassy, a young Slovak, revealed his communist background in the critical days of February 1948. He frankly admitted that he had entered the party to efface his wartime sins of being active in the fascist youth movement.

In frequent negotiations with the Yugoslav government on trade and various financial settlements I sometimes opposed the Yugoslav requests or claims. The Yugoslav negotiators would immediately complain to Gottwald or to the communist Minister of Finances, who then intervened to force concessions for their Yugoslav comrades.

From the evidence it is more than apparent that communists should never have been appointed to civil service positions. However, it is likewise apparent that once the party had joined the government it was impossible to deny its members participation in public administration. After the first fatal step, the second was inevitable.

In the National Assembly

On October 14, 1945, half a year after the war, National Committees of the Provinces "elected" a three-hundred-member Provisional National Assembly. The membership was, in fact, based on an agreement among the political parties. Each of the six parties sent forty deputies to the Parliament, an arrangement which gave the communists a double representation because of their device of a technically separate Communist Party of Slovakia. The remaining sixty seats were allotted to such special-interest groups as trade unions and cultural organizations. With one exception, all of these special representatives joined established political parties. Consequently, in the final political distribution of parliamentary seats, the communists had 98 deputies, the National Socialists and Social Democrats 50 each, the Catholic Party 49, the Slovak Democratic Party 47, and the Ukrainian political group 5.

The Provisional National Assembly met on October 28, the Czechoslovak national holiday. It approved the measures which the government had introduced during and shortly after the war. Its first major legislative act was the nationalization of industry. This, however, as well as other parliamentary acts, was merely a rubber-stamp procedure since the composition of the Assembly reflected directly the distribution of political forces in the provisional government. Such a Parliament could not be taken seriously as a representative democratic body, and all democratic parties looked forward eagerly to elections. Once again they failed to anticipate communist strategy.

The electoral law was strictly democratic, differing in no essential from the basic legislative measures of Western democracies. It contained one unusual provision: voters were given the opportunity to vote for a so-called empty ticket if they did not wish to cast a ballot for any of the recognized political parties. The communists were the authors of this strange provision. It was their hope that people who used to support the conservative parties—particularly the Agrarian Party, which had been forcibly dissolved—would rather "vote" for the empty ticket as a sign of protest than for a non-communist party.

The registration lists were made public. The people were invited to object to any person known to be a former collaborator. Under this pretext between 250,000 and 300,000 persons were struck off the electoral lists. Notices of such objection were sent to many of these prospective voters only three days before the election date. The overwhelming majority of them was cleared of the accusation—after the elections.[29]

The election campaign was vigorous and outwardly free from pressures. However, the Communist Party enjoyed a material advantage since through the Ministry of Information it controlled the radio as well as a large number of newspapers. This control not only gave the party direct access to voters but produced a psychological impact upon them as well. Some local offices which were in communist hands are reported to have stamped their official correspondence with the text, "It is the duty of everyone to vote the CPC. We shall finish off the people who will not do so."[30]

The party platform spoke about freedom and democracy and promised that "small and middle-sized enterprise, particularly the property of farmers, remains and will remain untouched and will receive support, and that the middle classes in cities and in the country will be guaranteed the security of their existence."[31] This sounded more like the program of a middle-of-the-road party than of revolutionary communism. The democratic parties were unable to outdo the Communist Party in national sentiment and in their voiced devotion to principles of liberty. They could only point to the excesses of the communist-controlled governmental offices. In economic matters, communists continued to conceal their expropriation principles by promises of the guarantee of private ownership while the democratic parties themselves sincerely supported the policy of nationalization which had been inaugurated in 1945. Here was another important field in which the democratic parties had no political weapons with which to campaign against the communists. Competing among themselves for undetermined voters they failed to concentrate their efforts against the true enemy in their pre-election activities.

The Ministry of Agriculture, under communist control, proved

29 Ripka, *op.cit.*, p. 38. I. Herben, from a manuscript, p. 16.

30 Laušman, *Kdo byl vinen? op.cit.*, p. 90.

31 *Deset let*, *op.cit.*, p. 329.

to be the single decisive instrument in the electoral campaign. It offered to farmers easy credit to buy agricultural implements and it distributed various minor and major favors. Communist speakers promised the farmers who attended their meetings with mingled feelings of suspicion and expectation that their land would be protected. According to one statement made by Gottwald, 1.7 million Czechs, mostly farmers, had moved into the lands from which the Sudeten Germans had been expelled, there to receive land under the most favorable of conditions. The communists claimed for themselves all the credit for this huge program of colonization. Gottwald stated in a message addressed specifically to these colonists that the land thus allotted to the farmers would soon be theirs with full title and that 10,000 artisans who had also moved into the area would receive special support.[32] In one district where a big forest estate was to be parcelled out and turned over to cooperative ownership a communist speaker pointedly stated that the change would materialize only after the elections, and then only if the right party was elected.[33]

When the results of the elections which took place on May 26, 1946 were announced, the democrats had received another shock and the communists a pleasant surprise. The Communist Party carried 38 per cent of the electorate; the Social Democratic Party, which continued to be led by the fellow-traveller Fierlinger, 13 per cent; the National Socialist Party, 18 per cent; the Catholic Party, 16 per cent. In Slovakia, however, the communists suffered a serious defeat at the hands of the Democratic Party, which received 62 per cent of all Slovak votes; the communists polled only half as many votes; the rest was shared by two small Slovak parties which had been formed shortly before the elections, the Party of Labor and the Freedom Party. The communist fury against the Democratic Party was unleashed in a series of violent actions which followed shortly after the elections. As a show of

[32] *Ibid.*, p. 302.
[33] Laušman, *Kdo byl vinen? op.cit.*, p. 90.

force they called a general strike in Bratislava on May 31. A communist leader, L. Holdoš, on June 6, 1946 was frank enough to outline publicly what might be expected: "The leaders of the Communist Party of Czechoslovakia have prepared a plan, consisting of fifteen points, aimed at destroying the Democratic Party and at taking power into [Communist] hands. We must at all costs prove the Democratic Party guilty of treasonable activities and then disband it."[34]

The communist victory in the elections can be ascribed to several factors. In general, the communists had successfully created the impression of being good Czechoslovaks, ardent patriots, outwardly independent from Moscow. They had been tolerant toward religion; they had abstained from Marxist radicalism. As late as May 1947 Beneš had said to Sir Robert Bruce Lockhart that "Gottwald was a reasonable man who believed in parliamentary democracy. . . ."[35] Even later, toward the end of 1947, he went so far as to believe that Gottwald would not lie to him.[36] He was not alone in this opinion; other democratic leaders shared his optimism. Small wonder then that the politically uneducated masses were likewise so thoroughly deceived.

There were certain specific reasons for the communist victory. It was not surprising that many workers voted for the communists. They had been exposed to fifty years of Marxist education and had received certain economic advantages. However, it was a shock when analysts reached the conclusion that the communist victory had been assured by the votes of the traditionally conservative element of the country—the peasants. Lured by promises, assured of land ownership, attracted by various benefits, frightened by the threats of persecution, they cast their ballots for the party which three years later collectivized their land.

In addition, the Communist Party was substantially benefited

[34] Lettrich, *op.cit.*, p. 242.

[35] Sir Robert B. Lockhart, "The Czechoslovak Revolution," *Foreign Affairs*, vol. 26, July 1948, p. 635.

[36] *Recollections and Reconstruction*, *op.cit.*, meeting November 9, 1949.

when the voting age was reduced from twenty-one to eighteen. Youth as a rule has tendencies toward radicalism and young people had enjoyed the particular attention of the party.

Another interesting device was used. The Soviet command in Vienna informed the Prague government that it intended to move certain Soviet forces from the Soviet zone of Austria and Hungary to East Germany *across* Czechoslovakia, the transports to start two days before the election date. At Masaryk's intervention the plan was postponed, but the psychological impact of what many interpreted as a veiled threat left its desired effect upon the voters.

In the Constituent National Assembly, whose term was to expire in two years, the seats were distributed according to the election results: the Communists 114 (93 Czech and 21 Slovak), the Social Democrats 37, the National Socialists 55, the Catholics 46, the Slovak Democrats 43, the Slovak Party of Labor 2, and the Freedom Party 3.

The struggle over the composition of the Council of Ministers was vigorous. Gottwald became Prime Minister, according to the democratic tradition of appointing to this office the representative of the strongest party. Fierlinger had to satisfy himself with one of five Deputy Premierships. In the end, of the 26 members in the government, 9 were Communists, 3 were Social Democrats, and 4 were representatives of the other parties—National Socialists, Slovak Democrats, and Catholics. Masaryk and Svoboda remained as experts, though the latter continued to side with the communists on almost all important issues. Thus the radical left bloc of Communists and Social Democrats plus Svoboda had 13 votes in the government against the 12 votes of the democratic parties; Masaryk remained strictly non-partisan. The democratic position was strengthened when the Ministry of Education was freed from the clutches of the cantankerous communist Z. Nejedlý, to be administered by a cultured man and a democrat, J. Stránský, and by the appointment of the chairman of the National Socialist Party, P. Zenkl, one of the most determined fighters against communists, as one of the Deputy Prime Ministers. The Ministry of Justice, the guardian of legality and the independence of the judiciary, remained in the hands of the indomitable democrat, P. Drtina.

The Constituent Assembly began its work; the new government continued in the path of the previous one. The cause of democracy was given another chance. With a good policy, a well-thought-out tactic, and above all, within the framework of a favorable international situation, the outcome of this struggle of political forces could yet be reversed in favor of the democrats.

In Mass Organizations

There was no institution, no sector of life, which the Communist Party neglected in its overall policy of infiltration. With strategy as devious as in other fields it launched a systematic drive to conquer the non-partisan mass organizations, the trade unions, organizations of youth, women, gymnasts, peasants, and various patriotic associations.

In the realm of power politics the trade unions were of paramount importance to the communist policy and aims. In the interwar period the trade union movement in Czechoslovakia, as in many other European countries, was split up into groups affiliated with major political parties. During the war the German authorities introduced their own nazi-controlled organization of workers, NOUZ (National Center of Employees), from which old-time trade union leaders, including communists, were excluded. However, in 1942, the party gave a directive to its members to enter the nazi trade unions and to activize the struggle for power from within these organizations.[37] This directive paid a rich dividend after the war. Shortly before its end a group of trade union leaders had founded ROH (The Revolutionary Trade Union) which then simply took over the structure of the nazi-controlled NOUZ. Communists, who had been in the

[37] *Za svobodu českého a slovenského národa, op.cit.*, pp. 204-08.

organization since the war, had an overwhelming majority from the inception of the new organization. The experience of the interwar period was to be avoided, as Gottwald stated in a secret letter in December 1944, and the new trade unions were to be united, purportedly in the general effort to unify the whole nation for the postwar tasks of reconstruction.[38] The principle of a unified trade union movement was accepted in the program of the government at Košice and was confirmed by the first proclamation of its leadership, URO (the Central Council of the Trade Unions) on June 13, 1945.[39]

Under the cover of unity not only manual workers but white collar workers, public employees, and even students as well were invited to enter the common trade unions, which were already under communist domination. Out of the forty members which comprised their leadership only three persons were national socialists and two were representatives of the Catholic Party. The rest were communists or fellow-traveller social democrats. Though an official declaration stated that "the united trade unions are independent of the political parties, but not politically neutral"[40] the composition of its Executive Committee and its practices left no doubt before long as to their political affiliation. By February 1946 URO spoke on behalf of over one and one-half million members, of which almost half a million were women and 116,583 young people of twenty-one years of age or less. It became the most powerful instrument of communist policy, in the name of an organization which was supposed to be non-partisan and in which many members were non-communists, indeed even anti-communists.

When the Provisional National Assembly on May 16, 1946 approved the law concerning the united trade unions it merely

[38] The letter of Gottwald to V. Nosek, Moscow, December 21, 1944. Veselý, *op.cit.*, p. 11.

[39] Antonin Zápotocký, *Nová odborová politika* (A New Trade Unions Policy), Prague, Práce, 1949, pp. 9-11.

[40] *Ibid.*, p. 44.

legalized the situation as it had been created in the revolutionary days by the well-conceived plan of communist leaders.

A parallel organization to the trade unions was that of the factory councils which were supposed to assist the manager in planning production and other managerial tasks. They, too, fell under communist control and exercised an influence which exceeded by far the powers allotted to them by law. They nominated candidates for the general management of the factory; they purged employees through the usual device of accusations of collaboration or even sabotage; they were, along with the trade unions, the real masters in the factories. Factory councils existed even in public offices, though their word there carried less weight than in industry.

According to the government's program "the trade unions and the factory councils [were to] represent legally the employees in their relations with the private entrepreneurs and the public offices." However, in a country where a widespread program of nationalization had affected the whole economic system the majority of gainfully employed people were employees of one or another category. What was once a legitimate task—to defend the social and economic interests of the working people—became a tyrannical whip used against any real or potential opposition to one political party. There was no question on which the URO did not intervene. It participated in the nomination of members to the National Administration of confiscated properties and in the appointments of managers of industries. It brought in verdicts concerning the integrity of persons employed in industry. It exercised control over private enterprise. It pushed women into work against their will. It put the government under pressure on all matters in which the communist leadership believed the other coalition parties were acting too slowly or too cautiously. It appealed to all sections of the population to form "voluntary" brigades to help on Sundays in harvesting wheat or to increase the production of coal. It attacked the traders whose small businesses escaped nationalization. It intervened in the preparation of the bill of national insurance. It demanded the "democratization" of the armed forces and their purification from "unreliable" elements. It was particularly aggressive in condemning bureaucracy and its old-time "bourgeois" spirit. It tried to influence even cultural affairs, vulgarly asserting that a people's democracy requires a people's culture. It frequently attacked the Ministry of Justice for acquitting people who were accused by trade unions of collaboration and subsequently detained by the communist Ministry of the Interior. Judges who insisted upon maintaining the independence and dignity of their office were exposed to constant denunciations and threats. The Minister of Justice, Prokop Drtina, was subjected to vilification. All this was done by the trade unions under the pretext of their duty to defend the new economic and social order of the Republic. It was no coincidence that though non-partisan in name the trade unions did not differ in one single question from the policy of the Communist Party of Czechoslovakia.

The activities of the trade unions aroused a great number of protests from all democratic quarters: from political parties, from journalists, business organizations, cultural institutions, women's and youth groups, and from such individuals as judges, high officials, artists, etc. The chairman of the URO, Zápotocký, answered the accusations with the now familiar designation—reactionaries—and called for greater vigilance and greater radicalism. Two collections of his speeches and articles bear the most eloquent testimony to the URO policy and the reaction it created.[41]

To undergird the policy of the trade unions with particularly telling force, major industries organized factory militia. Originally, in the immediate postwar days, they were supposed to defend factories against the danger of destruction by scattered remnants of the enemy. However, the party and the trade unions tried to maintain them as permanent organizations.

Under the cover of national unity the Communist Party tried to subdue other national organizations. The method was always

[41] *Po staru se žít nedá, op.cit. Nová odborová politika, op.cit.*

the same: first, they created a leadership composed of their own members and fellow travellers; second, they appealed to people to join and then, speaking in their name, they created a "non-partisan" public opinion which, without exception, was identified with the policy of the party. Thus, they founded and dominated the Association of the Liberated Political Prisoners, though according to reliable informants there were far more political prisoners from the democratic ranks in concentration camps than from those of the communists. They infiltrated and finally controlled the Union of the National Revolution. They founded the National Association of Partisans and accepted as members people whose partisan records were highly dubious. Taking over the name of the famous illegal wartime newspaper published by the leaders of the democratic underground, *V boj* (The Fight), they gave initiative to the foundation of an organization of underground fighters. When some persons who were really closely associated with the newspaper joined the organization, its already established communist leadership expressed astonishment and even went so far as to accuse some of them of collaboration and treachery.[42]

The tactic of creating unified national organizations and seizing their control was less successful in some other areas. Though a united Association of Youth was instituted and endowed with money and a special daily newspaper (*Mladá Fronta*) was issued, young people, particularly university students, soon saw through the communist game and in their college associations publicly demonstrated their opposition to communist aims and methods. They became a vanguard of the democrats' struggle for freedom. When the democratic students, after a thirty-hour uninterrupted session, won the elections in the Association of Students of High Learning, communist students simply left.[43] Equally unsuccessful were communists in their attempt to turn the traditional organization of Czechoslovak gymnasts, *Sokol*, to their use. They also

[42] From interviews and letters of I. Herben and J. Drábek.

[43] *Svobodný zítřek*, February 20, 1947.

failed to establish control over the Association of Czech Peasants. It was only after the communist putsch that the youth, the *Sokols,* and the peasants association were forcibly converted into totalitarian communist organizations.

The Communist Party did not limit itself to the struggle for people's minds through mass media, mass organizations, political campaigns, and elections. The struggle for a man's stomach is equally important in such contests for power. Such organizations of force as the police and the armed forces provide the necessary framework for success in such contests. The communists did not neglect any of these considerations.

In Agriculture

The Presidential Decree of June 21, 1945 provided for the confiscation of the land owned by Germans and Hungarians in Czechoslovakia as well as that of traitors. This land was taken over by the National Land Fund, which was set up in the Ministry of Agriculture. It was to be distributed among agricultural workers and small farmers in the amounts of 9 hectares of arable or 12 hectares of agricultural land. Forests of over 100 hectares were to be the property of the state's National Forest Administration; local communities were to receive forests of less than 100 hectares. Of the confiscated land, some 3,023,000 hectares in all, 1,772,000 were agricultural and 1,251,000 forest lands. Of the agricultural land about 1.5 million hectares were distributed among some 170,000 families; over 200,000 hectares were turned into pasture cooperatives. Most of the agricultural property was located in the frontier area from which the Germans had been forcibly evacuated.

On July 11, 1947 the Assembly passed a bill which provided for the revision of the land reform of 1920 and the expropriation of land holdings of over 50 hectares. The bill was accepted after an intensive political battle but its communist-controlled implementation created great bitterness. Whenever the democratic parties defended the letter and spirit of the law against communist abuses they were accused of sheltering landlords and squires.

The control of agricultural policy was to the Communist Party a unique opportunity for gaining the support of the peasant population. Party members received preferential treatment in allotments of land, with the result that others were understandably eager to join to share in these privileges. About 80 per cent of the voters who moved into the frontier region voted communist. The party's Secretary-General Slánský explained at the Cominform meeting in September 1947 that the party in Czechoslovakia had paid special attention to the peasants. The Ministry of Agriculture, he stated, helped small and middle-sized farmers by paying them an adjusted price for wheat: those who owned less than 20 hectares of land received the highest prices; those who owned over 50 hectares received the lowest. In the spring of 1947 the price of agricultural machines was reduced by 30 per cent, that of fuels by 40 per cent, work clothing and shoes by 20 per cent. Slánský failed to mention that the population as a whole had to carry the financial burden of this policy of concessions which, however, were distributed as communist favors.

As a result of the laws of 1945 and 1947, there were in 1947 2.16 hectares of land distributed per capita among the agricultural population, in comparison with 1.67 hectares after World War I. The inevitable result of this deliberately excessive implementation of the laws was the breaking up of the land into large numbers of small, unproductively managed, properties. Inevitably, for economic reasons, these parcels of land were brought together into cooperatives, and after the Communist Party had seized power in February 1948 it was easy to turn them into collective farms. This was done in spite of repeated assurances to the farmers by the party that Czechoslovak agriculture would not be collectivized.

The communist Ministry of Agriculture had still another means to hold the farmer captive. Though he was allowed to cultivate the newly acquired land, he was not permitted to sell or rent it.

Furthermore, the legal transfer of his right to the property, registered in the land books, was delayed to keep the farmer in suspense and uncertainty and to make him even more dependent on the will of the Ministry of Agriculture.[44]

The democratic parties fought against these malpractices in the government, in the Parliament, and in the press, but with little effect. Once the communists were established in a position of power, arguments had only academic value.

In Industry

The Presidential Decree of October 24, 1945 nationalized the following industries: mines, electric power plants, metal production, armament works, and certain other industries declared essential to the national interest. All of these industries were nationalized regardless of size. Some others were taken over by the state if they employed more than 120 to 500 workers, depending upon the kind of production. Banks and insurance companies were also nationalized. The law provided compensation to former owners, but as a consequence of the communization of the country in 1948 it was never implemented insofar as Czechoslovak citizens were concerned.

There was no quarrel about the principle of nationalization. However, an intense controversy developed among the political parties about its extent and the methods of its implementation. President Beneš advised a phased process which would allow for adjustments based on the experience acquired by the first step. The social democratic Minister of Industry, B. Laušman, however, defended the idea of an immediate and total nationalization. Communists associated themselves with the idea of immediate action, but as to its totality they still proceeded with some caution; Gottwald sent to Laušman a message saying that

[44] A. Rozehnal, *Pozemkové reformy v Československé republice* (Land Reforms in the Czechoslovak Republic), New York, National Committee for a Free Europe, September 1952, pp. 18, 19, 32. *Czechoslovakia, op.cit.*, pp. 247, 249, 250. *Zasedání devíti komunistických stran, op.cit.*, p. 110.

a total nationalization "is today a madness."[45] He opposed a phased nationalization because, as he stated publicly, the party wished to establish once and for all a clear-cut boundary between the nationalized and private economic sectors and insure "juridical security."[46]

The democratic parties for the most part fought bitterly against the Communist Party policy although it was supported by the radicals among the Social Democrats. As might be expected, they lost the battle. The Social Democrats, whose constituents were mostly workers, found it particularly difficult to oppose communists on an issue in which the bulk of their voters shared the opinion of the communist comrades; they themselves had deep roots in Marxist ideology. Thus, the left wing had a majority, slender as it was, in the government and in the Parliament. The trade unions were always willing to use threats to assure the broadest possible nationalization. The chairman, Zápotocký, stated openly that "without nationalization no one will today get workers to work."[47]

The press and the radio did all they could to mold public opinion. Communist newspapers and communist-controlled radio broadcasts were always ready to accuse the democratic leaders of sheltering capitalists and collaborators whenever they opposed the nationalization of any particular enterprise. When, for instance, the Catholic daily, *Lidová demokracie*, asked on September 26, 1945 for a thorough consideration of the nationalization bill, for less demonstrations and more solid work, Zápotocký, the communist chairman of the powerful trade unions, attacked both the paper and the author of the article in a broadcast, accusing them of being reactionaries. The trade unions protested frequently and Zápotocký delivered several speeches attacking the lack of speed in the government's program of nationalization.[48]

In fact, of course, most of the steps leading to nationalization

[45] Laušman, *Kdo byl vinen? op.cit.*, p. 80.

[46] *Deset let, op.cit.*, p. 293.

[47] Zápotocký, *Nová odborová politika, op.cit.*, p. 25.

[48] *Po staru se žít nedá, op.cit.*, pp. 22-28, 48-51.

had been taken before the law was enacted. As noted before, the property which belonged to the enemy or was abandoned by the owner was taken over in the revolutionary postwar days by a provisionally established National Administration in which as a rule communist workers had a decisive voice. However, as is frequently the case in such situations, what begins as provisional or temporary tends to become permanent. It proved extremely difficult, for example, for a former landholder, if he returned after the war or if he was acquitted of collaboration with the enemy, to be given back his full rights of ownership. Since in the case of businesses, the National Administration had been introduced at the proposal of factory councils and trade unions, communist speakers agitated that even if former proprietors conformed with the law the authorities should not be allowed to return them to the owner without a hearing by the communist-controlled factory council and trade unions.[49]

The law had other features making it difficult for small enterprises to escape nationalization: it stated that whenever the national interest required, several small enterprises of one kind could be combined into one. The next step, of course, was its nationalization. At the end, about three-fourths of all industries employing two-thirds of all industrial workers were nationalized, a policy which was certainly not envisaged by the democratic parties. Still, it was "a national revolution, not a social revolution," as Zápotocký stated with his continuing deceitful semantics. "It [the national revolution] does not socialize, it nationalizes. It does not set aside private capitalist undertakings, it puts them under control."[50]

After the communists seized power, all plants employing more than fifty persons were nationalized; other factories, still left in private hands, were simply denied raw materials. The inevitable result was that they participated "voluntarily" in nationalization. Such was Gottwald's understanding of establishing once and for

[49] *Ibid.*, pp. 34-36.
[50] *Ibid.*, p. 66.

all the position of private enterprise. As to how sacredly the communists viewed their pledge of juridical security, Zápotocký admitted openly, after the communist putsch, that "had [the party] not begun in the revolutionary period with the nationalization decree regardless of established laws and decrees, we would have never succeeded in getting promulgated the decrees of nationalization." "We had to teach people," he stated, "that it was not possible to maintain the old legality . . . in fact, just the opposite—that it was important to violate it."[51]

Along these same lines, in the nationalized industry, the banks, and insurance companies the party was able to infiltrate the entire fabric of the economic life of Czechoslovakia. Managers of nationalized enterprise were appointed at the party's request; other members posed as technicians or businessmen but maintained secret contacts with the party secretariat. Managers who were truly non-partisan were under the control of Factory Councils in which the party members were, as a rule, in the majority. There was no escape from the pattern.

In the Army

The officers' corps of the Czechoslovak armed forces was a heterogeneous body in the period following the end of hostilities. It consisted chiefly of four elements: the group of officers who came from the Soviet Union and who were in command of the Czechoslovak forces there; officers who served with their units in England and France; those who were active in the underground movement; and, finally and most numerous, those who, after the dissolution of the Czechoslovak Army in 1939, lived during the war in a sort of anonymity, performing various jobs, but with no wartime record. It was the first and last group on which the Minister of National Defense, L. Svoboda, and the Chief of Staff, General B. Boček, both Moscow-made and Moscow-supported commanding officers, built the new structure of the

[51] *Rudé právo*, January 31, 1953.

officers' corps. The first were communist-indoctrinated, aware of the promising careers which awaited them in the liberated country; the last, their military futures now shattered by their wartime inactivity, would grasp even such an opportunity to remake their lives as submission to communist orders. The fine group of Western officers, with distinguished combat experience at Tobruk and Dunkirk—particularly the pilots who had fought many battles over London and Germany—was sidetracked in spite of Beneš' initial insistence that they be appointed to positions of high command. Such distinguished officers as General S. Ingr were even accused of planning a fascist putsch, the sole purpose of the accusation being to exclude them from any position of influence. Only General H. Pika, whose patriotic work in Moscow during the war consisted mostly of combatting the subservient attitude of Fierlinger and Svoboda toward Soviet and communist policy, was at Beneš' insistence rewarded by appointment to the position of Deputy Chief of Staff. But he was isolated and limited to formal duties and soon after the communist putsch executed on charges of treachery.

As to the officers who took a valiant part in the underground movement, most of them were killed in action or were executed by the nazis. None of the small number who survived the war received an appointment of prominence or importance.

In addition to the Ministry of National Defense and Chief of Staff, two other key positions were under communist control. The first, the department of Defense Intelligence (OBZ), through which passed all messages, was headed by a Bedřich Rejcin of Sudeten German origin. He had lived in the Soviet Union from the 1930's until 1945. The other position, the chief of the Army Educational Service, which was another term for the Soviet-inspired institution of Political Commissar, was in the hands of General Jaroslav Procházka. He had lived in Russia since 1924 and had received training for this important assignment during the war as the chief of the "enlightenment service" in the Czechoslovak army there.

Educational officers were appointed to every unit of the newly organized army as second in command. Not only were they responsible for the political education of soldiers in an understanding of the spirit of the new "people's democracy"; they also had a decisive voice in appointments and promotion of officers. Colonel Rejcin's department of Defense Intelligence had its appointees in every unit also, thus together establishing a wide net of counter-espionage which enabled them to remove any unreliable—meaning, largely, democratic—elements.[52]

In spite of this initial success of the Communist Party in establishing its own members or fellow travellers in key positions (it was thought by some that Svoboda and Boček themselves were possibly secret adherents of the party) the Czechoslovak armed forces were not completely subject to communist control. The party leadership was aware of this problem. From time to time, therefore, various "non-partisan" organizations, such as trade unions and the Association of Political Prisoners, carried resolutions requesting purges and a greater democratization of the army. As late as January 1948 Slánský, the Secretary General of the party, asked publicly "that the army be cleansed of reactionaries" who "do not like the new people's regime, who admire Western imperialism, who are enemies of the Soviet state and who criticize and speak ill of our republic."[53]

Because of their uncertainty as to the "reliability" of the army, communists organized a special military group, the SNB (the National Security Corps), within the Ministry of the Interior; in fact, it was a regular military establishment.[54]

In the Police

Contrary to expectations, the communist Minister of the Interior, Václav Nosek, did not proceed immediately after the war

[52] Gracchus, "Memorandum on Czechoslovakia," *op.cit.*, p. 178.

[53] *The New York Times*, January 10, 1948, p. 5.

[54] Unless otherwise stated, the material on the army is based on Ithiel de Sola Pool, *Satellite Generals*, Stanford, California, Stanford University Press, 1955, pp. 28-54.

with the reorganization and unification of the police forces. He realized that the democratic parties would watch closely the activities of this powerful office. He first named only a few members of the party to key police positions and quickly organized the SNB, regiments of National Security Corps, to send them to the frontier area where chaotic circumstances required special security measures. This organization proved to be a body of armed men completely under the control of the Communist Party, both by its activities in the area and later in the decisive days of the national crisis. Next, the Minister of the Interior established a special corps of mobile police under the pretext of liquidating the remnants of the nazi army still in the country. This special corps, too, was composed chiefly of communists.

In other fields of maintaining public order, although the Minister of the Interior preserved the institution of local police and of the state-controlled gendarmes, he also added to them special province and district security commissions. He also supplemented the intelligence services of the Ministry of National Defense and of the Ministry of the Interior with a new agency, the *ZOB*, the Provincial Security Detachments, which were subordinated to the three Provinces' National Committees, all of these, of course, under communist control.

The chaotic situation created by this multi-track organization of police and intelligence services was useful in a number of ways. It could camouflage its activities from the watchful attention of the democratic parties; it could also establish nuclei of power in various communist-controlled organizations, an important tactical step as long as the Ministry of the Interior was not safely in communist hands and as long as the armed forces were not thoroughly purged of "unreliable" officers.

The methods of the communist police investigators equalled those of the Gestapo and NKVD, the Soviet secret police. They specialized in denunciations of democrats who stood in the way of communist infiltration in all sectors of life. General Bartík, a non-partisan expert of long standing in intelligence work, chief of that service in the Ministry of the Interior, was removed in January 1946 on the basis of a forged document.

The democratic leaders attacked these practices and the organization of the police forces on frequent occasions. They presented their complaints and protests, supported by collected evidence, in the Ministerial Council, in the National Assembly, and in the press. The Minister of the Interior would always promise an investigation, but no positive results were achieved. In July 1947 the Parliament voted a law which established a legal framework for the powers of the police forces and envisaged their reorganization before the end of 1947. Also, the intelligence services were to be centralized, removed from the competence of the Ministry of the Interior, and attached to the six-member Presidium of the Ministerial Council in which sat three democratic Deputy Prime Ministers.

The law was never implemented and the intelligence services were never unified. The communist Minister of the Interior sabotaged the plan and instead proceeded speedily with the elimination of non-communist police officers and with their communist replacements. It was finally the question of the police forces which, at the beginning of 1948, became the central point in the national crisis and precipitated the communist putsch.[55]

The Gruesome Story Continues

It has already been noted that the wartime resistance record of the Communist Party is doubtful; that some of its prominent members were even in the service of the Gestapo. (See pp. 57-67.)

Aware of their members' deficiencies or indeed crimes, the Ministry of the Interior was anxious to efface any trace of such wartime history; it spared no effort to collect documents which might disclose the truth. Moreover, the party wished to establish the legend that activity in the underground movement had been

[55] The information is based on Ripka, *Le coup de Prague*, *op.cit.*, pp. 153-68; I. Herben, from a manuscript. See also *Svobodný zítřek*, May 8, 1947; *Svobodné slovo*, December 18, 1947.

limited to communist efforts and that the democratic groups, in fact, had cooperated with the Germans.

On January 2, 1946 a certain Captain Pokorný, who replaced General Bartík in the intelligence service of the Ministry of the Interior, circulated a secret instruction to those persons charged with the investigation of imprisoned members of the Gestapo. The circular stated that these investigations must not only serve to establish responsibility in war crimes but must also be used to collect information about the activities of individual Czechoslovaks during the war. The person under investigation, the instructions read, was to be won over by friendly appeals and increased rations in cigarettes and food. If the member under investigation was willing to sign a statement that prominent democratic patriots collaborated with the nazis during the war, he was to be spared execution. The least these investigations were to achieve, the circular ordered, was to establish that, based on these prisoners' testimony, the democratic underground was a farce and of no concern whatever to the Gestapo.

The Ministry of the Interior had organized a special department in charge of the preparation of defamation reports about democratic groups which were then passed on to the police for further investigation, according to the same secret circular. These reports included such names as Jaroslav Kvapil, a famous theater director and one of the country's greatest national figures since World War I; Kamil Krofta, former Minister of Foreign Affairs and a noted historian; Ivan Dérer, a prominent Czechoslovak statesman and patriot; Petr Zenkl, who spent six years in the Buchenwald concentration camp; Arnošt Heidrich, distinguished diplomat and close aide of Dr. Beneš; Vladimír Krajina, generally recognized as the most courageous man in the underground movement.

As a result of these police investigations, on April 6, 1946 Captain Pokorný convened an off-the-record press conference at which he praised the glorious deeds of the communist underground; as to the activities carried on by other groups, "they were just playing 'cops and robbers' with the full knowledge of the Gestapo." In his list of collaborators were names of prominent persons, some of whom, such as General Eliáš, had been executed by the nazis.

This statement, released by the Ministry of the Interior, caused a thunderous reaction. The Minister, Nosek, was immediately questioned in the Ministerial Council. Under attack, he retreated and withdrew the list.

Some individual cases will go down in history as pathological examples of political chicanery. A certain sergeant, Ryšánek, at the beginning of the war was a member of the democratic underground *Obrana národa* (The Defense of the Nation). He was caught by the Gestapo, which compelled him to pretend a continuation of his underground activities. Before his role was uncovered, several leaders had been denounced and had lost their lives. After the war, the sergeant was arrested. Mr. J. Drábek, the prosecutor general for punishment of war crimes, writes: "The Ministry of the Interior's investigation proceeded in the case of Ryšánek according to the directive. They offered him various advantages, even to spare his life if he were willing to testify according to their needs. A protocol was prepared with him—I read it—and it contained several hundred pages, in which were listed the most merited members of the non-communist underground as Gestapo collaborators or as stupid non-entities with whom the Gestapo just played a game."

Again, the case provoked intensive indignation. The Minister of the interior stated in an informal, jovial manner that it was based on a misunderstanding. "Nevertheless," writes Mr. Drábek, "his intelligence groups continued in their perfidious activities."

The case which created the greatest anger concerned Professor V. Krajina. The Ministry of the Interior accused him of collaboration with the Gestapo, basing its accusation on the testimony of no less important a witness than K. H. Frank, the chief German representative in Prague during the war. At the end of hostilities Frank was taken prisoner by the American Army and handed over to the Czechoslovak authorities as the principal war criminal in Czechoslovakia. In August 1945 the police investigators questioned him about Krajina. His Czech was poor and the investigation had been conducted until then in German. However, in the case of Krajina, a document was prepared for Frank's signature in Czech and, assured that it contained exactly his statement, he was asked to sign it for purely technical reasons to hasten up the procedure. After some reluctance, Frank agreed. However, being himself a nazi investigator of long experience, he became suspicious of this unusual step. Back in prison, and meanwhile handed over by the Ministry of the Interior to the custody of the regular departments of justice, he wrote a statement in German in which he recapitulated exactly what he had said to the police investigators. "When comparing the two protocols the result was devastating," writes Mr. Drábek and continues: "The protocol written in Czech contained two allegations: (1) that Krajina denounced to the Gestapo a group of parachutists; (2) that a group of people whom Frank toward the end of the war transferred from other concentration camps close to Prague—and there were among them the most merited people in Czechoslovakia—in fact cooperated with the Gestapo. There was nothing about these two points in the German text of Frank's protocol; nor did it mention any other treacherous activities of Krajina as Frank had supposedly stated according to the Czech text."

The Ministry of Justice immediately ordered Frank's confrontation with Krajina. He admitted that the police investigators had tried to induce him to make statements against Krajina and to sign a document in Czech and he confirmed that he had never made the allegations contained in the Czech protocol.

The Minister of Justice, P. Drtina, brought the scandalous affair before the Ministerial Council. At his insistence a three-member commission was entrusted to investigate Krajina's wartime activities. The commission, of which one member was a communist official of the Ministry of the Interior, unanimously recognized that Krajina's conduct during the war was beyond reproach. He was bestowed with the highest order of merit by the President of the Republic.

The finding of the commission did not, however, prevent the communists from reopening Krajina's case in September 1948, after they had seized power, and condemning him *in absentia* to twenty-five years imprisonment for high treason.

There were other instances of Gestapo men "testifying" before the police that democrats had collaborated with them. When transferred to the regular organs of justice, they boasted with malicious joy that the communists were obviously trying to liquidate—as Goebbels had predicted—their former democratic allies. Among those who made statements about the methods and purpose of the investigations conducted by the Ministry of the Interior were three men, the mention of whose names during the war made Czechs tremble: Heinrich Joekl, the commander of the concentration camp at Terezín; Pfitsch and Hornischer, two Gestapo investigators in Prague. "The latter was in the prison hospital in Pankrác with TB," writes Mr. Drábek. "A few hours before his death he asked to make a declaration. He stated that he was aware of his life coming to an end and wanted to relieve his conscience."

As all these excesses of the Ministry of the Interior became known, the democratic parties revealed them to the public and asked the government for remedy. Their protests were of no avail. The communists made promises only to bypass them; they did not withdraw measures already taken; they continued with their communization of the police forces.

The government still called itself a government of a united National Front; there was still agreement among the parties on basic issues but, in actual fact, under the surface of this unity bitterness and suspicion seethed. It was concentrated around the communist-controlled Ministry of the Interior and the democratic Ministry of Justice, but the struggle stretched far beyond the work of the two governmental offices. It was a struggle for principle between totalitarianism and freedom.

Democratic leaders came to realize the futility of their complaints or requests once the Communist Party was established in positions of power. In a country which still maintained some signs of democracy there was only one way to stop its tragic descent into the abyss of lawlessness. This was to change, with the help of public opinion, the power relationships of the two contending forces. The Constitutional Assembly had been elected in May 1946 for a term of two years. New elections seemed to offer the best—and perhaps the last—opportunity for such a change.[56]

[56] The chapter is based on J. Drábek, a letter of May 7, 1958; Ripka, *op.cit.*, pp. 163-68.

A MUTUAL OFFENSIVE

THE YEAR 1947 augured well for the cause of democracy. People were increasingly critical of communist policies. Many farmers now suffered from the ill-advised support they had given the party in the 1946 elections. Students became more and more vocal in their opposition to communist methods. The intelligentsia chafed at their curtailed freedom. Even workers, supposedly the backbone of the Marxist program, became hostile to constant communist appeals to increase their labor and to give freely of their hours of rest for so-called voluntary work. Practically everyone, except the functionaries of the party, detested the activities of the Ministry of the Interior.

Democratic newspapers raised their voice in protest against communist tactics in politics, economy, and cultural affairs. Democratic deputies spoke against them in the Constituent Assembly, and there were frequent clashes in the government itself. Increase in the circulation of democratic dailies and the enthusiastic response of audiences at public meetings of democratic leaders indicated unmistakably the direction in which the pendulum now swung.

This developing democratic offensive was, however, accompanied by some disconcerting features. Even as the masses turned to the democratic parties for leadership, no common plan of action, not even methods of consultation, were developed. The National Socialists were at the head of the struggle, followed closely by the Catholics. The Social Democrats were split into the radical left led by the fellow-traveller Fierlinger and the wing which followed V. Majer, with the opportunist Laušman in between. The Slovak Democratic Party, though commanding a preponderant majority among its constituents, was hamstrung by its attitude toward matters of Slovak autonomy, an attitude as radical as that of the communists themselves.

There was, therefore, no natural leadership of the democratic forces. Even worse, their leaders still clung desperately to the illusion of possible cooperation with the communists within a framework of democratic liberties and carefully avoided any overt acts of cooperation that might in any way be interpreted as an anti-communist bloc.

In contrast to this heterogeneity, the Communist Party of Czechoslovakia, with key powerful positions already under its control, possessed every characteristic which the democrats lacked: a preconceived plan, a homogeneous leadership, and discipline. Above all, however, it had the support of a powerful ally, the Soviet Union.

An International Setback

In 1947 the international situation deteriorated visibly. Peace treaties with the smaller defeated countries—Hungary, Bulgaria, and Rumania—had been signed in February, but no sooner had the signatures been affixed than the communists, with open Soviet support, violated both their political and military clauses. Poland went through elections in January 1947 which carried every imprint of communist totalitarian methods. Yugoslavia was safely in the hands of Tito, at that time Moscow's most devoted follower. Greece was on the verge of collapse under the burden of communist-instigated civil war. Turkey was exposed to repeated Soviet blackmail. East Germany was rapidly being drawn into the Soviet sphere. A network of bilateral alliances between the East European countries and the Soviet Union itself laid the foundations for a Soviet bloc which threatened directly an unarmed, disunited, and exhausted Western Europe. In France and Italy powerful and well-organized communist parties still held important positions in government at the beginning of 1947.

Against the backdrop of this international situation Czechoslovakia continued to display an uneasy balance. She was the only country in the area still struggling to maintain the basic principles of democracy but at the same time to preserve friendly relations with the Soviet Union. All parties were unanimous in their determination to remain Russia's faithful and loyal ally. The democratic leaders answered communist attacks alleging anti-Soviet intentions with repeated assurances to the contrary and with assertions that friendship with the Soviet Union was not the monopoly of the Communist Party. At the same time, however, the democratic leaders did their best to maintain and improve Czechoslovakia's relations with Western democracies. Her delegations at the Paris Peace Conference in the summer of 1946 and at the United Nations manifested some measure of independence; cultural ties with the West were renewed; her expanding foreign trade reopened old contacts with the West while trade with the Soviet Union remained negligible; UNRRA assistance was highly appreciated.

A treaty of alliance with France, designed to balance in a way the impact of the alliance with Russia, was keenly desired by President Beneš and the democratic parties. The Communist Party agreed with this step as long as the Communist Party of France remained in the government. It was in all probability Stalin's hope that France would succumb to communism and that her alliance with Czechoslovakia might speed up the process. The negotiations, however, were protracted and in the spring of 1947 not only were the French communists ousted from the government but also France signed a treaty of alliance with England, the Dunkirk Treaty. Czechoslovak communists immediately lost interest in the treaty with France, though an exchange of views between Prague and Paris continued through diplomatic channels for some time.

During this period the communist press kept up its harangue, insisting that on all questions of importance to Czechoslovakia, political and economic, the Soviet Union was the only big power ready to give assistance. The West was either disinterested or actively against Czechoslovakia's aims and desires. The West unfortunately often confused such communist tactics with official policy and reacted to these accusations with unnecessary bitterness.

Secretary of State James Byrnes, for example, relates how he cabled instructions to the State Department from the Paris Peace Conference sometime in the summer of 1946 to stop the extension of credit of 50 million dollars which had been allotted to Czechoslovakia for the purchase of surplus property because two Czechoslovak delegates—both communists—among ten heartily applauded Vyshinsky's charges "that the United States was trying to dominate the world with 'hand-outs.'" At the same time negotiations with the Export-Import Bank for a 150-million-dollar loan were suspended.[1] The reaction in Czechoslovakia was exactly that which the communists and the Soviet government wished: shock, disappointment, a feeling that the West had failed to understand the country's problems in its struggle for independence.

In one other matter of vital importance to Czechoslovakia many people became convinced of the truth of the communist line—that the Soviet Union, after all, was the only reliable ally. This was the question of the transfer of 100,000 Hungarians from Czechoslovakia to Hungary. At the Paris Peace Conference the United States and Great Britain openly opposed the Czechoslovak request. The Soviet Union gave the impression of supporting it, and this impression had a marked effect upon public opinion. The bitter truth, of course, of the actual Soviet position was not known. This is revealed by an episode which throws an illuminating light on Soviet political practices and which deserves to be told here, probably for the first time. The former Secretary General of the Ministry of Foreign Affairs, Arnošt Heidrich, writes:

"I was present when, towards the end of June, 1945, Stalin agreed with the suggestion which Clementis put before him

[1] James F. Byrnes, *Speaking Frankly*, New York, Harper and Brothers, 1947, p. 143.

to exchange the Hungarian population in Czechoslovakia for Slovaks in Hungary. If I said that he agreed, it is an understatement because Stalin showed great enthusiasm for the proposal, promised all necessary help, and ended, 'Kick them in the teeth!'

"When, after our return in Prague, there was no political and diplomatic help coming for some time, Dr. Clementis followed the matter up and he found out from some of the leading representatives of the Soviet Union in Budapest, that at about the same time Stalin was giving his promise to Dr. Clementis, Dekanosov was assuring the leader of the Hungarian Communist Party, Rákosi, of full Soviet support to Hungary in her opposition to the exchange of the population."[2]

This fact did not deter Vyshinsky, of course, from making the public statement that he was "authorized by the Soviet government to say that Czechoslovakia [had] grounds for ridding herself of part of her Hungarian minority."[3] The political effect in Czechoslovakia was as Vyshinsky expected it.

Within the framework of increasing international tensions the question of the Czechoslovak-French treaty became a testing ground not only for the conduct of the Czechoslovak foreign policy but also for broader Soviet intentions in Europe. Again Mr. Heidrich offers an enlightening insight:

"In June 1947, Gottwald came with a new and quite surprising interpretation of our treaty of alliance with the Soviet Union. The provisions of this treaty are identical with the provisions of many other previous treaties which obligate the signatories towards mutual assistance in defense against an aggressor. The treaty, therefore, does not allow for any other interpretation than the one which was given to similar previous treaties. In spite of this, Gottwald came with the interpretation according to which the treaty would be the foundation of a kind of common action against Germany and all other western powers as Ger-

[2] From a letter of Mr. Heidrich, April 22, 1958.

[3] *The New York Times*, September 21, 1946, p. 2.

many's potential allies. He did it, of course, at the instruction of Moscow. When the democratic members of the government and President Beneš refused to identify themselves with this interpretation, Gottwald suggested that a special governmental delegation be sent to Moscow to negotiate about the question and about the envisaged treaty with France with the Soviet representatives. I am mentioning this episode in order to illustrate how dangerous in the hands of the Soviets are the treaties, even with standard provisions about the sense and consequences of which there was never before any doubt."[4]

July 1947 was a black month in the history of postwar Czechoslovakia. The story of what transpired that month is well known and needs to be retraced here only briefly. It is the story of Czechoslovakia's experience with the Marshall Plan.[5]

The Czechoslovak government, including its communist members, had accepted unanimously the invitation to attend the opening conference in Paris, even though Molotov had already left the preparatory session attended by the Soviet Union, Great Britain, and France, and had rejected Soviet participation. The communists were encouraged in their desire to participate by their belief in Soviet consent, by the assurance of the Polish government that it would attend the Marshall Plan conference, and also by strong indications of Yugoslav and Rumanian participation.

As had already been planned, the Czechoslovak governmental delegation, led by Gottwald, left for Moscow on July 9 to negotiate the interpretation of the Czechoslovak-Soviet treaty of alliance, to consult with the Soviet government about the pact with France, and to discuss Soviet-Czechoslovak trade relations. Discussion of the Marshall Plan was not even on the agenda. However, one ominous sign accompanied their departure: a few hours before taking off the delegation was informed that the Polish

[4] From a letter of Mr. Heidrich, April 22, 1958.

[5] Ripka, *op.cit.*, pp. 43-65; Stewart Alsop, "Stalin's Plans for the U.S.A.," *Saturday Evening Post*, vol. 224, no. 1, pp. 17ff.; D. A. Schmidt, *Anatomy of a Satellite*, Boston, Little, Brown, 1952, pp. 100-02.

government had rejected the invitation to Paris. The Yugoslav and Rumanian governments had done the same.

On the afternoon of July 9 Gottwald was called in secrecy to Stalin. What transpired became apparent that evening when Stalin received the whole delegation. He told them that the Marshall Plan was directed against the Soviet Union and that Czechoslovak participation would be a hostile act against the Soviet Union. To him, as he put it, the Czechoslovak attitude was a matter of principle, upon which would depend Soviet friendship toward Czechoslovakia. Finally he asked for a change of the Czechoslovak government's decision. He was obviously not impressed by a memorandum which Beneš had sent to him emphasizing the significance of Czechoslovakia's participation in the American assistance plan.[6]

Late that night, immediately after the conference with Stalin, the democratic members of the delegation—Masaryk, Drtina, and Heidrich—admitted their defeat, and Gottwald telephoned to Prague asking for a meeting of the Ministerial Council and for withdrawal from the Marshall Plan conference. He also instructed Clementis, the Deputy Foreign Minister, to inform Dr. Beneš. At 4:00 a.m. members of the government in Prague were convened for an emergency morning session. Clementis, who meanwhile had seen President Beneš, had found him in bed, gravely ill. In the early hours of the morning Dr. Beneš had suffered a brain hemorrhage which was accompanied by a loss of speech. Clementis could not even understand what he was trying to say. When the democratic members of the government attempted to consult him by telephone, the President could not speak with them. The democratic Ministers, shocked, confused, and humiliated, after a heated discussion with the communists, agreed to revoke the original acceptance of the Marshall Plan.

On July 10, 1947 Czechoslovakia lost her independence. The Soviet Union had arrogantly dictated to her government a course of action on a matter of paramount importance to her future.

[6] Smutný, *op.cit.*, vol. 1, p. 7.

It had violated flagrantly and viciously its assurance, solemnly given and guaranteed by treaty, that it would never intervene in Czechoslovak national affairs. As Masaryk said to his friends upon landing in Prague on July 12, "It is a new Munich. I left for Moscow as Minister of Foreign Affairs of a sovereign state. I am returning as Stalin's stooge."[7]

There are observers who believe that President Beneš and the democratic parties should have insisted on maintaining the original decision of the government at whatever the cost and whatever the consequences. But they did not.

Toward a Showdown

The Czechoslovak experience with the Marshall Plan clearly indicated the lengths to which Moscow was ready to go in matters of importance to the Soviet Union. As far as the internal political struggle was concerned, it was a serious setback for the democrats. Nevertheless, they soon resumed the offensive.

The Communist Party had indicated early in 1947 the tactics it intended to follow in its election campaign. Gottwald spoke on January 22, 1947 before the Central Committee of the party; attacking the "reactionary" forces in the National Front, he stated that the only way to remedy the situation was to strengthen the party by gaining, not 40 per cent of the votes, "but an absolute, overwhelming majority." To achieve this goal, the party's policy must be, he stated, "a policy of active struggle against reaction, of gaining new position after new position, of consolidating conquered positions and pushing the enemy into the defensive."[8] He repeated the appeal a few days later and, pointing significantly to the favorable international situation, promised that the forces of reaction would be beaten.[9]

From that time on the target of achieving 51 per cent of the

[7] I. Herben, "Comment Staline empêcha la Tchécoslovaquie de participer au plan Marchall," *Le Figaro*, August 12, 1948.

[8] Gottwald, *Spisy*, *op.cit.*, vol. I, pp. 120.

[9] *Ibid.*, p. 124.

votes in the election became the chief slogan of communist agitation. Soon a pattern emerged. The communists attacked every move which appeared to them to be a strengthening of democratic processes or positions. Gottwald, for instance, called it a reactionary act when Professor K. Engliš, a noted conservative economist, was elected Rector of Charles University in Prague. He attacked the Parliament for its attempts to amend the government's draft bills.[10] But the chief target was the Slovak Democratic Party, which had gained 62 per cent of the votes in the last elections. It was exposed to concentrated accusations of harboring fascists; in June 1947 the *New York Times* correspondent, Albion Ross, rightly predicted that "the communist-led campaign against the Slovak Democratic Party will be presented to the Czechs as a matter of crushing seditious separatism in Slovakia. . . ."[11]

Simultaneously with the policy of compromising the Slovak Democratic Party, communists staged acts of violence. In the summer months of 1947 a few units of the so-called Bandera army crossed the Czechoslovak boundary in northern Slovakia. The army consisted of Ukrainian nationalists and some desperadoes who attacked scattered Soviet and Polish military establishments. To repel them was a matter of administrative police action. However, the Communist Party requested the government to allow the rearmament of former partisan units to help the regular army in the mopping-up operation. A secret party circular ordered its members to join the partisan units on the pretext of fighting the Bandera troops but in fact to organize "an armed militia for the forthcoming struggle with capitalist reaction."[12] The communist device was foiled by calling partisans to the colors but incorporating them at the same time in the regular army.

In the fall of 1947 two events occurred which compelled the

[10] *Ibid.*, pp. 188-89.

[11] *The New York Times*, June 29, 1947, sect. IV, p. 6.

[12] I. Herben, "Benešovy porady s Gottwaldem v Moskvě" (Beneš' Consultations with Gottwald in Moscow), a manuscript, p. 24.

communists to reconsider their general strategy of gaining 51 per cent in the elections which were to take place in the spring of 1948.

A public poll showed that the popularity of the party was decidedly on the wane and predicted considerable losses in the forthcoming elections. The party leadership reached the same conclusion on the basis of its own survey.

The other event was an international development. The Marshall Plan had served as a first warning to the Soviet Union that the United States would not look on passively at the process of economic disintegration in Western Europe, with communist agitation flourishing on the soil of her economic misery. Moscow decided to fight back. The first blow fell on Czechoslovakia. The Soviet Union decided, one can assume, that in view of the critical international situation it could not afford to let the Communist Party of Czechoslovakia lose the elections. It was probably sometime in September that the decision was made to communize the country by the old established bolshevik method—by violence.

In September 1947 the Cominform was founded. The step was probably the result of Stalin's experience in July when the East European allies of Russia had apparently intended to join the Marshall Plan. This, it appears, led Stalin to the decision that he must at all costs tighten his control over them.

The first meeting of the Cominform marked the opening of a new aggressive policy of the international communist movement. The speeches and resolutions were characterized by an analysis of the international situation that was filled with the old concepts of class struggle and class hatred. The Secretary General of the party, Slánský, reporting on the situation in Czechoslovakia, indicated certain of the things to come, something of the policy to follow. He stated that reactionaries were increasingly aggressive; that there was no unity in the leading circles of the National Front; that there was, however, a unity among those people who were organized in the powerful trade unions, in the Association of Youth, in cooperatives, and the United Association of Peasants. "These organizations, particularly the trade unions, can in the future play a more active role in the National Front. They can help more actively in its strengthening," said Slánský.[13] He further expressed the expectation that with the increasing tensions in international affairs there would develop an increasing struggle of forces within the individual parties of the National Front. He assured the communist leaders from other countries that the "democratic elements" in the non-communist parties would undoubtedly follow the Communist Party. "It will be necessary to throw reactionary forces out of the National Front," he stated quite plainly, and thus "bury forever the hopes of international and internal reaction. . . ."[14]

This is exactly what happened in Czechoslovakia during the fourth week of February when the struggle between democracy and communism reached its denouement.

Meanwhile the party staged a series of measures designed to prepare the situation for the final showdown. It started with a systematic campaign against the United States which was accused of "dollar diplomacy" and of preparation for war against the Soviet Union. Anti-communism was identified with friendship for the United States, which was thus "dragged into the center of the ideological struggle within the country. . . ."[15] The Soviet Union, which had offered Czechoslovakia 200,000 tons of wheat as a sort of compensation for the loss suffered by her non-participation in the Marshall Plan—an inadequate compensation for an irreparable loss—was pictured by the communist press as the savior of the country. Then, a number of political explosions followed, one after another, well-timed bombs which had been planted as a result of the Cominform's decision.

The serious financial situation into which farmers had fallen as a consequence of a severe drought was to be settled, according to a communist proposal, by imposing a special tax on all property

[13] *Zasedání devíti komunistikých stran*, *op.cit.*, pp. 113.

[14] *Ibid.*, p. 118. [15] *The New York Times*, September 29, 1947, p. 4.

exceeding the value of one million crowns (20,000 dollars). Communists called it provocatively "the millionaire tax," aware of the fact that such properties under the nation's inflated currency in many cases did not represent any appreciable wealth. The proposal was sheer demagoguery. When the government majority rejected the communist draft, the communist daily, *Rudé právo*, published on its first page the following day the names of the Ministers who had voted against the bill and presented them to the public as protectors of millionaires. Jan Masaryk, who was not present at the government's meeting, subsequently published a statement in which he declared that he too was against "the millionaire tax" and condemned the "quite unusual and entirely propagandistic indiscretions" of the communist press.[16]

Then began a series of events and movements which eventually was to make inevitable the use of force and violence by the Communist Party, for they clearly indicated that if the democratic processes were to be followed, communism in Czechoslovakia was doomed to suffer vast reverses and eventually lose its leading position in the government.

These events took many forms. A few days later, on September 10, the nation was shocked to learn that three democratic Ministers, Jan Masaryk, Petr Zenkl, and Prokop Drtina, had received three identical packages, marked "perfume," which in fact contained explosives. This attempt on their lives was thwarted only by the timely detection of the contents of the packages. The police, under communist control, began investigations which seemed to lead to Prague but which yielded no real results. With such police negligence, the public became increasingly suspicious that the communists had arranged the affair themselves. Soon another sensational discovery was made, one that was to rock the nation and eventually bring about its downfall.

On the same day that the attempted assassination was announced, it became known that the Social Democratic Party and

[16] *Svobodné noviny*, September 5, 1947.

the Communist Party had reached an agreement to proceed in the future in full solidarity "along the socialist line" and that the National Socialist Party had been invited to join them. However, not only did the National Socialists refuse to sign, but it was also disclosed that the agreement between the Social Democrats and the Communists had been made by fellow-traveller Fierlinger without the knowledge of the majority of the Social Democrats' leadership. That leadership immediately issued a declaration that their party would continue to conduct an independent policy. This, to the Communist Party, was a serious defeat.

The party therefore concentrated all its efforts on Slovakia, where the Democratic Party for months had been under constant communist fire. At the end of September the communist-controlled police searched the office of the secretary to the Deputy Prime Minister Ursiny, the leader of the Democratic Party. On October 6 the Commissioner of the Interior in the Slovak autonomous government announced the discovery of a plot of high treason, and 380 people were arrested. On October 30 a mass meeting of the Slovak trade unions, accompanied by violent demonstrations, asked for the expulsion of the Democrats from the Slovak government. Its chairman, the communist G. Husák, immediately submitted the government's resignation without even consulting the Democrats, the majority party. A meeting of the National Front of the Slovak parties was convened to discuss the crisis. It was attended, as Slánský had predicted at the Cominform session in September, by representatives of the communist-controlled trade unions, peasants, and resistance organizations. The Democratic Party refused to participate. The same attempt was made by Gottwald a few days later in Prague, on November 4, to create a new, communist-oriented majority in the National Front. All democratic parties refused to attend the Prague meeting. When the National Front met again, the so-called non-partisan representatives were absent. When the Slovak government was reorganized, the Communist Party was still in the minority.[17] The tactic had failed. The party had suffered a double defeat.

Another blow to communist policy was administered by the party which the communists hoped was already their servant. Between November 13 and 16, 1947, the Social Democratic Party had its congress at Brno. After an intensive battle Fierlinger was unseated from the chairmanship and, by a vote of 283 to 182, was replaced by B. Laušman. He was an opportunist who had sided with the communists but, sensing well the anti-communist trend in his party, he switched to its right wing; his election was therefore an anti-communist manifestation.

Fierlinger's defeat reverberated beyond the borders of Czechoslovakia. He himself had stated angrily to the visiting mayor of Schafhausen, Walter Bringolf, who attended the congress, "In four months I'll be back."[18] A Soviet official said to Ripka that "comrade Fierlinger was [to the Soviet Union] a guarantee of [Czechoslovakia's] friendship for the Soviet Union. His defeat indicates the anti-Soviet tendencies of Czech and Slovak reactionaries" he stated, and threatened that the Soviet Union "considered this intolerable." Ripka encountered a similar reaction in Warsaw, and a Yugoslav communist leader told him directly, "What you have just done against comrade Fierlinger is an unbearable provocation. . . ."[19]

What happened was in fact the democratic process in action. There was behind it no thought of an anti-Soviet move. But the Czechoslovak communists were furious: the hope of achieving the 51 per cent majority was gone for good. On November 27 Gottwald admitted in a speech before the Central Committee the seriousness of the situation. According to him, the international situation was worsening: foreign reactionaries allegedly were exercising pressure on Czechoslovakia and reactionaries were active in the National Front; in Slovakia a dangerous

[17] Lettrich, *op.cit.*, pp. 248-51. Ripka, *op.cit.*, pp. 110-17.

[18] *Recollections and Reconstruction*, *op.cit.*, meeting November 26, 1949.

[19] Ripka, *op.cit.*, pp. 124, 125.

fascist plot of the Democratic Party had been uncovered and had received support from National Socialists and the Catholic Party. The Social Democratic Party must be watched, he stated; utmost vigilance was required against the reactionary circles which contemplated replacing the present government of the National Front by a cabinet of officials. At the end Gottwald asked for the inclusion of non-partisan organizations in the National Front, a demand which had been refused before.[20]

The party's Politburo sat permanently in these somber days. At one meeting its secretariat submitted a report that it had lost popularity among the masses and there was no hope of receiving 51 per cent in the next election. It is reported that a representative of the Cominform also read to the Politburo a directive from the Secretariat of the Communist Party of the Soviet Union asking that Gottwald's slogan about the special Czechoslovak road toward socialism be subdued as it was throwing the party into dangerous waters of "right wing deviation."[21]

Immediately thereafter, the speeches of communist leaders became more radical and violent. They identified the democratic parties with capitalism and incited in the workers familiar sentiments of class hatred. In the elections for factory councils communist agitators used terror as well as various deceitful devices to achieve majorities. However, even the Social Democrats, freed now as they were from Fierlinger's leadership and believing themselves to have significant following among the workers, openly denounced these methods. Their chief organ, *Právo lidu,* now dared to denounce "all the questionable practices [which] were used and calculated to upset the democratic forms of election. . . ." It continued: "The meetings are usually called after working hours when the majority of workers are leaving or have left. Furthermore, the methods of voting are controlled which is practically equivalent to direct intimidation."[22] The

[20] Gottwald, *Spisy*, *op.cit.*, vol. 1, pp. 266-82.

[21] Laušman, *Kdo byl vinen? op.cit.*, pp. 98-99.

[22] *The New York Times*, January 10, 1948, p. 5.

terrorist practices of the Communist Party became an object of frequent interpellations in the Parliament.

When communists were not in a position to terrorize, electoral results were indicative of the forthcoming national elections. Before the end of 1947, students' organizations met for their annual meetings. In all colleges communist candidates failed to achieve more than 20 per cent of the votes. The faculty, too, was largely opposed to communism, and the communist Minister of Information threatened publicly that it must be purged.[23]

Two more events, however, brought the atmosphere, already filled with tension, to the point of explosion.

Krčmáň

Krčmáň is a small village in northern Moravia. Few people in Czechoslovakia would know about its existence had not the Communist Party of Czechoslovakia brought it to their attention in the autumn days of 1947. It is now connected in their minds with the attempted assassination of three democratic ministers.

After a desultory investigation, the communist Ministry of the Interior reported that it had been unable to trace the crime beyond finding the manufacturer of the three wooden boxes in Prague. It now seemed certain that the investigation would be brought to an inconclusive end. Meanwhile, the communist press and even the Secretary General of the party, Slánský, publicly ridiculed the democratic Ministers with the suggestion that they had sent the explosives to themselves.

The communists did not know that although the police had tried to conceal the real origin of the attempt by deliberately following a false lead to Prague, a certain Ladislav Loveček, on September 30, 1947, had secretly informed the Secretary General of the National Socialists Party, Dr. V. Krajina, that the crime was initiated in the village where he lived, Krčmáň, and that the

[23] *The New York Times*, December 8, 1947, p. 9; Jan Novotny, "How the Reds Took Over Our Faculty," *Vital Speeches of the Day*, vol. 22, pp. 535-39.

wooden boxes were manufactured in the workshop of a Jan Kopka.

Krajina passed the information on to the regional police in Brno, to Dr. Alois Přikryl, who was known not to be a communist. He immediately opened an investigation. He brought Kopka and his wife to Brno for interrogation. The couple, both members of the Communist Party, confessed that Kopka produced the boxes upon orders from the party local organization at Olomouc and that they were aware of the purpose for which they were to be used. At this moment, Přikryl arrested Kopka and informed his superior, Dr. Goerner, a communist, about the examination. Kopka was shown the boxes, identified them, and repeated the confession. Goerner, however, insisted that the real manufacturer was located in Prague, though his products looked obviously different from the boxes in question. Goerner then released Kopka and declared the affair closed. At the same time by a secret telephone call—which however was tapped—he ordered the police at Olomouc to cover up all tracks leading to Krčmáň.

In every orderly democratic country the police, having discovered a crime, pass the results of its investigation on to the organs of justice. In this case the police did just the opposite. Seeing this, Krajina then filed a charge with the District Court at Olomouc. The District Attorney opened his own investigation and issued a warrant for the arrest of Kopka. Kopka repeated the statement he had made before the police and admitted further that the boxes were ordered and taken from him by an A. Zapletal, the janitor of the building in which the offices of the Communist Party local organization at Olomouc were located. An inspection of Kopka's shop revealed hidden guns, hand grenades, and a considerable quantity of ammunition. In the course of the investigation of the Krčmáň affair, 89 guns, some light and four heavy machine guns, and several boxes of ammunition and hand grenades were found in the apartment of another communist, Opletal. The discovery led to another name—J. Jura-Sosnar, a communist member of the National Assembly, who had ordered the transfer of the arms to the apartment from communist headquarters at Olomouc. When Opletal, a railroadman, hesitated to hide the arms Sosnar threatened him, "If you ever breathe a single word, it might be that you would be crushed between two cars or fall off a train without anyone knowing how it happened."[24] Moreover, Kopka revealed through an intercepted letter sent out of prison to Sosnar asking for immediate help and threatening otherwise to denounce him and other prominent members of the party, that Sosnar was also mixed up in the Krčmáň affair. Further investigation showed that Sosnar himself put the explosives in the boxes and that he acted at the instruction of Dr. Alexej Čepička, chairman of the county executive committee of the Communist Party. Even as the investigation was in process, the party on December 3 proposed Dr. Čepička as Minister of Interior Commerce instead of A. Zmrhal, who, it was said, was in poor health. Beneš nominated him immediately after he had been assured by the Prime Minister, Gottwald, that the nomination had been agreed to by the government. In actual fact the proposal was never brought before the government because Gottwald realized that the democratic Ministers would not have approved the appointment of such a person.[25]

The political atmosphere was now unbearable. One day at the beginning of January 1948 Gottwald said to Drtina, the Minister of Justice, who was responsible for the court investigation, "Drtina, you will meet with a bad end." When asked what he meant Gottwald repeated, "You will remember my words. I am telling you again you will meet with a bad end."

When the Ministry of the Interior continued to state that its own investigation gave no results and even blamed the Ministry of Justice for hampering further procedure, Drtina made a detailed statement to the Parliament on January 21, informing the deputies about the progress of the investigation. He also disclosed

[24] Ripka, *op.cit.*, p. 175.

[25] *Recollections and Reconstruction*, *op.cit.*, meeting November 19, 1949.

that illegal deposits of arms had been found at places of persons connected with the Communist Party. The statement had the effect of a bombshell. A trial was to take place in a short time, just before the spring national elections were to be held.

The chain of proof appeared closed, except for finding the person who took the boxes to Prague to mail them. Then he, too, was identified. A Joseph Štěpánek, a railroad employee and chairman of the communist organization at Krčmáň, was known to be in Prague during the days of the assassination attempt, wearing the garb of a priest. The comparison of his handwriting with the addresses of the three Ministers showed a distinct likeness and its identity was confirmed by two Prague graphologists, though the communist police subsequently tried to make them change their finding.

The trial was to open in March 1948. It never took place. The Communist Party on the eve of the elections could never allow such a revelation to the public of the criminal methods with which it tried to liquidate its opponents. Nor did it, with its seizure of power. A. Čepička, himself a culprit in the Krčmáň affair, was appointed Minister of Justice. He released all suspects and had imprisoned all persons who had conducted the court investigation.[26]

A Staged Plot

After the fall of 1947 communist speakers and press had hurled attacks against the democratic parties, particularly against the National Socialists, accusing them among other things of contacts with Western imperialist powers. They then set about to manufacture and produce their proofs. On October 20 the police released from prison a Vladimír Podivín and took him to a private apartment. There, two officers from the Ministry of the Interior

[26] This information is based on a copy of the letter (thirteen pages, single spaced, typewritten) which J. Drábek sent to Justice Robert H. Jackson, January 4, 1949. Ripka, *op.cit.*, pp. 169-78; statement by Dr. Drtina in the National Assembly, January 21, 1948, *Hlas Československa*, vol. III, no. 2, pp. 33-36.

indicated to him that he would be acquitted if he rendered certain services; if not, his mother and brother would be arrested. A few days later, Podivín, accompanied by his newly acquired "friends," went to Teplice-Šanov, a town in northern Bohemia, to seek out a real friend of his, Pravoslav Raichel. He introduced the two men with him as Americans of Czech origin. The men carried identification cards of American journalists, stamped by the Ministry of the Interior, and with an attached permit to search out the graves of American airmen. They then introduced themselves as Tony and Eddy. The group visited a local inn. Here Podivín told Raichel in a confidential manner that they were all actually sent to see him by a political anti-communist center in Prague whose members were prominent democratic leaders and, also, by the American military attaché in Prague, Major Richard S. Steffel, and First Lieutenant Hartig. The visitors told Raichel that communists were preparing a violent upheaval and that the political center in Prague entrusted him with the important task of organizing a military group for counteraction. At the following meeting they promised him assistance by the delivery of arms and a place was chosen where they would be deposited. Raichel then collected the names of Czechoslovak officers who were known as anti-communists and particularly those who were stationed with the garrison at Most, another town in northern Bohemia.

On November 6 the two supposedly American friends took Raichel to Prague to meet members of the political center. They reached the capital after 2 a.m., took him to a private apartment, and promised to come in the morning.

Raichel had not been asleep one full hour when he was awakened by a sharp beam of light. It became immediately clear to him that he had fallen victim to an act of *agents provocateurs*. Widespread arrests followed. Raichel was promised freedom if he stated that he organized a plot against the Republic at the request of the democratic leaders and the American espionage service.

Toward the end of November the Minister of the Interior announced in an official communiqué that his office had uncovered a network of espionage. Little did he know that the agents of the Ministry of Justice had turned up proof that the two "Americans" were indeed undercover agents of the Minister of the Interior, Müller and Kroupa, and that the whole affair had been staged by the communist-controlled police. On January 17, 1948 Dr. Drtina, the Minister of Justice, made a full and detailed statement of these facts to the Ministerial Council. The participants were stupefied. The Minister of Education, J. Stránský, exclaimed, "I don't know whether these are the ways of the Gestapo or the GPU; but in any case I know that these are not methods of the Czech police!"[27]

It was decided that the Ministry of Justice should proceed with its investigation. When, however, it asked the Ministry of the Interior to instruct its officers to present themselves for examination, the Ministry refused. The investigation was never brought to an end. Three weeks later the communists seized power. In May Raichel was condemned for life, but on January 2, 1952 he escaped and crossed the border; he lives now in the United States.[28]

As the new year, 1948, dawned, heavy clouds were hanging over Czechoslovakia. The air was charged with electricity. Communist methods had been exposed and their offensives dissipated before the determined will of the democrats.

When Jan Masaryk stopped in London in December 1947 on his way home from the General Assembly of the United Nations, he met his good friend Sir Robert Bruce Lockhart. He intended, he told Lockhart, to take part in the election campaign. He did not lack confidence in the outcome. "If they were fair," he said, "the communists would lose seats. Whatever happened, Gottwald would not get his 51 per cent majority." Then he added

[27] Ripka, *op.cit.*, p. 183.

[28] This information is based on a memorandum (six pages, single spaced, typewritten) by P. Raichel; Ripka, *op.cit.*, pp. 179-83.

gravely, "That is, of course, if the Russians do not interfere." Masaryk also spoke well of Gottwald, "whom he had always liked."[29]

The leaders in Prague were of the same opinion, both about communist intentions and about the sincerity of the joviality with which Gottwald dealt with his political opponents. Within a few weeks lightning struck. The illusion vanished, and with it vanished Czechoslovak freedom.

[29] R. B. Lockhart, *op.cit.*, p. 639.

THE CRUSH

I WAS IN PRAGUE at the beginning of January 1948. The political battle between the democratic and communist parties had reached its highest pitch. I met many political friends; they were in good spirits, confident of the forthcoming elections. Since the previous September the Communist Party had lost one political fight after another: the "millionaire tax," the Krčmáň affair, the staged plot and espionage hoax. Communist methods being now thoroughly exposed, people were turning away from them.

Witnessing as I had the more violent politics of the Communist Party of Yugoslavia, I conveyed to my friends my uneasy doubts about the certainty of the outcome of the struggle in Czechoslovakia though I had shared their belief that one might cooperate with Czech communists. They brushed my fears aside, saying that Gottwald was not a Tito and that Czechoslovak communists were Czechs and Slovaks first, communists second.

On January 12 I was received by President Beneš. He spoke only with great difficulty as a consequence of two strokes which he had suffered the preceding year. He was obviously a gravely ill man; intellectually, however, he was as alert as ever. The audience lasted almost four hours, two in the morning and two in the late afternoon. President Beneš was extremely worried about the international situation and in strong terms fixed the responsibility for the crisis on the Soviet Union.

Then he turned to the situation in Czechoslovakia and said: "As much as I am pessimistic about the international development I am calm about the internal situation. The elections will be held in the spring. Communists will lose, and rightly so. People understand their policy and will not be duped as they were in May 1946. They will lose something like 10 per cent and the

National Socialists and Social Democrats will gain. That will bring a just balance." Smiling slightly, he added, "I don't want them to lose too much. That would arouse Moscow's anger."

I mentioned that perhaps the communists could not afford to lose in this election, that Moscow must already be angry that they had not as yet succeeded in overthrowing democracy in Czechoslovakia. I then asked Dr. Beneš if he was not worried lest the prospect of losing the elections might lead the communists to a putsch. He answered: "They thought of a putsch in September 1947 but they abandoned the idea and will not try any more. They found out for themselves that I enjoy certain authority in the nation. And not only that. They know that I have numerous supporters among the working class, even among many communist workers. They have come to realize that they cannot go against me. A putsch would be directed against me as well, and they cannot afford it. I shall not move from my place and I shall defend our democracy till the last breath. They know it, and therefore there will be no putsch. Besides that, the police is not fully in their hands. Half of it stands behind me, and the army is on the whole fully behind me."

I again expressed my doubts as to whether the communists would fully evaluate all those facts and I told him that, as seen from Belgrade, I could sense how difficult it must be for Gottwald to explain to the Cominform why he had not yet pushed the democratic parties out of the government. Czechoslovakia was the last country of the Soviet bloc which had not gone under, and almost daily in Belgrade I heard the opinion expressed that Czechoslovaks were semi-reactionaries, not wholly reliable in the struggle between the West and the East.

I asked the President what he thought of General Svoboda, the Minister of National Defense. He replied that Svoboda was reliable as well as Generals Vicherek, Pika, Klapálek, and some forty younger generals. I asked him whether he knew that Vicherek, the commander of the Air Force, was a member of the Communist Party, as I had heard. He was astonished to hear this, but remarked that he was reliable all the same. Then I asked him about the Chief of General Staff, Boček. "He is a chameleon who changes with each development to be on the winning side," answered the President. "He is a careerist who would kill even his own grandmother if it helped him in his career. Don't be worried, the danger of a communist putsch has passed. Return to Belgrade and carry on." Those were President Beneš' last words to me. I saw him no more.

The democratic leaders were full of confidence in those early weeks of 1948. The government coalition was breaking up, but they believed, having pushed the communists to the wall, there would be a new coalition, with communist participation but with communist strength cut to more modest proportions. There was no thought that their opponent might employ other than constitutional ways to acquire power. There was, therefore, for such an eventuality no plan. Neither, however, was there any plan for coordinating the democratic parties' political activity.

The Social Democratic Party held the key position to the democrats' majority in the government. Though its leadership was not quite freed from fellow travellers by the Congress in Brno, most of its members did show the courage to fight communist encroachment, and some attempt was made to bring its leadership closer to the National Socialist Party leaders. Toward the end of December 1947 (probably December 22) an informal meeting between the representatives of the two parties was held. The sense of the discussion was according to Majer, who took part in the meeting, "that the time has come not to retreat before the communist terror. It was decided to march together, and Laušman was entrusted to inform the Catholic leaders."[1] However, it was two months before the next meeting was held—too late for any common action.[2]

One of the reasons why there was no plan for common action, not even of common consultations among the two parties, or

[1] *Recollections and Reconstruction*, *op.cit.*, meeting December 4, 1949.

[2] Smutný, *op.cit.*, vol. 1, p. 13.

among any democratic parties, was their preoccupation with the idea that they must avoid any suspicion that they were creating an anti-communist bloc or that they intended to exclude communists from the government. It so happened that the Communist Party accused them of such a policy anyhow and finally excluded them from the coalition.

Certain ominous moves on the part of the Communist Party should have warned the democratic parties not to put complete trust in the democratic procedures, or at least to "keep their powder dry." Even toward the close of 1947, for example, information had started to reach Social Democratic headquarters that cases of arms were being delivered secretly to the communist members of the former workers' militia, which in 1946 had been dissolved at the insistence of the democratic parties.

There were also the words of Fierlinger, now the defeated social democratic fellow traveller, who said once to Majer, his opponent in the party, "Don't play with the communists. They will not tolerate it, nor will the Soviet Union." And those of Gottwald himself, who threatened Majer, saying, "So you succeeded in throwing the Social Democratic Party into the camp of the reactionaries, but it will end up very badly. Your behavior does not surprise us; you have always been a reactionary. But we'll settle our accounts with Laušman; he betrayed us."[3]

J. Stránský, one of the leaders of the National Socialists, noticed, at the beginning of 1948, that Gottwald, with whom he had always had friendly relations, had become, as he described it, "an enigma," concealing something grave and serious. However, he felt it was only part of the communist policy to frighten democrats.[4]

On January 5, 1958 the Secretary General of the Communist Party, Slánský, sent a circular, No. 2485-48, addressed to the secretaries of the party in the Prague district. It came to the attention of the Security Committee of the National Assembly

[3] *Recollections and Reconstruction, op.cit.*, meeting November 19, 1949.
[4] *Ibid.*

and was hotly debated on February 12. The circular read: "I order that in the interest of successful elections you take under control all secretaries of the Catholic Party, at all places. It is of particular importance that these servants of the reactionary movement in the country be followed when making public statements and that all means be used to separate these secretaries from their reactionary party in the pre-election period. By making impossible any activity of the secretaries of the Catholic Party we shall secure a smoother course in the elections as we can expect that chaos among its functionaries will ensue."[5] One can assume that such or similar circulars were sent to communist functionaries all over the country and that they concerned not only the Catholic but other democratic parties as well.

At the same time, at the beginning of January, the Cominform held a meeting in Milan. The daily *Lidová demokracie* reported that, according to a news leak, the first secret session was devoted to the situation in Czechoslovakia. The Communist Party of Czechoslovakia was in the process of strengthening its power, the delegates were informed, to guarantee its unshakable position, "and this should be done before the elections in the Parliament. The offensive of the Communist Party of Czechoslovakia is supposedly prepared in all details and its execution should be already launched by January," stated the report of the Prague daily.[6]

Toward the end of January, in the midst of the mounting crisis, Gottwald left Prague for Štrbské Pleso, a health resort in the Tatra Mountains close to the Polish border. Officially he went for health reasons but it was viewed with some astonishment when his villa was surrounded by the police and his visitors kept in deep secrecy.

In Gottwald's absence an important communist came to see Ripka, the Minister of Foreign Trade and one of the leaders of the National Socialists. He told Ripka, undoubtedly with in-

[5] *Ibid.*, meeting January 31, 1950.
[6] *Ibid.*, meeting January 3, 1950.

structions from the party, that tensions had reached such a point that "the worst" might happen, and that the two camps would inevitably have to measure their forces in an open conflict. Ripka asked him, "Do you mean to say a violent upheaval, a revolution?" The man answered after some hesitation, "It may go that far."[7] Ripka saw in his words another threat, another attempt at intimidation, and, as he later indicated to Gottwald, a product of the communists' own weakness and their fear of the outcome of the elections. He also received information from Budapest that Hungarian communists made no secret about a forthcoming change in Czechoslovakia which would produce communist mastery of the country.[8]

Daily, the infiltration of key posts in the police and security organizations continued. Most of the important posts of the Ministry of the Interior were in the hands of communists. "In the division of security, five heads of departments out of nine were communists. Three branches of the SNB were headed by communists. . . . In one of the most important divisions (division 111/2) there were fourteen communists out of nineteen. Heading the security corps there were nine communist officers out of thirteen. In the central office of the political police, the three commanding posts were all in communist hands. In the intelligence service the communists dominated even the inferior positions. At the province level of the SNB in Prague four superior officers out of five were members of the Communist Party. Out of seventeen regional directors of the SNB in Bohemia twelve were communists. Out of a total of seventy superior officers of the SNB, about sixty were members of the party."[9] Some 1,500 police without regular duties were kept in Slovakia. Some political police organs which supposedly had been dissolved by a governmental decision still operated under a different name.[10]

All this and much more the democratic leaders knew, yet they

[7] Ripka, *op.cit.*, pp. 188, 189-92, 193.
[8] *Ibid.*, pp. 190, 193. [9] *Ibid.*, pp. 203-04.
[10] *The New York Times*, February 1, 1948, p. 16.

could not bring themselves to believe in a communist revolution and they failed to make preparations to counteract such an eventuality. They thought that it was all part of communist tactics of intimidation, not by physical force but by psychological impact. They were resolved to fight the intimidation—but with arguments, with majority rule. These were not enough.

Events moved swiftly, as in the government violent political and economic quarrels erupted, one of which was to trigger the final catastrophe. The communist-held Ministry of Internal Commerce in January of 1948 unleashed an attack against private business and proposed the nationalization of the wholesale textile trade. The democratic parties opposed this policy and were immediately accused of sheltering black marketeers.

In the wake of this campaign, the communist Minister of Finances proposed the fusion of all banks into one central institution, a move which would have facilitated the communist control of the whole system of financial transactions. The Ministry of Agriculture, led by a communist, then introduced into the long-debated proposal for a new land reform the concept that the land holdings, regardless of size, should be distributed if they were not cultivated personally by the owner.

Both these proposals were of an economic nature though they had obvious political connotations. The communists, by presenting them as matters of social justice, hoped to separate the Social Democratic Party, with its own Marxist heritage, from the other democratic parties. Their tactic was successful; social democrats voted on these questions with communists and the opposing democratic parties were attacked in the communist press as champions of the capitalists and reactionaries.

Then, early in February, the government began debate on an issue that on the surface was a relatively innocuous one—the problem of state employees, their high numbers and low salaries. The Communist Party knew that the civil service was still overwhelmingly anti-communist. It proposed an overall and thoroughly beggarly increase of 300 crowns (6 dollars) a month to employees of all categories. This time the Social Democratic Ministers voted with the other democrats and the proposal lost. Then V. Majer, a social democrat, submitted a new scheme, more favorable to civil servants; at the ministerial session of February 6—against vigorous communist objection—it was accepted. The chairman of the trade unions, A. Zápotocký, who was present at the meeting in the capacity of an expert, protested vehemently and stated that the trade unions would never accept the government's decision. He immediately convened a national congress of the trade unions' delegates to be held February 22 in Prague.

This was the issue picked by the communists to trigger the explosion. Three weeks later, on February 25, this vote on the question of the salaries of civil servants was to culminate in a violent seizure of power by the communists.

Several major sources permit a fairly complete reconstruction of the events of these three fateful weeks which shattered all the hopes and dreams, all the calculations and expectations, all the strenuous working and planning of the democrats, which led to final and complete defeat all those who for their own reasons and in their own way had pursued the will-of-the-wisp of co-operation with the communists.[11]

That the issue of salaries was only a convenient pretext is seen by the fact that toward the end of January the trade unions' leaders had already sent out confidential information that a congress was planned as a part of the communist campaign.[12]

A few days later, February 15, Zápotocký threatened openly, "If the Parliament does not fulfill the program of the trade unions, away with it!"[13] F. Jungmann, another trade unionist, went even further. "If they do not like the slow road, then we

[11] H. Ripka, *Le coup de Prague*, *op.cit.; Recollections and Reconstruction*, *op.cit.*; J. Smutný, *Únorový převrat*, *op.cit.; Frankfurtský záznam* (Frankfort Memorandum), a collection of reports written by some fifteen political persons who were connected with the crisis in various capacities; Veselý, *Kronika únorových dnů 1948*, *op.cit.*

[12] Ripka, *op.cit.*, p. 198.

[13] *Recollections and Reconstruction*, *op.cit.*, meeting November 26, 1949.

can go the quick road," he declared and continued, "We have never said that nationalization is over. On the contrary, we shall go on with it. . . . A meeting of General Confederation of Labor delegates February 22 will decide which road we will take to socialism. The decision taken by the Rightist parties is provocation. Labor is the power in this state that will decide."[14]

The following day, February 16, the threat was substantiated by confidential information which leaked out of the communist headquarters and disclosed their program of action. The trade unions Congress, so the program read, was to vote a program of radical socialization; all enterprises with more than fifty employees were to be nationalized. Foreign trade was to become a state monopoly. The Social Democrats were expected to agree, unable as they were to oppose the trade unions. Other political parties would then be in the minority and if they opposed the sweeping measures a new government would be formed without them and composed of communists, social democrats, and representatives of the trade unions. This move would assure the new government of victory in the elections. The Cominform, the information revealed, agreed with the plan.[15]

The convening of the trade unions Congress was accompanied by threats in the press that the patience of the labor movement and the toiling masses had reached its end. The position of the democratic parties appeared to be seriously menaced if the communists succeeded in this plan to corner the social democrats. However, there was still one outstanding issue on which the democratic parties could swing the social democratic votes in the Ministerial Council to their side. It was the crucial problem of the communization of the police. They decided to use it as a weapon for a decisive offensive.

The day was Friday, February 13, 1948. The Ministerial Council met to consider a number of issues, one of them another communist proposal, a new national insurance bill. However, the

[14] *The New York Times*, February 18, 1948, p. 12.
[15] Ripka, *op.cit.*, pp. 208-09.

agenda was changed, and the Minister of Justice, Dr. Prokop Drtina, presented a detailed report about the developments in the Krčmáň affair and the so-called plot against the Republic. He accused the Ministry of the Interior of hampering the regular procedure of investigation. He accompanied the report by concise information about the extent of communist control of the police. Even as he spoke, a report came in that the Minister of the Interior, V. Nosek, had the preceding day removed another eight commanders in the province police force in Prague and had replaced them by communists. They all held positions which allowed them to distribute arms and ammunition to the ranks. During the session three proposals were made: that a special government commission investigate the situation not only in the police organization but also in the Ministry of Justice and report to the Ministerial Council on or before February 24; that until that day no changes or appointments be made in the Ministry of the Interior or Justice; that the eight commanders be reinstated and that the Minister of the Interior's order be revoked.

A heated debate ensued. The communists maintained that the Minister of the Interior, who was absent from the meeting for reasons of ill health, acted within his powers. On all three issues social democrats voted with other democratic parties. Only the first proposal was accepted unanimously, and on the other two the communists were defeated. It was decided to hold the next meeting on February 17, at which time the Minister of the Interior was to report on his implementation of the Council's last decision.[16]

Immediately after the meeting the Politburo met and, as Laušman was later told by a participant, it decided to inform the Soviet representative with the Cominform, Yudin, and the Czechoslovak representative, Pexa-Voda, about the situation without delay. It was further decided "to call, in an appropriate form, the party members to a state of permanent alertness." The Polit-

[16] *Recollections and Reconstruction*, *op.cit.*, meeting November 26, 1949; Ripka, *op.cit.*, pp. 202-06.

buro was to meet twice a day, at the lunch hour in Gottwald's office and in the evenings in his villa. The villa was immediately connected by direct wire with the security department of the Ministry of the Interior and with the residence of the Soviet Ambassador.[17]

The ministerial meeting, held February 17, was as tense as the preceding one. Gottwald represented the still absent Minister of the Interior. On the question as to whether the government's decision on the police had been carried out, he stated he did not know and that, at any rate, the decision was not constitutional because it intervened in an affair which was in the exclusive domain of the Ministry of the Interior. It transpired during the meeting that the decision had not even been transmitted to the Ministry. The session was suspended at noon, and Gottwald called on President Beneš to inform him of the seriousness of the situation. He accused the democratic parties of making governmental work impossible and even of plotting against the Communist Party by proposing the device of installing a government of officials not responsible to political parties. Beneš assured Gottwald that he would under no circumstances nominate a government of such officials, nor would he appoint any new government without communist representation.[18] The meeting of Ministers was resumed in the afternoon but again it led to no results. The democratic representatives insisted that their previous decision be carried out if for no other reason than respect for a governmental resolution. The communists remained adamant in their attitude. Another meeting was fixed for February 20.

I happened to be in Prague again in those days. A conference had been unexpectedly called to be attended by the Foreign Ministers of Poland, Yugoslavia, and Czechoslovakia to protest against the West's policy on Germany. It was the strangest international conference I ever attended. When Jan Masaryk gave a reception on the evening of February 17, the guests were left

[17] Laušman, *Kdo byl vinen? op.cit.*, pp. 106-07.

[18] Smutný, *op.cit.*, vol. 1, pp. 15-16.

almost entirely to themselves and one could see the democratic ministers in one corner of the large reception hall, the communists in another. Gottwald gave a lunch the following day but suddenly in the middle of it excused himself and left.

Both sides were taking battle positions. As it was subsequently described by a communist writer, the Politburo met immediately after the afternoon session of the Council of Ministers, on February 17. It decided "to mobilize the nation for an effective defense against the reactionaries' attack which was in preparation, [and] to call the party to a state of alertness." To meet the situation the Politburo issued that same evening a declaration in which it accused the anti-communist leaders of creating a governmental crisis in order to install by an anti-constitutional and anti-democratic process a non-parliamentary government of officials. The declaration called on all people to stand in readiness to "frustrate through all necessary force any subversive intentions of the reactionaries right at the beginning, and to safeguard the interest of the state and nation." At the same time, "couriers of the Central Commitee of the Communist Party of Czechoslovakia set out for all regions and more important districts. . . . The million-member colossus of the Communist Party with all its transmission belts to mass organizations was set in motion."[19] This same communist author describes further the formation of the workers' militia in individual factories. He also admits that the party decided "to wage the main battle not in the elections, as it had originally intended, but on the occasion of the national Congress of the trade unions to be convoked in Prague on February 22."[20]

Meanwhile, in an attempt to preserve at least some semblance of democratic procedure, the communists turned their attention to the Social Democratic Party. On February 19 they met with the social democratic leaders and asked them to join with the Communist Party in "battle solidarity." Should the democratic

[19] Veselý, *op.cit.*, pp. 76-77.
[20] *Ibid.*, p. 68.

parties force an open crisis, they proposed that the social democrats and the communists create a new government together. The social democrats refused. Instead they submitted to Gottwald a list of sixty social democratic police officers who had been dismissed and asked for their reinstatement.[21]

The democratic leaders now also took battle positions. For perhaps the first time since September 1947, when the situation started to show signs of impending crisis, they consulted each other and agreed on common action. However, the plan was limited to the National Socialists Party, the Catholic Party, and the Slovak Democratic Party. As to the Social Democratic Party, some of its leaders were kept informed but it appears that they were not directly invited to join the forces because of their politically delicate and complex position. Their leadership was still riddled with fellow travellers, led by Fierlinger, and it was also handicapped in its openly anti-communist attitude by its predominantly socialist following.

The democratic leaders decided to press hard on the issue of the police. They knew how widely unpopular were the practices of the communist police, whereas they were not so sure that the population at large was aware of the totalitarian character of the new economic measures proposed by the Communist Party. Moreover, on the police question they could count on the solidarity of the Social Democrats. Since the meeting of the trade unions was bound to bring to the forefront the economic and social problems and push into the background the police situation, they decided to force the crisis before the trade unions Congress.

The day after the last critical meeting of the Ministerial Council, on February 18, the National Socialists' leaders, Zenkl and Ripka, visited President Beneš. The conversation was long and appeared to them most encouraging. Beneš informed the visitors about his conversation with Gottwald the preceding day. It was established beyond any doubt that no one in the demo-

[21] Smutný, *op.cit.*, vol. 1, p. 24; Veselý, *op.cit.*, p. 82; Laušman, *Kdo byl vinen? op.cit.*, p. 114.

cratic camp had the remotest idea of establishing a cabinet of independent officials or of ousting the Communist Party from the coalition government. What the democrats wished was to compel the communists to respect the government's decision. Beneš encouraged them to remain firm and assured them he would not give up either. "You can count on me," he told them.

It is not quite clear what ensued at the end of the audience. Ripka, as he recorded it, said to Beneš that the crisis should be brought into the open before February 22 and that not only his party but also the Catholics and Slovak Democrats might submit their resignation to the President within two weeks, perhaps within the next forty-eight hours. He added that there was a good chance that the Social Democrats would take the same course. Beneš agreed, insists Ripka.[22]

On the other hand, Jaromír Smutný, the Chancellor of the President's office, who had the opportunity to follow intimately Beneš' policy as one of his closest associates, emphatically denies that the President ever agreed with the plan; he maintains that the National Socialists' leaders did not even tell the President about their intention to submit their resignations.[23]

It is probably correct to assume that the democratic leaders would not have undertaken such a step had they not been convinced of Beneš' approval. The controversy, therefore, assumes an aspect of historic importance.

Four major sources available to date, which deal with all details of the crisis, bring out the evidence that those national socialists who were direct participants in the crisis and who engaged in discussions with President Beneš agree that he fully endorsed this political plan, or, to say the least, did not suggest anything to the contrary, and that he assured the leaders of the three democratic parties of his own determination not to submit to the Communist Party pressure. This is also confirmed by a statement of Dr.

22 Ripka, *op.cit.*, pp. 223-31.

23 Smutný, *op.cit.*, vol. I, p. 14ff., his several statements at the meetings of the Group of Democratic Leaders.

Lettrich, the leader of the Slovak Democratic Party. Mr. Smutný, on the other hand, insists that the President was surprised by the resignation, and the social democratic participants are generally inclined to support Mr. Smutný's view on this fateful question.[24]

However, according to even Mr. Smutný, once the resignations were submitted, the President was still determined to support the democratic Ministers: "The President was against the communists 100 per cent, but he did not agree with such a tactic; he did not advise it. Once it happened, he backed up fully the Ministers who submitted their resignation; he was resolved not to accept the resignation; he wanted to compel Gottwald to reach an agreement with them."[25]

However, for a study which attempts to compare democratic and communist methods, even more important than the controversy is the attitude of the democratic leaders in the days of crisis and their awareness, or lack of awareness, of the adequacy, or the inadequacy, of the means at their disposal. It was in their minds that the threat of early elections might force the communists to accept the government's decision concerning the police, might create, as Stránský later described it, a properly functioning government. It now seems that they gave little thought to the actual strength of this perfectly constitutional maneuver, conducted as it was in what was clearly a revolutionary atmosphere, and even less to the eventuality of their further procedure should this alternative fail. This appeared to be true of all democratic leaders, including President Beneš.

Convinced of Beneš' full support, the democratic Ministers launched their plan on February 20. The same day the morning newspapers carried on the front page the story that the Deputy Foreign Minister of the Soviet Union, Valerian Zorin, had

[24] *Recollections and Reconstruction*, *op.cit.*; Ripka, *Le Coup de Prague*, *op.cit.*; *Frankfurtský záznam*, *op.cit.*; Petr Zenkl, "Historie komunistického puče v Ceskoslovensku" (The History of the Communist Putsch in Czechoslovakia), *České slovo* (Munich), vol. 4, no. 2, February 1948, p. 4; Smutný, *op.cit.*

[25] *Recollections and Reconstruction*, *op.cit.*, meeting February 21, 1950.

arrived in Prague in the afternoon of the day before. He had been startled at the airport by a governmental press agency reporter who asked him the purpose of his visit, since apparently it was entirely unexpected by government officials. He had taken aside the Deputy Foreign Secretary Clementis and after a whispered exchange of views had stated that he came to supervise the imports of Soviet wheat and to take part in the ceremonies of the Association of Soviet-Czechoslovak Friendship to be held three days hence, February 22.[26] It was a strange explanation. Top Soviet diplomats do not usually supervise such purely technical procedures as the delivery of goods nor do they arrive three days in advance of an event without letting anyone in the Ministry of Foreign Affairs know about their plans.

The same afternoon, February 19, the American Ambassador, Laurence Steinhardt, landed at the Prague airport, returning from Washington. It was later reported that the American government had indicated through him to the Czechoslovak government its willingness to give it a $25,000,000 credit.[27] The offer was supposedly meant to give political support to the democrats in their struggle with the communists. It was not only too little and too late, but also ineffective in kind. Zorin's arrival signified a different and much more positive type of assistance.

The democratic Ministers were disturbed by Zorin's arrival. They realized immediately that a new element, the powerful Soviet Union, had entered the scene of the struggle between communism and democracy, that now the Communist Party might expect support from the East while the democratic parties knew they would receive none from the West. If Zorin's visit was meant to intimidate them further, however, as was undoubtedly the case, the reaction among the democratic leaders whose policy had been fully approved by their respective representative bodies was one of even greater determination to proceed with their plan.[28]

[26] From an interview with A. Heidrich, June 13, 1958.

[27] Schmidt, *op.cit.*, p. 110. [28] Ripka, *op.cit.*, pp. 236-37.

On February 20, at 10:00 a.m., the Ministers of the three democratic parties were assembled in the office of one of the Deputy Prime Ministers and the chairman of the National Socialist Party, P. Zenkl, determined to carry out their first decision. When Gottwald let them know that he was about to open the meeting of the Ministerial Council they answered that they would not participate unless the resolution of the government of February 13 concerning the police had been implemented. Gottwald answered in writing, advising them evasively that the Minister of the Interior was present and would make a statement. He notified them further that the Minister of National Defense was prepared to make a statement about the Raichel affair.

The democratic Ministers insisted that they would not participate in any meeting until the government's decision had been effectuated.[29] The social democratic Ministers who until then had been in the cabinet room decided not to participate in the meeting either in view of the absence of other democratic members of the government. Gottwald threatened them saying, "If you do not march with us you will be liquidated the same as the others."[30] With both sides adamant in their positions, the Ministerial Council did not meet. The Ministers of the three democratic parties decided to resign. They informed the social democrats of their decision and expressed the wish, through their spokesman Ripka, that they too would resign.

In the afternoon, between 4:00 and 6:00 p.m., the President received letters of resignation from twelve democratic Ministers. Monsignor Hála, who handed to Beneš the resignation of the Catholic Party members, was the last caller that day. The President's last words to him were: "It was the only decision to take. Naturally, I will not accept your resignation; it is necessary that the communists capitulate. This time they calculated poorly. Now it is important to speed up the elections. The communists'

[29] For the text of exchanged letters, see Smutný, *op.cit.*, vol. 1, pp. 25-26.
[30] Ripka, *op.cit.*, pp. 237, 238.

losses will surpass their expectation. You can count entirely on me. I will not compromise."[31]

Having taken this step, the democratic leaders sat back and with feelings of considerable satisfaction awaited more or less passively—with the exception of some public meetings and private consultations—the outcome of this most dramatic and fateful governmental crisis. Their confidence seemed justified; three democratic parties had withdrawn from the government, which, however, still maintained a majority of fourteen over the twelve resignations. They were hopeful that the three social democratic Ministers would also resign, and that Jan Masaryk, always loyal to Beneš' leadership, would be advised by him to follow suit. If this happened, then Gottwald, representing a minority, would be compelled, according to constitutional procedure, to submit the resignation of the whole government. Should the social democrats still remain in the government, the President's promise not to accept the resignations of the representatives of the three parties would still compel the communists to reconsider their stand on the police issue. The government would then resume its work and the democratic parties would enter the election campaign with another victory, the communists with another defeat on their respective records. Sound reasoning, this, by these great democrats as they faced this crisis as good constitutionalists should—with principle. As strategists face to face with revolutionary, unscrupulous communists they had much to learn.

The communist leadership reacted to the democratic resignation with a series of blows. That noon, immediately after Gottwald had learned of their decision to resign, the Central Committee was called into session. It did not require any special intelligence to realize the key position of the social democratic leaders in this crisis. Even as the democrats hoped that they would submit their resignation, the communists saw with equal clarity that "the first task was not to permit the social democratic Ministers to join in the resignation." Zápotocký met immediately with

[31] *Ibid.*, p. 238.

the chairman of the party, B. Laušman, and appealed to him to "create with the communists a revolutionary majority government. . . ."[32] Laušman rejected the offer. Later that same day, Gottwald said to Vilím, the Secretary General of the Social Democratic Party, "If you do not go with us we shall crush you."[33]

At the same time, February 20, the first crack appeared in the democratic dyke. A Catholic Party deputy, Plojhar, telephoned Gottwald that he was at his disposal; a National Socialist deputy, Najman, did the same the next morning. Neither of these men had informed their respective party leadership about this step. The implications were enormous. Indeed, one communist writer asserts that the day the resignations were submitted, "Klement Gottwald was in fact already assured of a majority in the Parliament and this even in case only Fierlinger's wing of the Social Democrats was to go with the communists."[34]

Though none of the few individuals who betrayed their parties played an important role, the breach was important for it enabled Gottwald to tell Laušman, the vacillating leader of the divided Social Democratic Party, that "he had a new National Front government already assured and now it was only the question whether the Social Democrats would be represented." Laušman, who reportedly refused at the noon hour, by then, in the evening, was "ready to negotiate."[35]

That same afternoon Gottwald saw the President and asked him to accept the resignations of the twelve ministers. He accused them of sabotaging the work of the government, of acting against the highest interests of the nation, of maneuvering to oust communists from the government and to create a government of independent officials. Beneš emphatically denied the charges and assured Gottwald, as he had done before, that he would not

[32] Veselý, *op.cit.*, pp. 88-89.

[33] *Recollections and Reconstruction*, *op.cit.*, meeting December 11, 1949.

[34] *Frankfurtský záznam*, *op.cit.*; *Recollections and Reconstruction*, *op.cit.*, meeting April 11, 1950; Veselý, *op.cit.*, pp. 89-90.

[35] Veselý, *op.cit.*, p. 90; Laušman, *Kdo byl vinen? op.cit.*, pp. 120-21.

nominate such a government and that in any new coalition Gottwald would remain as Prime Minister. He advised patience and prudence in negotiations and emphasized that he himself would proceed strictly according to the Constitution. Gottwald refused to negotiate with the men who had excluded themselves from the government.[36]

Before the night descended upon the tense and excited city of Prague, the communist action had developed into an all-out offensive: "the Party stood ready, mobilized from the Central Committee down to the last communist cell." The Politburo ordered the whole apparatus to take battle stations. It prepared a proclamation which was immediately and repeatedly broadcast by all radio stations, as well as published in leaflets and special newspaper editions. The proclamation denounced democratic leaders for having "put themselves outside the National Front, outside the platform of the governmental program, and for taking up positions of an anti-state opposition." It appealed to all "good Czechs and Slovaks" to close their ranks in a firm National Front centered around Gottwald.[37] The news was spread through all available channels that Gottwald would speak the next day, February 21, at the ancient Oldtown Square.

The Politburo issued the same evening "detailed directives to the regional and district committees of the Party which ordered, among other things, . . . to make preparations for purging the National Front of the reactionaries, to begin in the factories with the organization of workers' defense corps, the workers' militia. Towards 11:00 p.m., couriers left Prague by cars in all directions. Bitter frost, snow drifts, blizzards could not deter them—directions had to be passed on time. Meanwhile teletypes transmitted orders to members of the party regional and district committees to convene and wait for instructions which were on the way."[38]

In Prague, Smrkovský, the deputy commander of the workers' militia—an illegal organization—reported to communist func-

[36] Ripka, *op.cit.*, pp. 268-70.
[37] Veselý, *op.cit.*, pp. 91-92.
[38] *Ibid.*, p. 92.

tionaries that "'a state of battle' for all militia is declared from 6:00 a.m. and that tomorrow 7,000 Prague militiamen will receive 200 cartridges each."[39]

The Presidium of the Social Democratic Party held a meeting that night. The cleavage within its ranks produced a dramatic clash. The fellow traveller, Fierlinger, supported the communist proposal to create a new government. Majer proposed that the Social Democrats join other democratic parties in resignation. Laušman took the opportunistic position and angrily criticized the National Socialists for not informing them ahead of time of their plans, nor asking them beforehand for their cooperation. Finally, the Presidium agreed on a statement which expressed the conviction that the National Front remained a good basis for the cooperation of the political parties and condemned both the hurried resignation and the subsequent declaration of the Communist Party.[40] The ambiguous position of the Social Democrats now left little hope that they would resign. Gottwald's position was strengthened.

The next day, February 21, brought the first fruit of the Communist Party's overnight activities. Thousands of telegrams, sent by communist-controlled factory councils and many other communist-led organizations from all over the country, were addressed and delivered to President Beneš. They all carried the unmistakable imprint of centrally organized action, asking in almost identical language that the President follow Gottwald's wish to appoint a new government and expressing full confidence in Gottwald's leadership. Simultaneously, scores of workers' delegations reached the Hradčany castle, the seat of the President, to convey to him their views and wishes. Other workers were ordered to leave factories and take part in a huge demonstration at Oldtown Square.

At that demonstration, Gottwald made a vitriolic attack on the democratic Ministers; he accused them of serving reactionaries

[39] Laušman, *Kdo byl vinen? op.cit.*, p. 124.

[40] *Recollections and Reconstruction*, *op.cit.*, meeting December 11, 1949.

abroad. He stated resolutely that the party would never release the police from its control and insisted that the Ministers who had resigned must not be allowed to resume their place in the government. At the end he appealed to "good Czechs and Slovaks" to found "Action Committees of the National Front"—a new device in the struggle for power.[41] The majestic monument of Jan Hus, erected in the center of the square, towered over the scene. The crowds, however, obscured the words inscribed on the pedestal: SEEK TRUTH, HEAR TRUTH, LEARN TRUTH, SPEAK TRUTH, UPHOLD TRUTH, DEFEND TRUTH UNTIL DEATH.

As the communist masses at the Oldtown Square applauded Gottwald's onslaughts, President Beneš discussed the situation with two leaders of the Social Democrats. He admitted that the resignation might have been a mistake, "but now it is necessary to hold on," he said, and continued, "I shall insist that the government be based on political parties." When the two leaders asked him what he would do if Gottwald submitted a new government, made without an agreement with the leadership of other parties, the President answered, "When the Prime Minister brings a list of a new government I shall put it before the leadership of the parties for their consideration. I will nominate a new government only in agreement with the leadership of the parties."[42]

From the meeting at the Oldtown Square a fifty-five-member delegation was sent to the President. After some pressure, he agreed to receive five spokesmen. The President tried to calm them down. One of them, a B. Kozelka, answered Beneš arrogantly, "Mr. President, I am a simple worker but I know this much, that if the majority of the nation wishes something, then even you as President must submit." Beneš retorted sharply, "We have not gone so far as yet that the street will decide whether I as President will or will not accept the resignation."[43]

[41] Gottwald, *Spisy*, *op.cit.*, vol. II, pp. 10-17.

[42] *Frankfurtský záznam*, *op.cit.*

[43] Veselý, *op.cit.*, p. 100.

The bitter truth was, however, that by now the country had gone that far. The communist machine of terror and propaganda worked at full blast. Factories were being taken over by workers' militia, guns and ammunition were being transported to Prague and distributed among party members, demonstrations were arranged in all towns, people were being arrested, messages and delegations continued to pour into Hradčany. The party Politburo at the end of the day sent a threatening letter to the President, as it "did not wish to leave [him] in doubt." Another letter went to the Social Democrats reminding them of their socialist responsibility and asking them to join the forces of progress. Also, Gottwald was entrusted to open "immediately, preliminary negotiations with the representatives of the opposition in the rightist parties of the National Front to seek out suitable persons for complementing the government."[44]

When the President expressed the wish to speak to the nation on the radio—the fact was even broadcast in the evening hours of February 21—the Minister of Information, the communist Kopecký, accompanied the news with the remark, "The government will decide if and when the President of the Republic will speak on the radio." And to his communist friends he added, "We will not allow Beneš to appear any more before the microphone."[45] The President never did.

In Slovakia, where the autonomous government was still formally in existence, the party solved the situation in a truly "constitutional" manner. Its chairman, the communist G. Husák, simply notified the democratic members who had a majority in the government that in view of the position of their fellow partymen in the central government they were dismissed, and he nominated other representatives from communist and fellow-traveller ranks to take their place. All positions of the Democratic Party, which in the elections had received 62 per cent of the votes

[44] Veselý, *op.cit.*, pp. 101-03. For the text of the two letters, see Laušman, *Kdo byl vinen? op.cit.*, pp. 128-29, 130-31.

[45] *Frankfurtský záznam, op.cit.*

as against 30 per cent for the communists, were liquidated with a stroke of the pen.[46]

What ensued needs no detailed description. The communist bulldozer rolled on. The pattern of events repeated the experience of other countries which had succumbed before: a combination of psychological terror, physical violence, and vulgar denunciation of opponents.

On Sunday, February 22, 8,000 delegates of the trade unions convened in Prague. There were among them some 400 national socialists, 500 social democrats, and 200 Catholics. The rest were communists. The Congress had supposedly been originally convened in connection with the question of civil servants' salaries. It turned into a violent communist demonstration. Gottwald repeated his dictatorial claims and, addressing President Beneš, without however mentioning his name, threatened, "And if someone thinks that when our people have in the last twenty-four hours so spontaneously, nay elementarily, expressed their demands that these agents of foreign and domestic reaction ought not to return to the government, that this demand can then be tossed to the winds, then that somebody is damn wrong. And I would like everyone to realize this soon."[47]

Any voice of opposition was silenced. When a resolution was put to a vote, ten lonely but courageous arms went up in the engulfing sea of madness.

The same Sunday morning Gottwald also spoke in the National Theater at the celebrations of the Association of Czechoslovak-Soviet Friendship. In the presence of the diplomatic corps and the democratic Ministers who did not wish to be absent from an official event, he delivered a violent speech in which he attacked the Western powers and promised eternal alliance with the Soviet Union. Valerian Zorin, the Deputy Foreign Minister, sat in the box with a sphinx-like face.

Zorin's moves in Prague were shrouded in deliberately dis-

[46] Ripka, *op.cit.*, p. 280; Laušman, *Kdo byl vinen? op.cit.*, pp. 125, 131-32.
[47] Gottwald, *Spisy*, *op.cit.*, vol. II, p. 27.

guised mystery. One hour and a half after his arrival he had visited Jan Masaryk, who had been confined to his bed during the critical days. As Masaryk reported the visit to the Secretary General of the Ministry, A. Heidrich, immediately afterward, Zorin was very cordial, "telling him that Stalin had full confidence in Masaryk but that on the other hand he must understand that the Soviet government cannot follow passively all the extravagances of the political parties in Czechoslovakia."[48] Ripka heard later that Zorin had gone even further and stated to Masaryk, "The events which take place at this moment in your country are intolerable and we shall not tolerate them."[49]

To maintain decorum, Zorin did visit the democratic Minister of Transportation, Pietor. It was reported that after the visit he mentioned to his secretary, Vilinský, that he failed to understand the attitude of the President, which had brought him into conflict with the will of the nation, and stressed that the USSR supported the action of the Communist Party of Czechoslovakia.

Zorin also paid a visit to Majer, the Minister of Food, though he was ill and declined to come to the office. At Zorin's insistence he saw him in his apartment and spoke to him about deliveries of wheat. However, as Mr. Majer relates, it became immediately clear to him that this was only a pretext to camouflage the real purpose of his presence in Prague. When Majer himself mentioned the political situation, Zorin did not react. He knew that Majer led the anti-communist wing in the Social Democratic Party.[50]

However, he knew equally well that Laušman, the chairman of the Social Democrats, was vacillating. Acting cautiously, he sent him a message on February 23. That afternoon Laušman was asked to come without delay to the apartment of a Dr. Srnka, the secretary general of one of the nationalized industries. There he was awaited by a Secretary of the Soviet Embassy, who asked him "if the party was going to support the efforts of Klement

[48] From an interview with A. Heidrich, June 13, 1958.

[49] Ripka, *op.cit.*, p. 330n.

[50] *Recollections and Reconstruction*, *op.cit.*, meeting February 7, 1950.

Gottwald to create a new National Front . . . as [Zorin] was eminently interested in the attitude of the Social Democrats because it interested Moscow."[51] When Laušman gave the man the requested information, he received an answer that "Zorin will not be enthusiastic, that at any rate Zorin had already informed Masaryk about [Moscow's] extraordinary interest and through Masaryk, Beneš, and he added diplomatically that 'this time Moscow will remain firm.' "[52]

The Soviet government did not wish to leave any doubt on what it meant by being firm. *Pravda* published an article which condemned the policy of the democratic parties and described the crisis as a result of intrigues of an international character. It praised the irresistible authority of the Communist Party. Describing the development of the crisis, it stated that it was provoked "by the instructions from abroad that placed the State, by its agitation, in a dangerous situation. . . . It is with their [the democratic parties] aid that foreign reactionaries try to divide the ranks of the people's democracy. This attempt will not be successful."[53]

The communist press and radio seized immediately upon the opportunity offered by the *Pravda* article and spread the news that 200,000,000 Soviet people were standing solidly behind the Communist Party in its struggle against domestic and international reaction.

Zorin's presence in Prague and the Moscow attitude sent shivers of fear down people's spines. Meanwhile, the democratic Ministers tried to maintain and even strengthen their positions. Apparently they did not know how terribly weak they were. When, for instance, Laušman, the social democrat, and Drtina, the national socialist, had lunch on February 21 with General Svoboda and Boček to feel out the position of the army in the crisis, the political counsellor of the President, Dr. Jan Jína, unexpectedly entered the room and in the course of the discussion stated "that

[51] Laušman, *Kdo byl vinen? op.cit.*, pp. 142, 177.
[52] *Ibid.*, p. 177. [53] Ripka, *op.cit.*, p. 283.

the President was deeply shocked by the resignations. . . ."[54] That, of course, was a serious blow to any hope for support from the armed forces.

Most of the democratic Ministers left Prague on Sunday, February 22, to hold public meetings and to encourage their adherents. At some meetings they received encouragement; other meetings were broken up by communist agitators. Their newspapers published special editions; the parties' leadership issued proclamations. But it soon became apparent to them and to the populace that words cannot stop sheer power. Wherever they looked, the sources of power—the police, the army, the factory, the radio, most of the press—were decisively if not fully in communist hands. The process of infiltration which had started in June 1941, after the Soviet Union had entered the war—a process which the democrats' own good will and loyal cooperation had facilitated—now, in February 1948, paid rich dividends. It could not be stopped by any weapons which democrats knew how to use. For that matter, it was probably by now also too late to use force against communist violence.

The crisis now centered around the person of President Beneš. Would he continue to keep the resigned Ministers in office; if so what would be the next move? Would he call upon the army, part of which he believed to have remained faithful to him; if so, would he face the risk, in fact, the reality, of a civil war? And, overshadowing all, what about the Soviet Union and the Red Army?

Mr. Smutný, who was at Beneš' side throughout the crisis, proposes answers to these questions. He is highly critical of the democratic parties, first for having precipitated a crisis that inevitably went far beyond their expectations; second, for having no common plan of action; finally, for leaving all the responsibility with the President. But Beneš, maintains Mr. Smutný, was necessarily above parties and politics; he was the constitutional head of state and as such he could not take sides. If his reasoning

[54] *Frankfurtský záznam*, *op.cit.*

was legally correct, events indicate that it was politically wrong. To observe the principles of strictly democratic procedures when democracy itself is crumbling beneath the blows of brutal anti-democratic force is to be manacled by one's convictions and can only invite disaster.

The dreary fact is that by now there was little or nothing that Beneš could do. There was not even recourse to armed resistance to the communists, had he chosen to try it. "If someone says," declares Mr. Smutný, "that he could call upon the army, *Sokols* [a traditionally patriotic organization of gymnasts—with no arms], legionnaires [by 1948 the remnants of the popular organization of Czechoslovak Legionnaires of World War I], etc., he is naïve. Everyone knew the condition of the army. How could he have given such an order? Everyone knows that such an order can be executed only through some staff or group of officers. But the President had not a single opportunity to give such an order. We must not forget that all army channels passed through the Second Department where Rejcin sat. . . . How was it possible for the President to launch a counter-revolution against his own Prime Minister, who, with his own [party] people had succeeded without resistance in getting hold of all positions right on the first day? . . ."[55]

The Sunday meeting of the trade unions weakened Beneš' firmness. He listened to its proceedings on the radio. Late in the afternoon he received the chairman of the Social Democratic Party, Laušman, whose vacillating attitude had a further depressing effect upon him. Then in the evening, through his counsellor, Dr. Jan Jína, he sent a message to the national socialist Ministers, asking them if it would not be better "to appease" the communists by accepting their resignations. He asked them to agree. The Ministers were dumbfounded. Their own information indicated a highly encouraging response of the population to their appeals and meetings. More and bigger demonstrations

[55] *Recollections and Reconstruction, op.cit.*, meeting January 17, 1950.

were in the process of preparation. The group sent a message to Beneš asking him to remain firm.[56] Minister Stránský then turned to Ripka and said, "I hope that you at least have no more illusions and that you know everything is lost."[57]

Meanwhile the Communist Party continued to develop its well-planned activities. The Politburo met in Gottwald's villa at the same time that the democratic group was discussing the message from the President. During the session it received a report concerning measures which the Ministry of the Interior was then taking against an alleged plot of a group of officers who were known to belong to the National Socialist Party. Numerous arrests were in progress. Offices of the National Socialists were searched. Gottwald issued to all police, SNB, and to the army an order declaring that a state of emergency existed, to occupy all public buildings, to transfer to Prague the crack police troops from the frontier areas, and to give arms to the workers' militia in Prague. As a communist source describes it: "At night, a convoy of trucks set out from the yard of Brno Zbrojovka [an armament factory] in the direction of Prague. It was accompanied by a battalion of SNB. . . . It carried 10,000 rifles and 2,000 automatic guns which the Brno armament workers were sending to their comrades, members of the workers' militia."[58]

As the military preparations during the night continued and the police occupied all important public objectives, Gottwald called to his residence the deviationists from the National Socialist and Catholic parties and reached an agreement with them about their entry into a new government. Then, late at night, he called the social democrat, Laušman, and briefly presented these alternatives: to take part in the new government "as a partner of communists" or as one of the satellites. Laušman promised to

[56] Ripka, *op.cit.*, pp. 260-63. See also a long memorandum by Dr. J. Jína about his carrying out the message, *Recollections and Reconstruction*, *op.cit.*, meeting March 14, 1950.

[57] *Ibid.*, p. 263.

[58] Veselý, *op.cit.*, pp. 118-20.

discuss the offer at the meeting of the executive committee which was convened for the next day, Monday, February 23.[59]

That day the growth of Action Committees mushroomed. They were created all over the country, in towns and villages, in factories and offices, in the political parties and in the Parliament, even in hospitals. They were composed of communists and a few fellow travellers. They even appeared in those ministries of the government which were still administered by representatives of the democratic parties. When on Monday morning the Minister of Transportation, Pietor, entered his office, the Action Committee gave him an ultimatum to leave it before 1:00 p.m. A similar action was taken against Ripka and Stránský. The Minister of Posts and Telegraphs, Monsignor Hála, received a letter stating, "We forbid you to enter the Ministry of Posts. If you do not obey we shall use all the means which the working class has at its disposal."[60]

The working class undoubtedly had many "means" of power, particularly since they now were in the hands of the communist party. The police had many other "means" even more convincing to the unarmed democrats and the horror-stricken public. In Bratislava, the capital of Slovakia, printers refused to run the Democratic Party presses. In Bohemia, workers in several paper mills refused to produce paper for National Socialist and Catholic newspapers; railwaymen refused to load and unload it. The police continued to search offices of the democratic parties and to arrest their members and secretaries. The borders were sealed. By Monday workers' militia were organized in some forty or fifty factories in Prague, its ranks numbering 15,000 men; its units, fully armed, paraded through the streets of the city.[61]

By Monday it became clear that the democratic parties could expect no help from the Social Democrats. Their executive committee continued to be split into three wings—left, right, and center. Every issue was carried by a different number of votes.

59 Laušman, *Kdo byl vinen? op.cit.*, pp. 135-36.

60 Veselý, *op.cit.*, pp. 122-23. 61 *Ibid.*, pp. 123-28.

The only unanimous decision was that the Social Democratic Ministers should not resign.[62]

At 4:00 p.m. a dramatic meeting took place at the Hradčany castle. The President, on several occasions since the resignations had been submitted, had seen Gottwald, the Prime Minister, who kept putting pressure on him by personal harangues, through delegations, threatening public speeches, organized mass telegrams, and mobs in the streets. He had seen the social democratic leaders who wavered between the two political belligerents. But he had had no further contact with those Ministers who had resigned—none except that message of the preceding night which had struck like lightning.

Now, on Monday afternoon, February 23, the four Ministers of the National Socialists Party—Zenkl, Stránský, Drtina, Ripka—were received by the President. They had known each other intimately for thirty years. They represented a party of which Beneš had been the leader until 1935, and which even afterward represented the chief pillar of his policy. Whatever his move, the National Socialists were behind him.

The five men met for a conversation which they seemed to realize was to seal not only their personal fate but also that of the cause of freedom in their beloved country. Zenkl, in his sixties, former Mayor of Prague and a member of several former governments, inmate of the Buchenwald concentration camp for six years, a relentless fighter against totalitarianism. Stránský, in his sixties, former publisher of the nation's most distinguished daily, *Lidové noviny*, member of Parliament, university professor, sensitive, cultured, the greatest orator of his time. Drtina, in his fifties, quiet, determined, unmovable as a rock in his faith, for years Beneš' political adviser and spokesman, with pathetic devotion to him, now the stubborn guardian of justice. Ripka, well over fifty, journalist, diplomat, seasoned negotiator, with a unique knowledge of world affairs, an attractive sense of *joie de vivre*, but deadly serious in matters of liberty, the best political

[62] Laušman, *Kdo byl vinen? op.cit.*, p. 141.

tactician of them all. And Beneš, statesman of world fame; Foreign Minister of his country for seventeen years, and its President for thirteen years; cold analyst, trained sociologist, democrat to the marrow of his bones, dedicated to reason and to peaceful means, but also the victim of Munich, a political stroke from which he never recovered, and now of two physical strokes, his alert intellect housed now in a broken body.

On that gloomy day of February 23, as Ripka records it, when they still thought themselves to be at least partly in control of the fast-breaking events that swirled around them, Beneš opened the conversation with the words, "I shall not give up. I said to Gottwald clearly: what you are doing is a state coup, a putsch, but I will not be pushed around. . . . I told him flatly: what you prepare is a second Munich."[63] He then told the Ministers the story of his conversations with the Prime Minister and about Gottwald's menacing demands, his accusations and his insults directed at the democratic leaders. "I did not react," said Beneš, describing the conversation with Gottwald. "It's up to you to defend yourselves. As far as I am concerned I must remain above the fight, above the parties."[64] He further related how he had rejected Gottwald's suggestion to appoint new government members and "to be content with a majority, achieved artificially by intimidation and deliberate disintegration of the present political parties. [His] task is to proceed in a strictly constitutional and democratic manner."[65] The President further insisted that he would negotiate only with authorized representatives of the parties and advised Gottwald to do the same. He was well aware of the device, experienced elsewhere, of handpicking puppets who are ready to serve communists, thus breaking the unity of the opposing parties. When Gottwald rejected his advice, the President then told him that he would "never attach [his] name" to a list of puppet Ministers. Should Gottwald not succeed in remaking the government in a democratic manner "the old govern-

[63] Ripka, *op.cit.*, p. 267.
[64] *Ibid.*, p. 268. [65] *Ibid.*, p. 269.

ment would remain in a caretaker capacity till the elections."[66] This sentence, reported by Ripka, is important in that it puts into words Beneš' concept of the central idea and aim behind the plan of the democratic leaders.

The five men then continued to discuss the situation. They were concerned, of course, with the reaction of the Soviet government. Ripka believed that it would not go beyond political support to Czechoslovak communists, that it would not intervene militarily. Beneš was not quite sure; he knew the Soviets, their fanatical beliefs, their blindness before reality, and he knew, too, that as far as the West is concerned "no one will help us."[67]

The audience was over. Ripka records Beneš' last words: "I repeat what I have told you. I'll act as I did in September 1938. I shall not give up; be sure of that."[68]

This, then, was the conversation of these five men, five idealists caught in a power play, still talking as they must of constitutional processes of law, of peaceful procedures. They did not even touch upon the question of posing force against force, though perhaps their silence on this crucial question signified their awareness that they had none.

That evening, February 23, some 10,000 university students, traditionally the flower of the nation's progressive thinking, moved in compact ranks to Hradčany castle. The President received the delegation, deeply moved by this courageous demonstration of loyalty. He told them that it was his "goal to preserve democracy in the spirit of T. G. Masaryk." It must have sounded like a voice from another world. The students' demonstration was the only public manifestation in support of democracy in the streets of the ancient capital which otherwise belonged to communist mobs.

At the same time, however, a meeting was taking place in the City Hall. It was attended by communist leaders, communist-controlled "non-partisan" organizations, and carefully picked de-

[66] *Ibid.*, p. 270. [67] *Ibid.*, p. 274. [68] *Ibid.*, p. 275.

fectors from the democratic parties. It founded a Renewed National Front and its Central Action Committee. It gave Gottwald another opportunity to exercise pressure on the President, for if Beneš had ever entertained the hope that the army commanders were loyal, this meeting dispelled that hope forever. The Minister of National Defense, Ludvík Svoboda, the commander-in-chief's subordinate, supposedly a non-partisan officer, participated at the gathering and, taking the floor, declared, "The army goes with the nation. Who disturbs the unity of the nation is a menace and must be removed!"[69]

Many people had already been removed; many more were to follow. The next day, February 24, mass arrests continued; Action Committees continued to spread; adherents of democratic parties continued to be thrown out of office. Democratic journalists were driven from their jobs and communist puppets were appointed by Action Committees in their place. Only a handful of defectors turned against their parties, the overwhelming majority expressing repeatedly during the days of crisis their confidence in their leadership; but this handful of collaborators was accompanied by armed police and assisted by the panic and fear which engulfed the country. The real leaders had the votes, the majority, and right on their side—but nothing more. Their newspapers did not appear, their voice could not be heard on the radio. Instead, they were accused of treachery, working for foreign powers, sabotage, espionage, as the communist-controlled press hurled accusations against them. They had no means to answer.

The leaders of the Slovak Democratic Party saw the President on the morning of February 24. He assured them, according to a statement by Dr. Lettrich, that he would not accept the resignations and would appoint a new government only after an agreement with all interested political parties had been reached. And should he fail "chaos may ensue and a similar situation occur

[69] Veselý, *op.cit.*, pp. 138-41; Ripka, *op.cit.*, pp. 299-301; Laušman, *Kdo byl vinen? op.cit.*, pp. 142-43; Gottwald, *Spisy*, *op.cit.*, vol. II, pp. 28-42.

as that which followed Munich." Lettrich felt from the audience with the President that "he had lost self-confidence and that he would eventually succumb to communist threats."[70]

Nor was there any help forthcoming from the Constitutional National Assembly, scheduled to convene on February 24; frightened by communist pressure, its Presidium decided the preceding day to revoke the session.[71]

At noon, 2,500,000 workers went on a one-hour strike as a demonstration of the strength of the communist-led trade unions. Those who declined to join the strikers were immediately thrown out of their jobs.

In this flood of violence, all organized and led by a minority, one small item of news appeared in the papers. It went almost unnoticed in the uproar of the political earthquake. The Supreme Court ordered that four factories be released to their private owners, for their nationalization was declared to be against the law.[72] It was like a late autumn flower suddenly seen on a drab and wintry hillside, neither noticed nor long remembered, but for a moment, there.

Wednesday morning, February 25, the newspapers published the following statement: "To all members of the Czechoslovak Social Democracy! Dear comrades, the events which have developed in the last period with ever-increasing speed caused differences of opinion in our party which have now been overcome by a mutual agreement and a united solution. On the basis of sincere socialist cooperation we have agreed on the proposal of a new government and the establishment of a new effective National Front on a broad basis."[73]

The statement sealed the fate of one of the oldest political parties in Europe. The Social Democrats were once again taken over by Fierlinger, with the wavering Laušman joining forces in the last minute. The decision had been preceded by hours of

[70] Smutný, *op.cit.*, vol. IV, p. 132.

[71] *Frankfurtský záznam*, *op.cit.*

[72] Veselý, *op.cit.*, pp. 143-51.

[73] *Právo lidu*, February 25, 1948.

wrangling. During the session of the Executive Committee, Fierlinger was heard calling someone, "It's not working here, so let's start giving it to them."[74] Within a short time the building was occupied by Fierlinger's henchmen and the police. Fighting ensued and several people were wounded, Minister Majer among them. When he went to his office a mob attacked him and tried to throw him out. He telephoned Gottwald for protection. It was refused. Leaving the office he was jeered and threatened.

Drtina, the rock of Gibraltar, when entering his office was received by a similar mob. In his Ministry, in which out of 350 employees only 8 were organized communists, he had defended the integrity of justice with unparalleled audacity. When the mob ordered him to leave, the indomitable jurist said with dignity, "I want to bring to your attention that you are committing a crime of insurrection."[75]

Beneš thought that there was still time to negotiate. When Gottwald sought him out in the afternoon of February 24 to tell him that he would submit the list of a new government the following morning, the President refused to consider it and continued to insist that the Prime Minister negotiate with the political parties. Gottwald refused equally emphatically.

Late at night, Beneš answered the Communist Party's letter of February 21. It opened, "You know my deep democratic conviction. I cannot but remain faithful to it at this moment as in my opinion democracy is the only solid and permanent basis for human life and honesty and dignity." He stressed again the necessity of solving the crisis in a democratic and parliamentary way. He emphasized the acceptance of a socialist economy, but to him liberty and concord could march along with socialism and "they [were] indispensable principles of the whole national life." He repeated that Gottwald must remain Prime Minister, and appealed to him to bring all the parties together and to resume discussions about a new, durable cooperation. "I

[74] *Recollections and Reconstruction*, *op.cit.*, meeting April 11, 1950.
[75] *Recollections and Reconstruction*, *op.cit.*, meeting February 28, 1950.

believe," ended the President's letter, "that a reasonable agreement is possible because it is absolutely necessary."[76] However, to the communists the agreement was neither possible nor necessary; to them it was not desirable.

The Politburo received Beneš' letter while in session in Gottwald's villa. At that time the self-appointed Action Committees of the democratic parties had already accepted the ministerial candidates picked for them by the Communist Party. Social Democrats succumbed and the proclamation of Fierlinger, which appeared in the paper early the next morning, had already been prepared.

Without any hesitation the Politburo rejected Beneš' letter. In its answer it refused again to negotiate with the true leadership of the democratic parties and asked the President for an immediate decision to nominate a new government which, Gottwald was convinced, would "in full agreement with the principles of parliamentary democracy appear before the Constituent Assembly, present its program, and ask for its approval."[77]

The President received the letter on the morning of February 25. At 11:00 a.m. the leaders of the Communist Party came to see him to ask him for an early decision, and Gottwald submitted a list of the new government. The communists had one-half of the portfolios; the rest included three social democrats, all Fierlinger's fellow travellers, and representatives of collaborators from other parties—and Jan Masaryk. He took with him to the grave the mystery of why he allowed his name to be included in the list. Gottwald also presented a list of 166 deputies in the National Assembly, a majority, that would vote for his new government. The conversation was a *Te Deum* to Czechoslovak democracy. In a tired and broken voice Beneš said that he must think it over, that the crisis must now be solved quickly, that he himself must take an honorable attitude, indicating that he might

[76] Smutný, *op.cit.*, vol. IV, pp. 137, 138-39.
[77] Veselý, *op.cit.*, pp. 157-58.

remove himself from office. He ended by saying, "At any rate, you will receive my answer today."[78]

In Prague, proclamations, arrests, demonstrations, violence went on and on. From the early hours of the morning, appeals went out to workers to convene at the St. Venceslaw Square at 4:00 p.m. At noon the radio announced that the President had accepted the resignations of the Ministers. It was not true—not yet—only a part of the campaign of pressure. When the National Socialists' leaders, hearing the news, asked the President's office to be received by him, they were given an evasive answer and waited for a call. It never came.

At 4 p.m. Gottwald drove to the Hradčany castle for the President's answer. Then, a few minutes later, he drove back to St. Venceslaw Square. He had a paper in his hands. It was the list of the new government, signed by the President of the Republic. His head was covered by a Russian sheepskin cap. Two hundred thousand mobilized workers awaited him. Police and workers' militia mingled with them. He announced the constitution of a new government and read the list. He expressed gratitude to President Beneš for respecting the will and wish of the people.

The mob accompanied Gottwald's every word with frantic applause and thunderous shouts. Somewhere close to the President's castle a few thousand university students were gathering to march again to his residence. The police fired on them. The deposed Ministers listened in their homes, surrounded by the police, to Gottwald's address. He was obviously drunk, drunk with alcohol, and with success. The day was bitterly cold. Gray skies obscured the sun. In Czechoslovakia, democracy was dead.

[78] For the composition of the government see Schmidt, *op.cit.*, p. 130; Veselý, *op.cit.*, pp. 161-62; *Recollections and Reconstruction*, *op.cit.*, meeting January 10, 1949; Smutný, *op.cit.*, vol. IV, pp. 156-60.

THE LONG NIGHT

As Edvard Beneš watched the striking of the presidential flag on the grounds of his villa at Sezimovo Ústí on that gray morning of June 7, he must have seen, too, the somber parade of the figures and events that had filled his life during the thirty years of the existence of his little Republic of Czechoslovakia. If, in addition to the grief that choked his heart, there was room for bitterness, then bitterness was there, for the events and figures which had brought his young Republic into the long night of communist totalitarianism were those that spoke of perfidy, of treachery, of broken promises and cynical disregard for truth.

Beneš and the other democratic leaders of Czechoslovakia had trusted, perhaps because there was no other choice for them, the promises of the Soviet Union and of the Communist Party. The broken shards of their hopes and dreams revealed now with utter clarity, though far too late, the folly of such trust.

The Soviet Union had guaranteed the territorial integrity of this small democracy, but it annexed through violent means her eastern territories, Subcarpathian Russia. It had promised not to intervene in her national affairs, but quickly broke that promise when these were not identical with Soviet interests. It had encouraged by word and solemn treaty Czechoslovak nationalism, but was quick to deny her the exercise of acts of sovereignty whenever such denial worked to Soviet advantage.

Still worse had been the acts of his fellow countrymen, the members of the Communist Party of Czechoslovakia. They had posed as protagonists of patriotism but as soon as the party seized power the last vestiges of national loyalty were quickly abandoned. Had Beneš lived beyond the three months left to him he would have seen fully demonstrated what now he could see only beginning: Czech culture, perhaps the most ennobling product of nationalism, sacrificed at the altar of Soviet "socialist realism"; Czech economic prosperity subjected to the needs of the Soviet Union; the conduct of public affairs perverted to the demands of a foreign ideology.

He could have seen, too, the continuation of communist perfidy and broken promises. The Communist Party had declared a coalition government to be a permanent feature of Czechoslovak politics. Once it had eliminated the democratic parties, it then described the coalition government as a temporary arrangement, only a step in the struggle for exclusive power. It had guaranteed, even in its own Constitution for the country, the preservation of private property and enterprise. Today all industry and trade is nationalized and sixty per cent of the land is collectivized.

All this Beneš came finally to understand. All this the remnants of his democratic colleagues who with him put their trust in the integrity of the Soviet Union and their faith in the essential patriotism of Czech communists now know—now that it is far too late.

The essence of democracy is faith, and the manner of free men is to trust. There are statesmen and writers in the free world who still today accept at face value the more alluring pronouncements of communist leaders as the changing face of communism from time to time takes on a friendlier guise. It is hard to change the habits of faith and trust even in the light of history or in the face of continuing communist ideological agility. "Communist morality is the morality which serves this [communist] struggle," wrote Lenin. He instructed his followers "to use any ruse, dodges, tricks, cunning, unlawful methods, concealment, veiling of truth" to achieve communist aims. In these two single statements lies the clarification for the history of seeming inconsistencies in Soviet and communist policies and for their intractable flexibility.

Thus the communist leaders find it possible to defend the principle of coexistence of various political and economic systems, the while Khrushchev is bluntly saying to the free world, "We shall bury you." Thus they are able to declare the right of each nation to follow its own path toward socialism but are also able to state that "every country's path to socialism cannot be different. To speak so is to deny the international significance of Bolshevism's experience." They profess to adhere to the principles of territorial integrity and non-intervention in the internal affairs of other nations while the record of the Soviet Union is replete with flagrant violations of these principles. They allege to have accepted parliamentary procedures as a valid road toward their goal only to dispose of it as an "historically obsolete" institution in the "era of the proletarian dictatorship." They plead constantly for disarmament, concealing the Leninist dictum that "the party never disarms," that it must be held "in a state of mobilization." They have high praise for the neutrality policy of some Middle East and Asian countries, and yet they define "the position of neutrality under all conditions [as] not only a dangerous illusion which does not to any extent really prevent the neutral state from being drawn into war but is indeed a factor aiding the unleashing of war."

Above all, the Soviet Union and the communists have become champions of nationalism and of the self-determination of nations. But numerous writings of their leaders include such blunt statements as "Marxism is incompatible with nationalism"; "the principle of the self-determination of nations . . . must be subordinated to the principles of Socialism"; "we are at liberty to agitate for or against secession [i.e., national independence], according to the interests of the proletarian revolution"; and we "must enter into a temporary alliance with bourgeois democracy in colonial and backward countries."

The Babel-like confusion of language continues without end, for it emanates from the semantics of Marxist dialectics and is meant to confuse. It allows communists to follow any course of action in a given situation, and still pursue with inflexible purpose the original directives of Marx and Lenin. The wolf is most dangerous when dressed in the clothing of the sheep.

The question posed by the tragic experience of the communist putsch in Czechoslovakia is one for which, no matter how difficult it may be, the democratic leaders of all nations must find a satisfactory answer. The events of the week of February 20, 1948 in Czechoslovakia were not a sudden, unexplainable, lightning-like stroke of violence. They were the inevitable result of a long struggle in which the weapons of democracy were shattered by the forces of communism. The question must therefore be asked: Can the civilized ways of free men hope to survive against the constant corrosion and deliberately deceitful intrigue of communist strategy? The communists themselves posed the question well when of Beneš they wrote: "Edvard Beneš was a typical bourgeois democrat of the old French-English school. His insistence on all appurtenances of democracy of the western European type became for him and with him for the Czech bourgeoisie, fateful. For it is an historical fact, and at the same time a peculiarity of the February events in 1948 in Czechoslovakia, that all the postulates of a formal bourgeois democracy were, through the developments of events, on the side of the communists. In the hands of that master of communist tactic and strategy, Klement Gottwald, and with him the whole Presidium of the Communist Party of Czechoslovakia, the principles of bourgeois democracy turned into a weapon through which the bourgeoisie was deprived with complete finality of all remnants of power and influence on further developments in Czechoslovakia."[1]

Perhaps in this study of the long history of communist design in Czechoslovakia and the nature of democratic defense, there has emerged some further understanding of the great dilemma of democrats everywhere as they face continuing militant communism. Everywhere, as in Czechoslovakia, the principles of democracy, bourgeois and otherwise, are turned by militant communism into effective weapons of war. True, in the case of Czechoslovakia, there were certain conditions that were quickly exploited to communist purpose: the economic and social upheaval

[1] Veselý, *op.cit.*, pp. 181-82.

of the period of occupation; the liberation by Soviet troops; the Teheran agreements and the memories of Munich; the Sudeten lands and the German estates, available for exploitation by communist agitators; the existence of an easily divided Marxist oriented Social Democratic Party; and, looming always on the horizon, the ever-present threat of the Soviet Army. All of these conditions, somewhat unique to the case of Czechoslovakia, were thoroughly exploited by the communists in their brutal assault on Czech democracy, but this probing of every chink in the armor is itself a universal technique of communism.

More important, however, is the "fixed" pattern, the exploitation for communist purpose by perfidy and faithlessness of the institutions of free men. The list of commmunist victims is long and the evidence is sadly eloquent: Estonia, Latvia, Lithuania, Poland, Hungary, East Germany, Yugoslavia, Rumania, Bulgaria, Albania, China. In the story of the dreary march of these countries into the communist night, certain universal patterns emerge, patterns which thinking men by now should begin to recognize whenever and wherever militant communism makes its bid for power.

In the beginning of any such campaign, the communists have been careful not to give offense to the specific cultural, religious, political, and economic traditions of the country concerned. Instead, there are assuring displays of patriotism, an outspoken tolerance of other political parties, a loudly professed loyalty to the principles of democracy and freedom, and pronouncements of respect for private property. So loud are their proclamations and so clever their masks that people are led to believe that the communists of *their* country have ceased to be true Marxists and that the Soviet Union has, in *their* case, abandoned the policy of communist expansion. With the people thus reassured, there follows the establishment of a coalition government. Then, though reassurances and displays of patriotism continue, the gates have been opened to a process of systematic infiltration into all spheres of national life and, particularly important, to an exclusive entrenchment in the command of the armed forces, the police, and mass communications. At the same time, as an almost inevitable design, there is the establishment of National Fronts embracing all parties, National Committees with vast local authority, trade unions unifying all working people, and other mass organizations. With almost equal certainty there is the courtship of the intellectuals, who are attracted by the seeming social justice of Marxist teaching, the purposeful division of the ranks of democratic socialists who share with the communists the theory of the abolition of private property, and the subtle conquest of those democrats who display some tolerance toward party objectives. There is also collaboration with individuals of most doubtful reputation. Thus, consciously or unconsciously, people of all walks of national life assist the communists as they breach the gates of democracy to admit this twentieth-century Trojan horse.

Simultaneously, and highly important to the entire design, is the maintenance under the same cover of patriotism, tolerance, cooperation, and devotion to democracy, of illegal military organizations and professionals in the techniques of seizure of government, the shock troops of the moment of "take over."

At all times and in every case, there is the duplicity of Soviet diplomacy, overtly friendly but in fact active in the direction of the policy of individual communist parties, and always to be relied upon for their open support at the culminating moment of violence. In the past (though happily not true today) there was a lack of understanding on the part of Western democracies of the nature of the struggle and the absence of any effective assistance to the threatened democrats.

Finally, and tragically, there is the appropriate moment, the masks fall, previous solemn promises are forgotten, friends and non-communist politicians are denounced, violence flares, the tightly organized communist machine is set in motion against the now disorganized and thoroughly infiltrated forces of democracy. The conquest is accomplished—conquest through coexistence.

Time after time the pattern has emerged; time after time it has been successful. The result is tragic: 750 million people brought under the shadow of communism in the short period of four years from 1944 to 1948. Their present agony could be at least partly redeemed if others will but listen to the unobtrusive but enlightening voice of history, a voice of warning that in the uneven struggle between the forces of violence and tolerance the good faith and trust of democrats is not the currency with which they may buy from communists the blessings of peace and freedom.

If this voice is ignored, if the inexorable pattern is not recognized, if—without sacrificing the democratic principles for which they live and fight—free nations cannot redesign their weapons and reshape their tactics to repulse the inevitable onslaught which one day they must surely meet, then the Benešes of all nations, all civilized men, all men of good will, can hope for little more than their own variation on the event of June 7 at Sezimovo Ústí.

≺ BIBLIOGRAPHY ≻

DOCUMENTARY MATERIALS

Beneš, Eduard, *Memoirs of Dr. Eduard Beneš*. Translated by Godfrey Lias. London: George Allen & Unwin, 1954.

Desať rokov. Československá otázka v Spojených národoch. S úvodom Jána Papánka. Chicago: Československá Národná Rada Americká, 1958.

Dokumenty o protilidové a protinárodní politice T. G. Masaryka. Prague: Orbis, 1953.

Dvořák, Josef, *Slovenská politika včera a dnes*. Prague: Pokrok, 1947.

Feierabend, Ladislav, *Paměti* (unpublished), 8 volumes.

Fierlinger, Zdeněk, *Od Mnichova po Košice*. Svědectví a dokumenty 1939-1945. Prague: Práce, 1946.

———, *Letter to the Leaders of the Social Democratic Party in London* (unpublished). Moscow, December 21, 1943.

———, *Ve službách ČSR*. 2 volumes. Prague: Svoboda, 1947, 1948.

Frankfurtský záznam (unpublished). A collection of statements by a group of Czechoslovak democratic leaders on the February 1948 crisis.

Gottwald, Klement, *Deset let*. Sborník statí a projevů, 1936-1946. 3 volumes. Prague: Svoboda, 1948.

———, *Letter to the Leaders of the Communist Party of Czechoslovakia in London* (unpublished). Moscow, December 21, 1943.

———, *Spisy*. Vols. I, 1946-1948; II, 1946-1948; III, 1931-1932. Prague: Svoboda, (n.d.).

Interviews and/or Letters: V. Bušek, J. Drábek, L. Feierabend, A. Heidrich, I. Herben, V. Majer, J. Papánek, H. Skala, J. Slávik, J. Stránský, P. Tigrid, P. Zenkl.

Kopecký, Václav, *30 let KSČ*. Prague: Svoboda, 1951.

———, *Tridsať rokov ČSR*. Bratislava: Poverenictvo informacií, 1948.

Krajina Archive. A collection of wartime documents; in possession of V. Krajina, Vancouver, Canada.

KSČ v boji za svobodu. Prague: Svoboda, 1949.

Laušman, Bohumil, *Kdo byl vinen?* Austria, (n.d.).

Lettrich, Jozef, *History of Modern Slovakia*. New York: F. A. Praeger, 1955.

Masaryk, Jan, *Memorandum on his conversation with K. Gottwald* (unpublished). Moscow, March 21, 1945.

Nazi-Soviet Relations, 1939-1941. Documents from the Archives of the German Foreign Office. Ed. by R. J. Sontag and J. S. Beddie. Washington: Department of State, 1948.

Nemec, F. and Moudry, V., *The Soviet Seizure of Subcarpathian Ruthenia.* Toronto: William B. Anderson, 1955.

Recollections and Reconstruction of the Czechoslovak February 1948 Crisis by a Group of Democratic Leaders (unpublished and untitled). Stenographic Report. London, 1949-1950.

Ripka, Hubert, *Le coup de Prague.* Paris: Plon, 1949.

Smutný, Jaromír, *Únorový převrat 1948.* 5 volumes, mimeographed. London: Ústav dr. Edvarda Beneše, 1953-1957.

Soviet Documents on Foreign Policy. Selected and edited by Jane Degras. Vol. III, 1933-1941. London: Oxford University Press, 1953.

Stránský, Jaroslav, *Personal Résumé,* Nos. 1-3, being a résumé of Recollections and Reconstruction of the February 1948 Crisis . . . (unpublished).

Únor 1948. Sborník dokumentů. Prague: Státní nakladatelství politické literatury, 1958.

U.S. Congress, The (81st, 1st Session). House Committee on Foreign Affairs. *The Strategy and Tactics of World Communism; Report, Subcommittee No. 5, National and International Movements.* Supplement III: Country Studies, A. The Coup d'Etat in Prague. House Doc. 154, Part 1. Washington: Government Printing Office, 1949.

Ustavení čs. vlády Národní fronty Čechů a Slováků a její první projevy. Prague: Orbis, 1945.

Veselý, Jindřich, *Kronika únorových dnů 1948.* Prague: Státní nakladatelství politické literatury, 1958.

Yiddish Scientific Institute, Yivo, *Attentat auf Obergruppenführer R. Heydrich am 27.5.1942 in Prag.* A report submitted by the Reichssicherheitshauptamt, Berlin, August 5, 1942.

Zápotocký, Antonín, *Nová odborová politika.* Prague: Práce, 1949.

——, *Po staru se žít nedá.* Prague: Práce, 1949.

Zasedání devíti komunistických stran. O založení informační kanceláře komunistických stran v Bělehradě. Prague: Svoboda (n.d.).

Za svobodu českého a slovenského národa. Sborník domumentů k dějinám KSČ v letech 1938-1945. Prague: Státní nakladatelství politické literatury, 1956.

Za svobodu. Do nové Česloslovenské Republiky. Prague: Knižnice Nové svobody, 1945.

GENERAL WORKS (selected)

Beneš, Eduard, *Czechoslovak Policy for Victory and Peace.* London: Čechoslovák: Lincolns-Prager, 1944.

———, *Democracy Today and Tomorrow.* New York: The Macmillan Company, 1939.

Betts, Reginald R. (ed.), *Central and South East Europe, 1945-1948.* London: Royal Institute of International Affairs, 1950.

Chmelař, Josef, *Political Parties in Czechoslovakia.* Prague: Orbis, 1926.

The Curtain Falls. Edited by Denis Healey. London: Lincolns-Prager, 1951.

Czechoslovakia. V. Busek and N. Spulber, eds. New York: F. E. Praeger, 1957.

Czechoslovakia, Twenty Years of Independence. Ed. by Robert J. Kerner. Berkeley: University of California, 1940.

Duchacek, Ivo, *The Strategy of Communist Infiltration: The Case of Czechoslovakia.* New Haven, Conn.: Yale Institute of International Studies, 1949.

Feierabend, Ladislav, *Agricultural Production in Czechoslovakia in 1953.* New York: Mid-European Studies Center (n.d.).

Friedman, Otto, *Breakup of Czech Democracy.* London: Gollancz, 1950.

Gyorgy, Andrew, *Governments of Danubian Europe.* New York: Rinehart, 1949.

Korbel, P., *Parliamentary Elections in Czechoslovakia.* New York: National Committee for a Free Europe, September 1952.

———, *National Committees in Czechoslovakia.* New York: Free Europe Committee, February 1954.

Korbel, P. and Vagassky, V., *Purges in the Communist Party of Czechoslovakia.* New York: National Committee for a Free Europe, October 1952.

Laušman, Bohumil, *Pravda a lož o slovenskom národnom povstaní.* Petrovec, Yugoslavia: Bratrstvo-Jednota, 1951.

Peroutka, Ferdinand, *Budování státu.* 4 vols. Prague: Fr. Borový, 1933-1936.

La Presse derrière le rideau de fer. Paris: (no publisher), 1948.

Reimann, P., *Geschichte der Kommunistischen Partei der Tschechoslovakei.* Hamburg-Berlin: Carl Hoym, 1929.

Rozehnal, A., *Pozemkové reformy v Československé Republice.* New York: National Committee for a Free Europe, September 1952.

Schmidt, Dana Adams, *Anatomy of a Satellite.* Boston: Little, Brown, 1952.

Seton-Watson, Hugh, *The East European Revolution.* New York: F. E. Praeger, 1951.

Seton-Watson, Robert William, *History of the Czechs and Slovaks.* Forest Hills, N.Y.: Transatlantic Arts, 1944.

Šíma, J. and Vergeiner, V., *Revoluční dělnické hnutí v Československu v boji za práci a životní úroveň pracujících, 1917-1952.* Prague: Práce, 1953.

Stránský, Jan, *East Wind over Prague.* New York: Random House, 1951.

Thomson, Samuel Harrison, *Czechoslovakia in European History.* Princeton, N.J.: Princeton University Press, 1953.

Zieris, K. F., *The New Organization of the Czech Press.* Prague: Orbis, 1947.

PERIODICALS

Gracchus, "Memorandum on Czechoslovakia," *Nineteenth Century,* vol. 140, pp. 114-20, 175-80.

Herben, Ivan, "Jak tomu opravdu bylo," a series of scripts for Radio Free Europe.

Horák, Jiří, "Českoslovenští sociální demokraté v druhém odboji," *Svědectví,* vol. II, no. 1, pp. 38-54.

Hulička, K., "Communist Anti-Masaryk Propaganda in Czechoslovakia," *The American Slavic and East European Review,* vol. 16, pp. 160-74.

Hunt, R., "Denigration of Masaryk," *Yale Review,* vol. 43, no. 3, pp. 414-26.

Josko, Matej P., "Slovenská účast v protikomunistickom boji," *Hlas Československa*, vol. 3, no. 2, pp. 10-14.

Klimek, Adolf, "Jak to dělali," *Hlas Československa*, vol. 3, no. 2, pp. 17-19.

Lockhart, R. B., "Czechoslovak Revolution," *Foreign Affairs*, vol. 26, pp. 632-44.

——, "Report on Czechoslovakia," *Foreign Affairs*, vol. 33, pp. 484-98.

Novotny, J. M., "How the Reds Took Over Our Faculty," *Vital Speeches*, vol. 22, pp. 535-39.

Skilling, H. G., "The Formation of a Communist Party in Czechoslovakia," *The American Slavic and East European Review*, vol. 14, pp. 346-58.

Taborsky, E., "Beneš and the Soviets," *Foreign Affairs*, vol. 27, pp. 302-14.

——, "Beneš and Stalin, Moscow, 1943 and 1945," *Journal of Central European Affairs*, vol. 13, pp. 154-81.

——, "Benešovy moskevské cesty," *Svědectví*, vol. 1, no. 3-4, pp. 193-214.

——, "The Triumph and Disaster of Eduard Beneš," *Foreign Affairs*, vol. 36, no. 4, pp. 669-84.

Zenkl, Petr, "Jak to dělali," *Svornost* (Chicago).

Zinner, P. E., "Marxism in Action: Seizure of Power in Czechoslovakia," *Foreign Affairs*, vol. 28, pp. 644-58.

NEWSPAPERS (some incomplete)

Čechoslovák, London, 1939-1945. *Kulturní zítřek*, Prague, 1946-1948. *The New York Times*, 1945-1948. *Rudé právo*, Prague, 1945-1948. *Svobodné noviny*, Prague, 1945-1948. *Svobodné slovo*, Prague, 1945-1948.

INDEX

Preissig, Vojtěch, 55